Brilliant
Mac Basics

Jerry Glenwright

Harlow, England • London • New York • Boston • San Francisco • Toronto • Sydney • Singapore • Hong Kong
Tokyo • Seoul • Taipei • New Delhi • Cape Town • Madrid • Mexico City • Amsterdam • Munich • Paris • Milan

Pearson Education Limited
Edinburgh Gate
Harlow CM20 2JE
United Kingdom
Tel: +44 (0)1279 623623
Fax: +44 (0)1279 431059
Website: www.pearsoned.co.uk

First edition published in Great Britain in 2008

© Pearson Education Limited 2008

The right of Jerry Glenwright to be identified as author
of this work has been asserted by him in accordance
with the Copyright, Designs and Patents Act 1988.

ISBN: 978-0-273-71706-5

British Library Cataloging in Publication Data
A catalogue record for this book can be obtained from the British Library

Library of Congress Cataloging in Publication Data

Glenwright, Jerry.
  Brilliant Mac Basics / Jerry Glenwright. -- 1st ed.
     p. cm.
  ISBN 978-0-273-71706-5 (pbk.)
  1. Mac OS. 2. Operating systems (Computers) 3. Macintosh
(Computer)--Programming. I. Title.
   OA76.76.063G587 2008
   005.4'4682--dc22

                                    2008023771

10 9 8 7 6 5 4 3 2 1
12 11 10 09 08

Set by 30 in 11pt Arial Condensed
Printed and bound by Rotolito Lombarda, Italy

The publisher's policy is to use paper manufactured from sustainable forests.

Brilliant guides

What you need to know and how to do it

When you're working on your computer and come up against a problem that you're unsure how to solve, or want to accomplish something in an application that you aren't sure how to do, where do you look? Manuals and traditional training guides are usually too big and unwieldy and are intended to be used as end-to-end training resources, making it hard to get to the info you need right away without having to wade through pages of background information that you just don't need at that moment – and helplines are rarely that helpful!

Brilliant guides have been developed to allow you to find the info you need easily and without fuss and guide you through the task using a highly visual, step-by-step approach – providing exactly what you need to know when you need it!

Brilliant guides provide the quick easy-to-access information that you need, using a table of contents and troubleshooting guide to help you find exactly what you need to know, and then presenting each task in a visual manner. Numbered steps guide you through each task or problem, using numerous screenshots to illustrate each step. Added features include 'See also...' boxes that point you to related tasks and information in the book, while 'Did you know?...' sections alert you to relevant expert tips, tricks and advice to further expand your skills and knowledge.

In addition to covering all major office PC applications, and related computing subjects, the *Brilliant* series also contains titles that will help you in every aspect of your working life, such as writing the perfect CV, answering the toughest interview questions and moving on in your career.

Brilliant guides are the light at the end of the tunnel when you are faced with any minor or major task.

Publisher's acknowledgements

The author and publisher would like to thank the following for permission to reproduce the material in this book:

Apple and iMac are trademarks of Apple Inc., registered in the U.S. and other countries. iWeb is a trademark of Apple Inc.; Broadband.co.uk screen image provided by Broadband.co.uk, with kind permission; Fetch screen images provided by Fetch Software, with kind permission; Google screen images provided by Google Inc.; iCalShare screen image provided by Patrick Crowley, with kind permission; Copyright 2005–2008 Mozilla. All Rights Reserved. All rights in the names, trademarks, and logos of the Mozilla Foundation, including without limitation, Mozilla®, mozilla.org®, Thunderbird™, as well as the Mozilla logo, and Thunderbird logo are owned by the Mozilla Foundation; OpenOffice.org is a registered trademark of the OpenOffice.org Community http://www.openoffice.org and is used with permission.

In some instances we have been unable to trace the owners of copyright material, and we would appreciate any information that would enable us to do so.

Author's acknowledgements

To Angela... here's to 20!

About the author

Author, editor and journalist, Jerry Glenwright is a mathematics and computer science graduate with 20 years experience writing about technology, motoring, music, photography, walking, women's issues, alternative health, homes and gardens and more.

Contents

Preface

With its rock-solid Unix foundation and highly intuitive, super-attractive graphic front-end Aqua, Apple's Unix, Darwin, offers high security and seamless networking and, allied with what is arguably the finet point-and-click interface ever created, form a virtually non-crashable operating system that is simple yet powerful, accessible and a true joy to use. There's a Mac for every need and a pocket too, from the whisper-quiet, tiny but fully-featured Mac mini, to the superuser Mac Pro and the MacBook range, thrown in (to a ruchsack!) for good measure. Once you use a Mac you will never want to return to the dreary days of hardware conflicts, and virus- and spyware-ridden operating systems

This book, the first Mac-oriented text in the hugely popular Pearson 'Brilliant' series, will take you on a journey of discovery through the delights that are the Mac and its OS, with tricks, tips and insights to get first-time owners and users on a par with seasoned Apple gurus – when Alt becomes Option you'll know you're there...

Introduction

Welcome to *Brilliant: Mac Basics*, a visual quick-reference book that gives you a basic grounding in the way the Mac works, introduces the OS X and demonstrates how to use bundled applications – a complete reference for the beginner user.

Find what you need to know – when you need it

You don't have to read this book in any particular order. We've designed the book so that you can jump in, get the information you need, and jump out. To find the information that you need, just look up the task in the table of contents or Troubleshooting guide, and turn to the page listed. Read the task introduction, follow the step-by-step instructions along with the illustration and you're done.

How this book works

Each task is presented with step-by-step instructions in one column and screen illustrations in the other. This arrangement lets you focus on a single task without having to turn the pages too often.

How you'll learn

Find what you need to know – when you need it

How this book works

Step-by-step instructions

Troubleshooting guide

Spelling

Step-by-step instructions

This book provides concise step-by-step instructions that show you how to accomplish a task. Each set of instructions includes illustrations that directly correspond to the easy-to-read steps. Eye-catching text features provide additional helpful information in bite-sized chunks to help you work more efficiently or to teach you more in-depth information. The 'For your information' feature provides tips and techniques to help you work smarter, while the 'See also' cross-references lead you to other parts of the book containing related information about the task. Essential information is highlighted in 'Important' boxes that will ensure you don't miss any vital suggestions and advice.

Troubleshooting guide

This book offers quick and easy ways to diagnose and solve common problems that you might encounter, using the Troubleshooting guide. The problems are grouped into categories that are presented alphabetically.

Spelling

We have used UK spelling conventions throughout this book. You may therefore notice some inconsistencies between the text and the software on your computer which is likely to have been developed in the US. We have however adopted US spelling for the words 'disk' and 'program' as these are commonly accepted throughout the world.

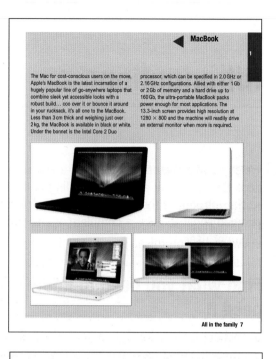

MacBook

1

The Mac for cost-conscious users on the move, Apple's MacBook is the latest incarnation of a hugely popular line of go-anywhere laptops that combine sleek yet accessible looks with a robust build... coo over it or bounce it around in your rucksack, it's all one to the MacBook. Less than 3 cm thick and weighing just over 2 kg, the MacBook is available in black or white. Under the bonnet is the Intel Core 2 Duo processor, which can be specified in 2.0 GHz or 2.16 GHz configurations. Allied with either 1 Gb or 2 Gb of memory and a hard drive up to 160 Gb, the ultra-portable MacBook packs power enough for most applications. The 13.3-inch screen provides high resolution at 1280 × 800 and the machine will readily drive an external monitor when more is required.

All in the family 7

All in the family

Introduction

Say goodbye to the misery of computer downtime and
maintenance, the endless threat of viruses, trojans and
spyware, compromised security and kludgy networking: you're
a Mac user! Unlike PC owners, who must be ever ready to
wield a screwdriver or else delve deep into the software
innards of their machines, those who choose Apple computers
do so safe in the knowledge that whenever they put fingertips
to keyboard it'll be for the purpose intended: powerful
computing using innovative hardware, the very best system
software and a planet's worth of free stuff stirred in for good
measure. Hyperbole? You'd think. Free advertising for Apple?
Absolutely, but you'll soon come to realise that it's entirely
justified and wonder how you ever managed without your Mac.

With the concepts, help and step-by-step instructions detailed
in this book, your new computer will be productive straight
from the box. The Mac combines hardware and an operating
system created at the outset to work perfectly together rather
than bolted on as an afterthought with all the concomitant
difficulties, mismatches and incompatibilities that an
afterthought brings. It's a computer with a pedigree that
reaches back to the early 1980s when the Mac Plus
crystallised and refined a number of ideas – principally the
twin concepts of an all-in-one hardware platform driven by a
graphical user interface (GUI) or graphic operating system –
which had appeared in earlier computers from Apple such as
the Lisa, the Mac 128k and the Mac 512k (and yes, those
figures really do denote memory size!).

What you'll do

Meet each member of the Mac family

Learn about the Mac's specifications and hardware options

Discover the Mac's operating system OS X

Thrill to the knowledge (well...!) that the rock-steady standard Unix is the engine that drives the Mac

And despite losing its way a little in the early 1990s when it seemed like the PC would squeeze any other computer out of the marketplace, the Mac returned to prominence with innovative new hardware (such as the visually stunning iMac) and an operating system built on the rock-solid foundations of Unix. Today, Apple's Mac offers an unparalleled computing experience and, with the company's ongoing online support and updates, your machine will continue to do exactly what you want it to long after lesser computers have limped their way to landfill.

Which Apple you pick(ed) depends, it's reasonable to suppose, on your computing needs. Domestic users and homeworkers will probably plump for a Mac mini or an iMac, whereas users on the move will select from the MacBook range. Power users have at their disposal the Mac Pro but I'm guessing that if you count yourself in that category you won't need this book. Let's take a closer look at the Mac family for those yet to make a choice …

For your information

Apple's Mac suite features a machine for every need whether you're a complete novice or count yourself among the ranks of the computing elite. Briefly, the family features:

Mac mini – cute cube little more than 6 inches (16.5 cm) square, sporting an Intel Core 2 Duo processor, DVD burner, up to 2 Gb of memory and a 160 Gb hard drive

iMac – continues Apple's long-standing all-in-one ethic in a chic high-res 20- or 24-inch LCD screen, which also contains a powerful computer. Comes with a super-sleek keyboard and wireless mouse

Mac Pro – traditional tower arrangement packing a powerful punch with the Intel Xeon Quad-Core processor for users whose needs go beyond the everyday computing experience

MacBook – prêt-a-processing in a sleek yet robust housing that will cheerfully stand up to a ride home in your rucksack

MacBook Pro – on-the-move computing with extra processing punch

The Mac mini is the distillation of 20 years of Apple's working towards the perfect all-round all-in-one desktop computer. Where other machines require acres of desktop real estate and bellow their presence with annoying cooling fans, at just 16.5 cm square and 5 cm tall the whisper-quiet Mac mini is arguably the world's smallest fully fledged desktop computer. It's certainly the cutest – unsurprising because Apple has always valued the combination of innovation and powerful aesthetic appeal. And don't worry that small equates to poorly specified: even the base Mac mini boasts the latest in processor technology, an Intel Core 2 Duo central processing unit (CPU) offering blistering speed and the power to manipulate your favourite applications with ease, 1 Gb of memory, an 80 Gb hard drive, and a DVD player/CD burner 'Combo' drive. Those with slightly fatter bank balances can pack a mini with a 2 Gb processor, 2 Gb of memory, a 160 Gb hard drive and double-layer multiformat DVD burner, the 'SuperDrive' (which also burns CDs); all minis come with fast built-in wireless and wired networking, and Bluetooth. The machine also sports four USB 2.0 ports to connect peripherals such as memory sticks, your mobile phone, digital camera and so on, and a FireWire port for digital video and super-fast backup drive access.

Mac mini (cont.)

Although the Mac mini neatly packs all you'll need within its diminutive case you will need to add a monitor of some sort. Apple's own range of high-resolution LCD Cinema Displays (starting with a 20-inch screen perfect for home desktops) will cheerfully link with the mini, or you can choose from an enormous range of third-party offerings.

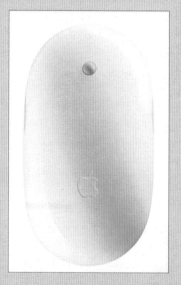

For your information

Time was when the humble mouse had a little rubber ball, which was forever getting snarled up with dirt, and a long trailing cable snaking around your desktop to connect it to the computer. Apple was among the first to do away with the rubber ball and rely on optical position recognition (essentially an LED, the light from which is collected by a sensor to detect *x-y* movement). Nowadays, Apple ships its computers with the Mighty Mouse, a ball-less but also Bluetooth-equipped wireless device featuring touch-sensitive right and left clicking, a touch-sensitive button for easy scrolling and squeezable sides for fast launching. It's the epitome of convenience and accuracy and, best of all, it's maintenance-free...

The iMac entirely captures the spirit of the very first all-in-one Macintosh computers such as the Mac Plus. With its built-in 20- or 24-inch LCD Cinema Display screen, which also houses the computer proper, its impossibly slender keyboard and fabulously ergonomic wireless Mighty Mouse, the iMac is a computer that's truly a joy to have on your desktop. Check the specs: in 20-inch guise, the iMac is just 46.9 cm high by 48.5 cm wide and 18.9 cm deep and weighs in at 9.1 kg.

At the heart of the iMac is the Intel Core 2 Duo processor running at 2 GHz or 2.4 GHz. The machine sports between 1 Gb and 4 Gb of memory and a hard drive between 250 Gb and 320 Gb as standard. There's also a SuperDrive optical disk burner. ATI Radeon high-resolution fast graphics cards are fitted as standard (in two guises, depending upon the iMac model).

Connectivity is provided by three USB 2.0 ports on the computer (plus two on the keyboard) and two FireWire ports.

Users with a need for raw computing power can choose an iMac with an Intel Core 2 Extreme processor running at 2.8 MHz and a hard drive with an incredible 1 Tb (i.e. one terabyte or 1024 Gb) capacity – ideal for intensive video and graphics applications.

All iMacs feature wired and wireless (AirPort Extreme) networking and enhanced data rate Bluetooth, an infra-red port, a built-in iSight camera for convenient image capture and a remote control handset.

Did you know?

Do you really need to know all these facts and figures? Does knowing the gigabyte rating of the hard drive or the megahertz rating of the processor really matter? After all, we're not talking PCs here, were talking Macs, built to match your expectations and needs – not the other way round. Short answer, then? No. Longish answer? Well, yes, but with a simple rule of thumb you can skip this chapter if you've already made a choice or simply couldn't care less: smaller numbers, cheaper computing, bigger numbers and faster, more powerful processing. Balance screen size against portability (or desktop space), memory and hard drive size against your likely applications, and – of course – price against what you can afford. But which ever machine you choose and what ever you throw at it, you can be sure your new Mac will handle the task well.

The Mac for cost-conscious users on the move, Apple's MacBook is the latest incarnation of a hugely popular line of go-anywhere laptops that combine sleek yet accessible looks with a robust build… coo over it or bounce it around in your rucksack, it's all one to the MacBook. Less than 3 cm thick and weighing just over 2 kg, the MacBook is available in black or white. Under the bonnet is the Intel Core 2 Duo processor, which can be specified in 2.0 GHz or 2.16 GHz configurations. Allied with either 1 Gb or 2 Gb of memory and a hard drive up to 160 Gb, the ultra-portable MacBook packs power enough for most applications. The 13.3-inch screen provides high resolution at 1280×800 and the machine will readily drive an external monitor when more is required.

MacBook
(cont.)

Depending on the model, burning is provided by the Apple Combo (CD) drive or SuperDrive (DVD and CD). All MacBooks feature wired and wireless networking, Bluetooth 2.0, an iSight camera, one FireWire 400 and two USB 2.0 ports.

For your information

Don't confuse memory with backing storage (that is, say, 4 Gb of RAM with 160 Gb of hard drive). What's the difference? Think of it this way: the memory in your head is like a computer's main memory (or RAM) and the notepad in your pocket equates to the computer's backing storage. The former is super-fast but limited and expensive; the latter is slow but relatively cheap and therefore plentiful. Although a small portion of the latter often substitutes for the former ('virtual memory'), nothing can aid speed and processing power like a large memory quotient. In a computer, memory is in the form of plug-in chips, whereas backing storage is the various drives (the hard drive, optical drives such as a CD, memory sticks and so on) that the machine can access.

The Mac laptop is for those with a requirement for desktop-like computing power and screen resolution. The basic MacBook Pro packs a 2.2-GHz Intel Core 2 Duo processor, 2 Gb of memory, a 15-inch screen, a 120 Gb hard drive and a SuperDrive for DVD burning. Choose the top-of-the-range model and you'll get a 17-inch screen behemoth with a 2.4-GHz processor, 4 Gb of memory and a 160 Gb hard drive.

All MacBooks offer excellent connectivity. There are two FireWire ports (400 and 800), up to three USB 2.0 ports, an ExpressCard/34 slot (the latest incarnation of the industry standard CardBus PC card), wired and AirPort Extreme wireless networking, and Bluetooth. All MacBook Pros sport highly respected NVIDIA GeForce graphics cards, external monitor ports and an iSight camera.

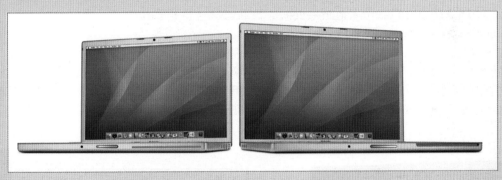

OS X

That's 'OS ten' not 'OS ex' by the way… OS X is Apple's Unix-based operating system comprising two layers: the underlying Unix foundation that you don't ordinarily see and the highly intuitive graphic interface that you do. Graphical OS interfaces have been around since the first computers climbed out of the primordial silicon soup, but few have bettered Apple's various renditions. Building on what he saw at PARC – the Palo Alto Research Center of copier company Xerox (where the R&D lab teams had invented the mouse, onscreen pointers, windows and the like), Apple boss Steve Jobs engineered his Apple II replacement, the Lisa, to enable it to become the first commercially available GUI-driven (graphic operating system) computer.

With an enormous price tag and operating concepts that went far beyond what ordinary users realised they might want, the Lisa remained on the shelves and became the prototype for Apple's next GUI outing, the Mac (initially sporting just 128 K of memory – a millionth of what the base machines ship with today). The computer in its various guises quickly built a huge following, which, despite a few wobbles in the mid-1990s, continues unabated to this day.

This early Apple GUI OS was known as the System and Finder (analogous to the underlying Unix and front-end graphics we see today) and continued in development from the early 1980s

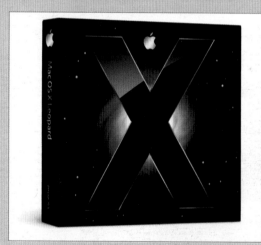

Did you know?

Notice how brand names are quoted (NVIDIA, ATi etc.) when graphics specs are mentioned? That's because, like the hard drive, DVD burner, memory chips and so on, the graphics chips (AKA 'cards') are made by leading developers in the field. Unlike unbranded, on-the-board graphics chips, branded cards use custom hardware and software algorithms to improve performance exponentially.

until around 2000, when Apple turned on to the Linux revolution (a non-commercial Unix-like operating system programmed and maintained by a worldwide army of users and enthusiasts – yes, geeks!), waved the System and Finder goodbye and embraced Unix in its stead (though the OS X desktop is still often called the Finder).

Apple's version of Unix is Darwin (Chapter 9 describes Darwin in detail and provides a handholding field trip for the uninitiated through its immense power). Together with Aqua, the GUI front end, the pair form OS X, arguably the best operating system on the planet. It is certainly the easiest to use and the most efficient in terms of power-to-resources quotient, and definitely the prettiest – exceptionally important when you have

to look at and manipulate the thing for any length of time! What's more, OS X is superstable, and you will never (well, almost!) see it crash … how's that for a pleasant computing experience?

See also

See the latest Macs and OS updates at **www.apple.com/uk**.

Did you know?

Each new release of Aqua is named after a big cat: Jaguar, Panther, Tiger and so on. The latest incarnation is Leopard (Aqua version 10.5).

Jargon buster

AirPort – Apple's take on the 802.11b/802.11g standard for wireless networking

Burning – the process of recording movies, music and data on to an optical disk such as a DVD or CD

Cache – special processor-only memory that 'remembers' recent operations, thereby improving processing efficiency

Hard drive – what's hard about it then? Difficult-to-understand drive? Inflexible drive? The epithet 'hard' hails from an age when flexible 'floppy' disks ruled the backing storage world because they were cheap and largely disposable. Hard drives had – yes, literally – inflexible disks and far greater capacity but phenomenally larger price tags

RAM – random access memory – a computer's memory chips

Welcome to the Finder

2

Introduction

As you learned at the end of Chapter 1, OS X comprises two parts: the underlying Unix that you don't see (but will later, when Chapter 9 teaches you how to manipulate it to good effect) and Aqua, the attractive GUI that you do see. In previous versions of Apple's operating system, those that predate OS X, the operating system and graphical front end were known as the System and Finder. Although not Unix-based, the System was the engine of the computer. It coordinated the screen display, spooled data to the hard drive, processed input from the keyboard and mouse, and managed all the other housekeeping tasks that turn a collection of electronic circuits into something tangible that you can work with. The Finder was the graphical front end, protecting you from the nitty-gritty of the System and enabling you to use applications, listen to music and surf the Internet without having to learn obscure commands.

Macs are now firmly in the twenty-first century OS-wise and use a stable and powerful version of Unix with the attractive Aqua, universally acknowledged as defining the best in GUIs. The concept of the Finder and the name remain an integral part of the user interface, providing, managing and facilitating your manipulating of the Desktop, the menus, the drive, application icons and so on. Think of it as a kind of interface to the operating system proper, the part of the OS you can see.

What you'll do

Meet the Finder and learn how to engage with it and return to it, whatever you're doing on the Mac

Learn basic Finder operations such as manipulating icons and windows

Set up basic system preferences to suit the way you like to organise your files and work

Discover how to restart and shut down the computer safely

Finder basics ▶

Shake hands with the Finder

1 The Desktop is your interface to the Finder. Think of it like your real-world desktop, which has the stuff that you need while working to hand: a pen pot, a notepad, a telephone and so on. From the Desktop you can manipulate system-level (computer stuff!) items such as windows and icons, view the contents of drives and initiate a network connection. This new version of Apple's OS X (10.5 AKA Leopard) sports a sleek new look that improves on what was already considered a leader in the field and many new features such as Spaces (Apple's take on the virtual desktops of the Linux world) and Stacks (a convenient and attractive way to display the contents of a folder).

2 This is the menu bar and to the left is the Apple menu, a staple of the Finder since its inception in the early 1980s. The Apple menu is the doorway to much-needed system functions and is always available, whatever you're doing on the computer. We'll look closer at the Apple menu and the other menus later in this chapter.

When you're working with an application such as a word processor and you want to copy a file from one location on the Mac to another, eject a CD or view the jobs in the print queue – i.e. perform a system-based task rather than an application-based one – the Finder is where you'll do it.

The Finder is up and running from switch-on and is always active in the background. You can return to the Finder at any time by clicking anywhere on the Desktop or selecting and clicking the Finder icon in the Dock (the smiling face at the far left).

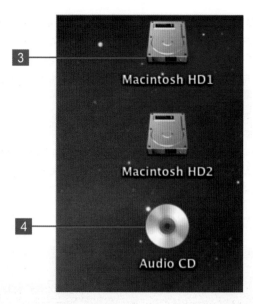

3 Unless you've moved it, this is the icon for the Mac's hard drive, the storage space for your applications and files, digital music, pictures, videos and so on.

4 Insert a CD, a memory stick or a DVD and its icon will appear at the right side of the Desktop alongside the hard drive icon.

At the foot of the screen is the Dock (though it can be relocated – you'll find out how on page 192), a kind of super-charged menu bar sporting a convenient and customisable selection of icons to provide access to your favourite applications and folders, the Finder itself (the Finder's icon is at the far left of the Dock), the Trash (US English for 'waste paper basket') where you dispose of the files you no longer want or need, and system functions such as the system preferences panel. Use the Dock to launch applications and switch between them on the fly.

Timesaver tip

Use the 'menu extras' at the right of the menu bar to get at-a-glance information such as battery life (for laptop users), speedy access to system settings such as the volume control, Bluetooth and AirPort settings, and functions such as Spotlight searches.

Finder basics
(cont.)

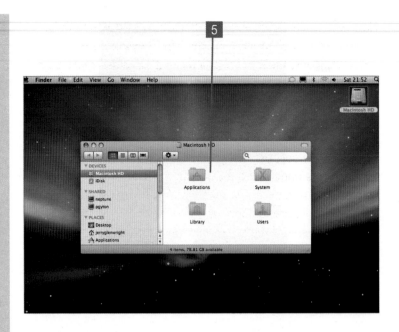

5 This is a Finder window – a snapshot of the available backing storage, your folders on the Mac's hard drive, the doorway to your Home folder and a Spotlight field for initiating a search for a file, folder, application or what have you on the Mac.

6 Windows have a number of controls, which you can use to resize, reposition, close, minimise and maximise them – more on this later.

Notice that you've met the fundamental elements of the Finder – windows, menus, icons and so on – but you're yet to see the Finder itself. In fact, it is these many elements and more which, together, constitute the concept that is the 'Finder'. When you work with the Finder you work with one or more of the elements that it's comprised of. The overall look and feel of the OS X GUI is Aqua, but manipulating its various elements is the process of working with the Finder…

For your information

Don't confuse the hard drive ('backing storage') with the computer's memory ('main' memory or 'RAM'), the short-term scratchpad that holds the stuff you're working on currently and the contents of which are lost when the Mac is shut down. Backing storage is the shoebox under the bed with your precious mementoes – your brain (main memory) might forget where the shoebox (backing storage) is, but its contents remain intact.

Time was when an introductory book to your new computer would have explained all about the WIMP system: the windows, icons, mouse and pointer that, together, make up a graphical user interface. Well, command-line-only computers have long since shuffled off to the silicon heaven that is landfill (though you can revive those halcyon days by turning to Chapter 9 and its explanation of Darwin, the Mac's Unix) and it's probably a safe bet that you've used a mouse previously and therefore understand the concept of moving an onscreen pointer, but possibly an explanation of windows and icons remains a valid proposition? If you've used Microsoft's Windows or one of the Linux desktops such as Gnome or KDE previously, you'll know that every user interface has its foibles. Mac OS X is no exception and, although all GUIs claim to be intuitive, faced with a screenful of 'clickables' it's easy to feel somewhat overwhelmed.

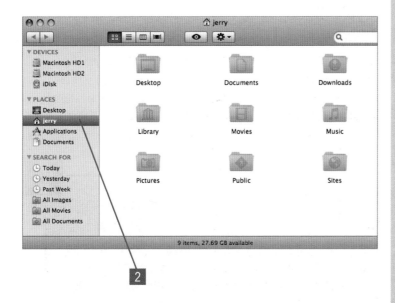

Open a window

1 That picture of a metal box in the upper right corner of your Desktop is the hard drive icon (for those who've never seen one before, that's kind of what the case of a hard drive would look like if you were to strip it from the machine). Direct your pointer to the hard drive icon and double-click it (i.e. press the mouse twice in quick succession ... but you know that, right?).

2 A Finder window opens on the Desktop showing (among other things) a list of folders and possibly files in the top-most level of the hard drive. To the left of the window is the Sidebar panel, window-based shortcuts to available drives, your favourite files, Home folders, applications and quickie searches. Under the Places heading in the Sidebar, click on your account name to see the contents of your Home folder. OS X organises folders into a standard Unix structure like this for your convenience, though you can customise it

Manipulating the Finder (cont.)

Did you know?

When Mac old hands refer to the Command key (as in 'press [Command] and [I]'), they mean the key to the left of the space bar that has both an Apple and a clover symbol on it. Similarly, the Option key is the one that has Alt and the 'squiggly line' symbol.

later when you become familiar with the Mac and how best you like to work. Notice how your account is now highlighted with a blue bar and the Finder window's title has changed to the name of your account…

3 In the upper part of the Sidebar panel a list of storage sources appears under the heading Devices: the hard drive and anything else inserted or attached such as a memory stick or CD. Below that is Shared (if your Mac is connected to a network) with a list of other computers you can communicate and share files with.

4 Click and drag (i.e. click the mouse, hold the click and drag the mouse) in the title bar or the information bar to reposition the window. Click and drag the resize grab handle to change its size.

5 Congratulations! You've survived your first encounter with icons and windows via the Finder.

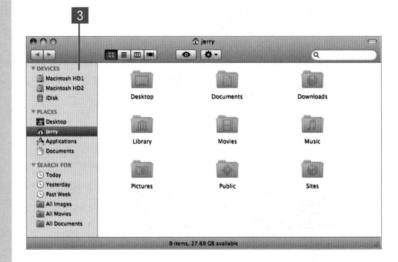

Timesaver tip

Keystroke Shortcuts:

Press [Command] and [N] while on the Desktop to open a Finder window on your Home folder

Press [Shift], [Command] and [N] while on the Desktop to create a new folder.

Budding power users might like to know that there are any number of keyboard shortcuts to replace mouse operations. For example: select the hard drive icon with a click and press [Command] + [I] to invoke the Get Info window. The Get Info shortcut works for any file or folder (in fact, any Finder entity).

Did you know?

Folders are stored in a tree-like structure. The first level is the root and branching from that are sub-folders, some of which are created and owned by OS X, and others by you. Your Home folder, for example, is a sub-folder branching from the Users folder that you can see in the top level of the hard drive window.

Contextual menus

1 [Control] and click (i.e. hold down the [Control] key as you single-click) the hard drive icon for a contextual menu of options associated with it. [Control] and clicking works like the right-click option on a two-button mouse.

2 For now, [Control] and click the hard drive and select Get Info from its contextual menu.

3 A window is displayed with information about the hard drive. Click the disclosure triangles to hide and reveal more or less of this information. From here, you can set permissions (determining who can gain access to your files), change the name of the drive and much else besides. We'll look closer at the important stuff later in the book.

4 Many OS X items have associated contextual menus, as do lots of applications – but not all.

Getting busy ▶

Positioning icons

1 To move an icon you click to select it and drag it to a new location, letting go of the mouse when the icon is where you want it ('drag and drop'). As you drag, the original remains in place while a transparent copy follows your mouse pointer.

2 You can move icons around the Desktop, clumping associated icons together, or put one or more into a folder. You can select multiple icons by 'lassoing' them. Click and hold on the Desktop slightly to the side of the first icon in what will be the selection. As you drag the mouse, a grey 'lasso' (box) will appear. Anything enclosed in this box when you let go of the click will be selected. Now click and drag any one of the selected icons to move them all.

3 You'll learn how to create new folders to store files later in this chapter.

Finder locates icons in predetermined areas of the screen – the hard drive, for example, will generally be displayed at the top right. Insert a CD or a DVD and it will appear at the right-hand side, as will files that you download and save to the Desktop. None of these icons is fixed, however, and you're at liberty to position them wherever and however you'd prefer.

Similarly, Finder windows have a number of buttons and other controls, some of which are highlighted as you scroll the mouse pointer over them. These buttons enable you to resize, reposition, close, minimise and maximise windows, toggle the Sidebar display, and generally customise your view of the files and folders displayed within.

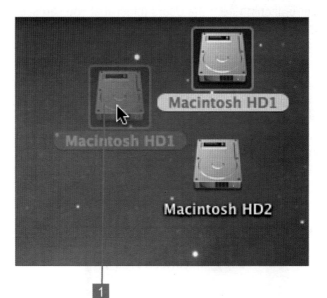

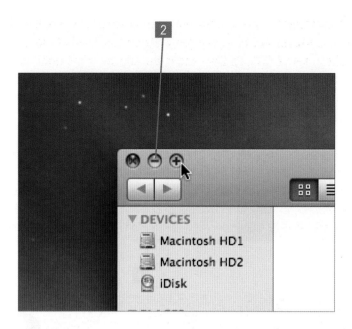

2

For your information

In List view, disclosure triangles are displayed alongside an entry in the list only when it contains nested items.

Manipulating windows

1 On the Desktop open a Finder window on your Home folder by pressing [Command] + [N]. The upper part of the window is called the title bar. [Command] and click the title in the title bar to reveal the file system path associated with the window. The title bar contains the toolbar, a Spotlight search field and traffic light buttons for closing and resizing the window. The toolbar icon enables you to navigate and customise the view of files and folders in the window.

2 Run your mouse pointer over each of the traffic light buttons in the upper left corner of the window. Each is highlighted with a symbol: x, – and +. Click the red button to close the window, the green button to toggle between two sizes, and the amber button to minimise the window, storing it temporarily in the Dock (click on it in the Dock to return it to the Desktop). You can also double-click in the toolbar area to minimise a window to the Dock.

Getting busy (cont.)

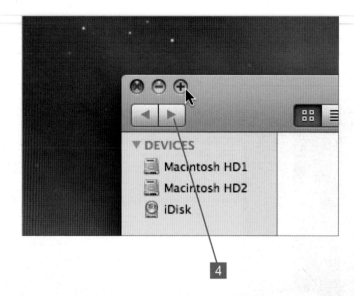

3 If you prefer an uncluttered window, use the toggle to switch the sidebar panel and toolbar on and off.

4 The back and forward buttons retrace your recent actions – they're greyed out (i.e. unavailable) when you first open a window (because you're yet to do anything). Double-click the Documents folder to open it. In effect, your position within OS X's folder hierarchy has changed to the Documents folder and you're viewing its contents. Notice that the back button is now available. Click it once to journey back a level in the folder structure (remember that it's organised like the roots of a tree) and return to your Home folder.

5 Now the forward button is available. Click it to move forward to the Documents folder again. Anyone who's used an Internet browser will find the back and forward buttons intuitive.

For your information

Select Show View Options from the Finder's View menu (or press [Command] and [J]) for a selection of customising options associated with the current window view type.

Window controls

1 The view controls switch between icons, a list, the column view, which shows the path to folders and files, and Cover Flow, which enables you to flip through a folder's documents in the same way as flipping through book covers or a CD collection.

2 List view is convenient when a folder contains many items. Use the disclosure triangles to display the contents of 'nested' folders (i.e. folders within folders).

3 Quick Look offers a super-convenient way to peek at a document without having to launch the application that created it or view information for a folder such as size and the number of items within it. Press [Command] + [Y] (or select Quick Look from the Action button) for a quick look. Use the resize handle to change the size of the Quick Look window or click the arrows to toggle full screen view. Click the close button (the cross) in the upper left to close Quick Look.

Important !

A path displayed in Column view is the route from one part of the file system (say, your Home folder) to an item somewhere else (say, a word processor document in a folder called Letters inside your Documents Folder, a path that might look like this: **Home>Documents> Letters>myfile.doc**. Each column to the right is a level further down the file system.

Getting busy (cont.)

4 The Action button provides a number of options associated with manipulating folders and files. Select a folder and click the Action button to reveal the options associated with it. You can Get Info or delete the folder ('Move to Trash'), make a copy ('Duplicate'), create a compressed archive ('Compress "filename"') or else change its colour to suit some organisational foible of your own. We'll examine some of these options in more detail in Chapter 3.

Use your Mac for any length of time and you'll accumulate a vast number of files, applications and other computer ephemera very quickly. Finding an item could be a nightmare, but not with Spotlight, the Mac's own search engine. To locate an item, enter its name into the search field. Almost immediately, Spotlight will display a list of matching items. Double-click to open or drag and drop the item, or use Quick Look for a preview. When you've finished searching, click the cross at the right of the field to return to window view.

Did you know?

You can customise the toolbar itself in a variety of ways including adding and removing shortcuts to your favourite files and folders – drag and drop a file or folder into a clear space on the toolbar.

Under Devices in the Sidebar you can see what backing storage is available to your Mac. Icons represent the hard drive, removable drives and any other data sources such as a memory stick. To view the contents of a memory stick, for example, click its icon in the Devices list. Its contents are displayed in the main window.

Customise the Sidebar by placing your most used applications, files or folders into the Places list. Select say, a file, and then drag and drop. As you drag, Finder highlights the Sidebar folders to indicate that dropping will place the item within that folder or else display a blue marker line to show that the shortcut will be created at that position.

You'll see something resembling a 'no entry' symbol when OS X won't allow you to drop a shortcut into a location that isn't suitable.

2

More windows (cont.)

Cover Flow is Leopard's funky new 3D window viewing option common to other Apple products such as the iPod and iPhone.

Managing the view with Cover Flow

1 Click the Cover Flow icon to switch to the new view. There are many ways to flick to and fro through the contents of a folder. You can use the slider bar at the foot of Cover Flow's display by clicking on the left and right arrows to move one item at a time. Click and hold to keep moving. You can also click and drag the slider left and right.

2 Alternatively, press the left or up arrow keys on the keyboard to flick left, or the right or down arrows to flick right.

3 When a cover appears that you want to access, double-click it to open it or launch the application that created it.

4 Press the [Return] key and Finder highlights the name of the item in the list below the Cover Flow window. Now you can type to change its name, pressing [Return] or [Escape] to rename the item or else retaining the original.

For your information

Remove an item from the Sidebar by dragging it. Release the mouse and the Finder displays a little puff of smoke to show that it's gone. However, only the shortcut is removed – not the actual file or folder that it represented.

For your information

Resize the Cover Flow window and the icons it displays with this grab handle. Move the mouse over it and the pointer changes to a hand. Click to grab and drag up or down to resize.

With two or three applications running at once and several windows open on the Desktop, it's entirely possible to become confused. Fortunately, OS X offers a simple solution, Exposé, which works in three modes: All Windows, Applications Windows and Desktop.

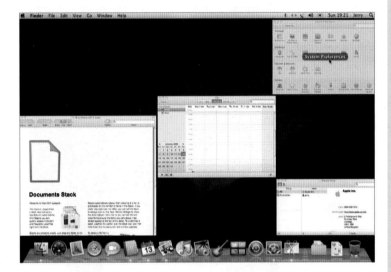

Whether you're at the Desktop or working within an application, press [F9] (i.e. the function key marked F9 on the keyboard) and Finder will reduce all the windows so that they fit together on the screen. Mouse over (move the mouse pointer over the item) any window to display its name, and then click to select. Press [F9] to close the All Windows view.

Timesaver tip

You can switch between windows in Exposé using the cursor (arrow) keys, and select by pressing [Return] or [Enter] on the keypad.

Managing windows with Exposé

2

1 To see only the windows associated with the active application, press [F10]. Move between and select windows as above. Press the [Tab] key to switch between the windows of running and inactive applications.

2 Press [F11] to hide all windows and reveal a clear Desktop. You can work at the Desktop as normal. Finder displays the shadowed edges of the hidden windows at the edge of the screen as a reminder. Press [F11] again to summon the windows.

3 Hold [Shift] when using the function keys and Exposé works in slow motion.

The menu bar

The concept of a menu bar is fundamental to graphical operating systems such as OS X, providing you with standard and application-specific menu options. The Finder's own menu bar provides controls for creating, manipulating and viewing files and folders, searching for and connecting to servers, acquiring system updates, restarting and shutting down the computer and much more...

Unlike previous versions of OS X, Leopard's menu bar is transparent – it's meant to look like that! When you launch an application, the menu bar remains available, though it's often extended and adapted to include options specific to the program you're using.

The Apple menu

1. The Apple menu is always available, regardless of whatever else is running, giving you access to important system functions. You'll see some of these options up close later in the book, but for now here's an overview of what's available...

2. Navigate to the Apple and click it to open the menu. The various options are grouped for similar functions. The first three give you information about your Mac and enable you to check for operating system updates and search the Apple website for downloadable goodies such as the latest versions of QuickTime and Safari.

3. Elsewhere on the Apple menu you can launch the System Preferences utility, see a list of recently accessed files, folders and applications, end an unresponsive application (Force Quit), put the machine to sleep if you plan to leave it for any length of time, restart, shut down or else log out and log back in to your own or another account.

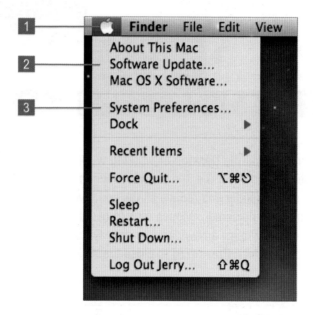

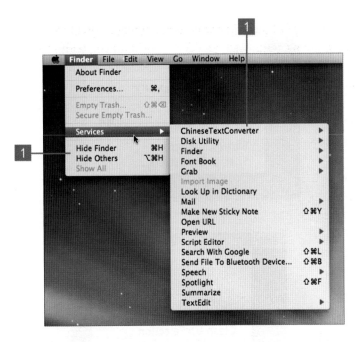

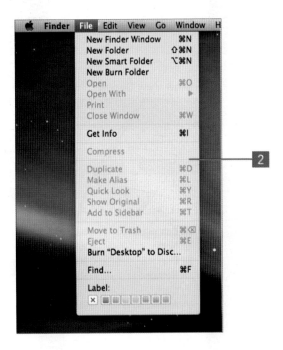

More menus

1 From the Finder menu you can set preferences that alter the appearance and behaviour of the Finder itself, empty the Trash (Secure Empty Trash overwrites deleted data to ensure they cannot be retrieved), or gain access to all kinds of useful system-level utilities from the Services menu (some of which you'll meet elsewhere). The Hide and Show features cause all open Finder windows to be cleared from the Desktop (select Hide Others or add the Option key to retain Finder windows while hiding applications windows).

2 The File menu provides access to common actions associated with files and folders. You can create a new folder, copy an item to the Sidebar or move it to the Trash (nothing is actually deleted until you select Empty Trash from the Finder menu). You can also eject a removable device such as a CD or memory stick or burn an optical disk (CD or DVD, depending on your Mac's hardware).

The menu bar (cont.)

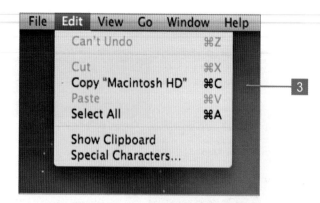

3 As a novice, one of the most useful features of the Edit menu is the Undo option. Use it to reverse typing and deleting blunders within applications or else reverse Finder actions such as returning a file or folder to its original location or undoing a renamed item. Elsewhere on the Edit menu you can select, cut, copy and paste text or a picture from one application or Finder location to another via the Clipboard (a holding place for cut and copied items).

4 Use the View menu to choose the way files and folders are organised. The Show Path Bar option adds a path display to the information bar in a Finder window (switch it off with Hide Path Bar). You can also access a number of Desktop customising options from the View menu via the Show View Options menu entry.

5 The Go menu is an aid to navigation offering direct routes to your Home folder, the Applications folder, other computers if your computer is attached to a network, iDisks (for those with .Mac accounts – more in Chapter 7) and so on.

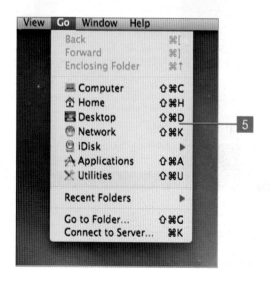

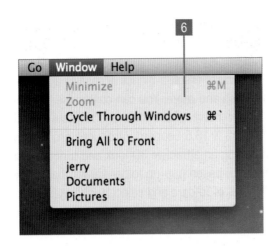

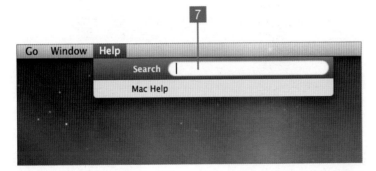

2

6 Using the Window menu you can switch between open windows on the Desktop, zoom (like the + traffic light toggle) and minimise a window to the Dock.

7 Use the Help menu to search for information about a feature of the computer or OS X that has you stumped or else select Mac Help to view an overview.

8 How (or whether) you use any or all of these menu bar options, combine them with navigational and editing shortcuts from other parts of the Finder or use them exclusively depends entirely on how you prefer to work. Most of the options feature keyboard shortcuts and, as you grow familiar with your Mac, you'll develop an operating style that's all your own.

For your information

Depending on whether there are several user accounts on your Mac or just yours, you may be required to log in after starting or restarting the machine. If only you have an account (and unless instructed otherwise), the Mac will start up direct to the Desktop, ready to work.

Important

You can check for system software updates by clicking the option under the Apple menu, but don't worry if you forget: by default, OS X makes periodic checks when your Mac is connected to the Internet.

The Dock

The Dock is one of the most appealing features of OS X, hugely useful for those new to computing and a speedy and intuitive starting point for anyone switching from another operating system. The Dock offers at-a-glance access to applications, folders, the Trash and more. You can customise the Dock, add your own stuff, remove what's there and relocate it on the Desktop. And OS X 10.5 Leopard introduces groovy new features including an attractive 3D look and functions such as Stacks, the Dock-based pop-up folder viewer that enables you to see the contents of folders and select documents without your having to navigate to them via layers of windows in the Finder.

Meet the Dock

1 Switch on your new Mac for the first time and there, at the foot of the Desktop, is the Dock, a 3D strip of colourful icons sitting on a shiny metal platform that extends 'backwards' into the screen. The Dock is a control centre that works as an application launcher and switcher and provides a shortcut to your folders and files. It's also home to the Trash and utilities such as System Preferences.

2 Additionally, there's Dashboard, which manages of widgets, mini pop-up applications offering everything from a calculator and clock to a flight tracker and movie clip previewer.

3 Whatever you're working with on the Mac, the Dock is always available.

OS X populates the Dock with what Apple believes is a representative selection of applications and utilities that you'll want to use 'out of the box' as it were. There's Safari, Mail and iChat for Web browsing, downloading and managing email, and talking online (more in Chapter 7), the universally popular music player iTunes, an address book and calendar (all featured in detail in Chapter 5), utilities such as Preview for viewing everything from a digital picture to a PDF document, access to the System Preferences accessory and Time Machine, the OS X backup utility. If your Mac shipped with the Apple applications suite iLife 08 preinstalled, you'll also see iMovie, iPhoto, iWeb, iDVD and GarageBand in the Dock.

Timesaver tip

Click and hold Dock icons to summon a contextual menu with shortcuts to associated files and options for hiding and quitting.

For your information

The names of items in the Dock are displayed as you mouse over them.

Working with the Dock

1 To launch an application from the Dock move your mouse pointer to an icon and click it once. The icon bounces up and down to indicate that it's launching and the application opens. You'll also see this icon bounce feature when an application running in the background wants your attention. Just click the bouncing icon to switch to the application.

2 The Finder places a small shiny marker beneath Dock icons of running applications.

3 Launch applications and switch between them by clicking the one you want in the Dock. Unix's efficient memory management means that you can open lots of applications and switch between them at will.

Universal Access

The Mac is designed to be easy and intuitive for all users. People with aural or visual impairments, or difficulties in using the keyboard or mouse can access a range of options (Applespeak: 'assistive technology') to help them with using the computer.

The easier option

1. Select System Preferences... from the Apple menu or click the System Preferences icon in the Dock.

2. Click the Universal Access icon in the System Preferences panel.

3. Tabs at the top of the panel give access to assistance with Seeing, Hearing, Keyboard, Mouse and Trackpad.

4. The Seeing tab enables you to zoom the screen, adjust the contrast and toggle white-on-black and greyscale displays. You can also turn on the text-to-voice utility VoiceOver.

5. From the Hearing tab you can swap visual feedback for alerts and the like usually associated with audio.

6. The Keyboard tab provides help for anyone who experiences difficulty in repeating or combining key presses.

7. Use the Mouse and Trackpad tab to substitute key presses for mouse clicks and scrolling and dragging actions and to increase the size of the mouse pointer.

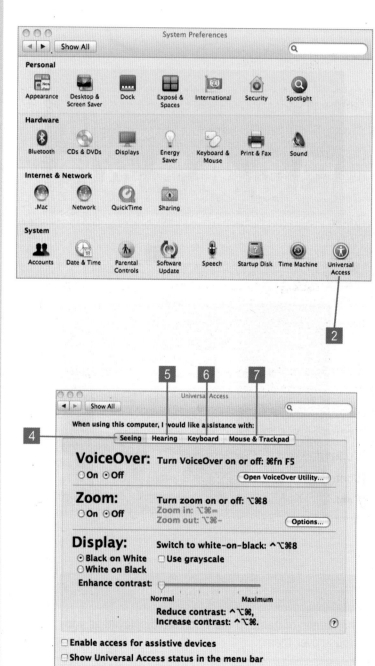

Timesaver tip

Keyboard shortcuts for Universal Access options:

[Option], [Command] and [8] – Turn on Zoom

[Option],[Command] and [+] – (plus) Zoom in

[Option], [Command] and [–] – (minus) Zoom out

[Control], [Option], [Command] and [8] – Switch to White on Black

[Control] and [F1] – Turn on Full Keyboard Access

When Full Keyboard Access is turned on, you can use the key combinations listed below from the Finder:

[Control] and [F2] – Highlight Menu

[Control] and [F3] – Highlight Dock

[Control] and [F4] – Highlight Window (active) or the window behind it

[Control] and [F5] – Highlight Toolbar

[Control] and [F6] – Highlight Utility window (palette)

[Command] and [F5] – Toggle VoiceOver

[Control], [Option] and [F8] – Open the VoiceOver Utility

[Control], [Option] and [F7] – Display VoiceOver menu

Talk to me

2

1 Enable the VoiceOver utility and your Mac will talk to you.

2 From the Seeing tab on the Universal Access Preferences, click the On button for VoiceOver (or press [Command] + [F5]) then click the Open VoiceOver Utility... tab to customise the way in which VoiceOver works.

3 Everything from a login greeting to the rate, pitch and volume of the available voices can be changed to accommodate your needs.

Fonts and Font Book

The Mac has always been blessed with excellent font capabilities – one of the reasons why the machine led the desktop publishing revolution in the 1980s – and the current family is no exception. OS X 10.5 Leopard ships with a large selection of fonts that you can readily use to style your word-processed documents, presentations, iApps projects and so on.

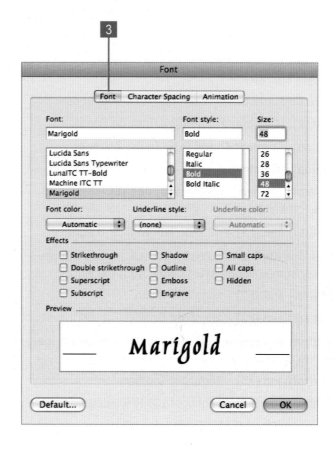

1 Fonts are stored in the various Libraries – yours (`Home>Library>Fonts`) where you add more fonts acquired from say, the Web, and the system's (`Macintosh HD>Library>Fonts`), which contains those fonts shipped with OS X and available to all users of the computer.

2 To view and manipulate fonts you use the Fonts panel available from the menu bar (standard across all applications that run under OS X) and Font Book, the system utility for organising fonts. It's stored in the Applications folder.

3 To choose a font family, style, size and colour, select Font from the Format menu within an application.

4 Familiarity with fonts breeds an ever-growing desire to collect more – and there's nowhere better to acquire them than the Internet (use your favourite search engine). Commercial fonts are vigorously protected by copyright law but there are

plenty of useful, interesting and fun font families available for free too.

5 To install a font that you've downloaded, click it on the Desktop. OS X launches Font Book. Click the Install Font button on the preview window to install the font in the Fonts folder in your Home Library.

6 With lots of fonts, you can gather them together into favourite collections or those specific to a particular project.

7 Click the Add button below the Font Book Collection column and type a name for the new collection. Click All Fonts at the head of the Collection column and drag and drop the fonts you want to the new collection.

Jargon buster

Font – (AKA typeface), the alphanumeric and other characters displayed on the computer's screen (and reproduced on a printer) in a variety of shapes (known as 'families', such as Futura, Gill, Din and so on), sizes and styles. The size of a font character is measured in points (and known as the 'point size'), 72 of which make an inch (e.g. Helvetica Bold, 12 point, italic).

Restart and shut down

Modern computers don't like to be switched off without you first performing a number of housekeeping tasks associated with cleaning up memory, closing user and system files and so on. The Mac is no exception and was the first computer to make switching off a menu option rather than requiring its users to scrabble for an off switch. You can also put the Mac into a power-saving Sleep mode or else restart it following system updates and software installation.

Put the Mac to sleep

1. Sleep mode puts your Mac into hibernation. The display and drives are shut down and the CPU runs at a tickover, saving power while remaining ready to work at the touch of a key or click of the mouse. Use Sleep mode if you plan to be away from your Mac for any length of time.

2. From the Apple menu select Sleep. There's no need to close applications, though it's probably a good idea to save open documents before entering Sleep mode.

3. If your Mac has a power light, it will gently pulsate after a few moments, simulating the relaxed breathing of sleeping.

4. Wake your Mac by pressing a key or clicking the mouse or trackpad. The Mac will recover and operate exactly as it was before sleeping. Your applications are ready to use and you can continue as before.

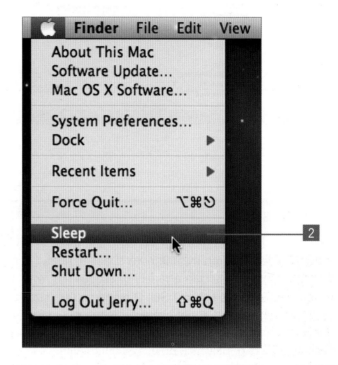

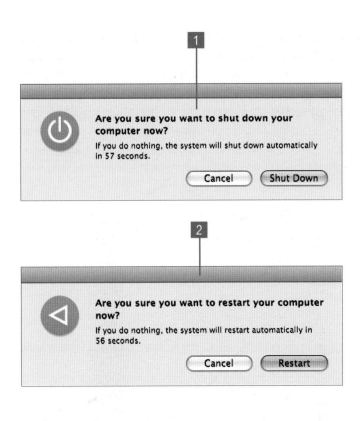

Shutting down

1 When you've finished computing, select Shut Down... from the Apple menu. Finder displays a warning dialogue for confirmation. You can elect to cancel the operation, do nothing (in which case the machine will switch off after two minutes), or else click the Shut Down button on the dialogue and the Mac will perform its housekeeping and, after a few moments, power down.

2 Use the Restart option when you want to reboot the system – cause it to start up afresh but without actually cycling the power.

3 Installing some software packages and system updates requires a restart. The function clears the Mac's memory and returns it to virgin state.

Important

Although you don't have to save your work and close applications before sleeping, restarting or shutting down it's a good idea: the Mac will prompt you to save before a restart or shutdown.

Timesaver tip

If you're using a Mac laptop, press the power button briefly and the Mac will ask whether you want to restart, shut down or put the machine to sleep.

Files and folders

Introduction

The stuff of computing is information. Word-processed documents, pictures, emails to friends, spreadsheets for your work and domestic finances, kids' homework, movies and music… it's all there as files on your computer and it's as real to you as anything you can hold in your hand.

Time was when backing storage totalling 20 Mb would be thought large, but today's terabyte behemoths offering a capacity greater by a factor of millions can store truly masses of data – your stuff. Combine that with the thousands of semi-visible system files and the possibility of having lots of users with accounts on the machine, all of which must be kept separate and secure, and you can see that the Mac has its work cut out managing everything. What's required is a strategy for data organisation and the Mac's – the Unix file system in the form of Apple's Darwin – is arguably the best available.

The Unix file system is rigidly organised. After a clean install of OS X (or when you first switch on your new Mac) there are a number of folders, some of which – System, Library and Users – are a necessary part of the underlying Unix. Others – Movies, Pictures and so on – are there to help you organise your stuff. You can use them as is or create new folders to suit your needs.

Finally, don't equate rigidity with inflexibility. Your Mac is as flexible in the way it will organise and store your data as any computer available and hugely more than most.

What you'll do

Learn about the OS X file and folder structure and how the system organises information

Create, copy, move, name and delete files and folders

Perform simple and complex searches

Compress and archive files and folders

Create and use Stacks on the Dock

The tree house

▶

The OS X file system – the files and folders that make up data, applications, music files, video clips and so on – are organised in a tree root-like structure with, at ground level (called the 'root'), four standard folders named Applications, Library, System and Users. Everything else (visible to you) branches off these four. There's a detailed explanation of the invisible Unix folders and file system in Chapter 9.

The OS X folders

1 The Applications folder is where programs installed on your Mac are stored. On the Desktop, open a Finder window (press [Command] + [N]) and double-click Applications in the Sidebar to open the folder.

2 Applications is already filled with programs such as Dictionary, DVD Player, iTunes and so on – the programs bundled free with your Mac. Any other applications you install – an image editing suite, perhaps – will also be located within the Applications folder.

3 There are several Library folders. At the root level, the Library is owned and maintained by OS X and contains system-wide applications support files, fonts available to all users, data caches and other essentials that wise users (especially novices!) steer well clear of. There's also a Library folder in your Home folder, which can contain fonts and certain other data accessible only to you.

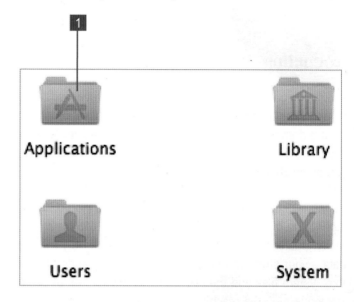

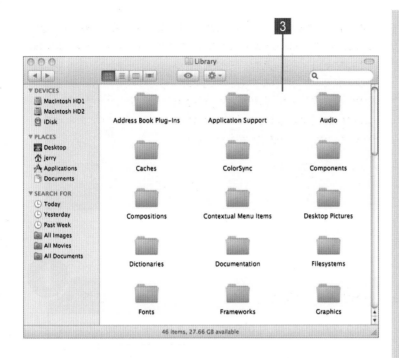

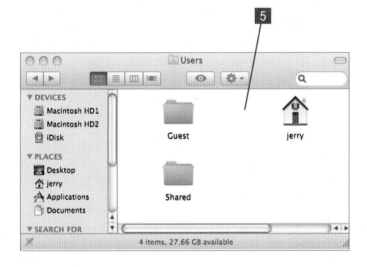

4 The System folder contains OS X itself and Darwin, Mac's Unix, and is best left well alone. Don't put anything into the System folder and don't take anything out of it.

5 The Users folder contains the personal workspaces of all the users with accounts on the Mac. If you're the only user there'll be just two or three folders inside: yours, denoted in lower case by the short name you entered when you created your account, Shared, a kind of open access workspace for any user (useful for swapping files between otherwise secure accounts) and Guest (if the Guest account is switched on.

6 These folders – Applications, System, Library and Users – are the Aqua representation of the underlying fixed Unix file system. There are many more but they're necessarily invisible to you – at least until you learn how to manipulate the machine from the Unix command line. For those users entirely uninterested in the nitty-gritty, however, there's really no need to move beyond the visible.

The tree house (cont.)

But what are folders for?

1. Folders contain and organise your files. And what are files? The documents, pictures, music, movies and any other data stored on your Mac.

2. Folders are created for you to store and organise files. Files are created when you use an application such as a word processor or a digital video editing suite, acquire downloads from the Internet, or upload pictures from your digital camera or iPod.

Important

If you have an administrator user account on your Mac (and you will if you're the only user) you have access privileges to move, copy and even delete essential system files from the System and Library folders. Be careful: what you move or delete could result in your Mac not working as expected or even at all...

For your information

Also contained in Applications is a folder called Utilities with many useful mini-applications for manipulating and repairing disks, calibrating the display, capturing a podcast and so on. We'll meet some of these utilities in later chapters.

Fundamental to the OS X and Unix experience is your Home folder. This is your personal space on the Mac and where the machine directs you after logging in. It's where you put your files and folders – even files placed on the Desktop are actually stored in a folder called 'Desktop' inside your Home folder.

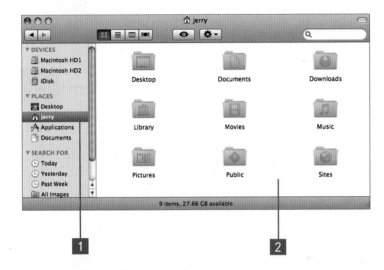

A Home from home

3

Timesaver tip

Press [Shift], [Command] and [H] from the Finder to open your Home folder at any time.

A Home from home (cont.)

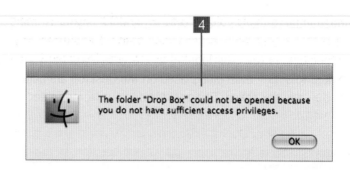

4

The folder "Drop Box" could not be opened because you do not have sufficient access privileges.

OK

3. Alongside these four are five other folders associated with your account on the Mac: the Desktop folder, which contains the items you see on the Desktop; the Library, which, rather like the Library at the Mac's root level, contains system-level data such as fonts and support files for applications, but which apply only to you; Downloads, a store for data from the Internet and other sources; the Sites folder, containing files associated with sharing data over a network using the same special protocols as the Internet; and the Public folder, a conduit for file sharing. The Public folder is a place for files that you want to share with other users who log into your machine or else connect to it across a network. These users can see the contents of your Public folder and can copy items from it.

4. Inside the Public folder is the Drop Box, a kind of one-way letterbox. Other users can put items in your Drop Box, but only you can view and manipulate them afterwards.

Jargon buster

Protocol – the word used to describe the way in which two or more computers connect and exchange information – if both are operating with the same protocols, data exchange is possible.

For your information

Log in as a different user and you'll see a Desktop that is nothing like yours, especially if you've used the Mac for a while and have files, folders and other stuff scattered about – each Desktop is unique to the user, hence the Desktop folder.

Alongside the existing folders created by OS X, you can create your own, naming them to meet your needs, and storing and manipulating them at will to suit the way you like to work. You can create new folders on the Desktop, within your Home folder or nested within any other folders in your Home folder – you might, for example, choose to create a folder called Letters located within your Documents folder or Holiday Pics Summer 08 in the Pictures folder.

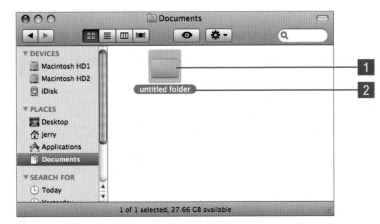

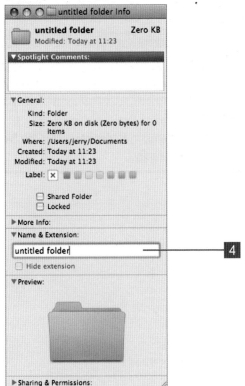

Making and naming new folders

1 Open a Finder window with [Command] + [N], click the Documents shortcut in the Sidebar and press [Shift], [Command] + [N] to create a new blank folder in the Documents folder. You can also select New Folder from the File menu in the menu bar.

2 A new folder icon appears in the window with the name untitled folder enclosed by a blue frame. This indicates that you can type a name for the folder immediately without having to select it. Name it My Test Folder and press [Return].

3 The folder is renamed. If you change your mind about the name, click it and pause for a moment. The blue frame appears again and you can overtype the existing name to rename it.

4 You can also rename a folder or file in the Get Info window. Click the item to select it and press [Command] + [I]. When the window appears click the Name & Extension disclosure triangle to reveal the name field and type over what's there. When you close the window the item is renamed.

3

Working with files and folders (cont.)

Moving files and folders

1 You move files and folders much as you would move any Finder icon: by drag and drop.

2 As you drag, a ghosted outline of the item follows the mouse pointer. When it's where you want it, drop to relocate.

3 Lasso or Shift-click to select multiple items. To select all the items in the window press [Command] + [A] (or choose Select All from the Finder menu). Click an icon again to deselect it.

4 After selecting multiple items, you can deselect one or more by holding down the [Command] key and clicking the item.

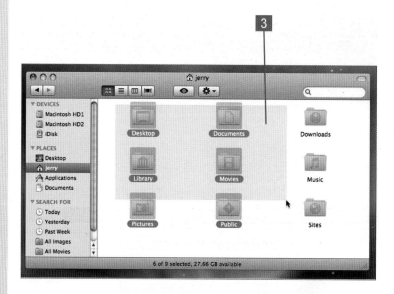

Timesaver tip

Drag and drop items to folder names in the Sidebar to relocate them instantly.

Spring-loaded folders

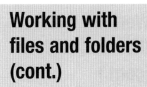

1 The Mac features 'spring-loaded' folders. Drag an item over a folder, pause for a moment and the folder flashes and then springs open.

2 When it opens, drop the item you're moving to relocate it or else hover over another folder to activate the spring and open it. You can continue to open spring-loaded nested folders in this way until you reach a destination for the item.

3 Change your mind while holding and dragging and you can move back to the source level by dragging over the original folder window (sounds harder than it is!).

4 Spring-loaded opening works with Sidebar items too. Drag and hold to a folder or volume in the Sidebar until it springs open and then drop the item in the window to relocate it (or else drag the item over another folder in the window to open it and so on).

3

Jargon buster

Volume – An attached drive such as the Mac's internal hard drive, a shared network drive, a pen drive and so on.

Did you know?

If you can't see all the items you want to select in order to lasso them, you can [Shift] and click them one after another instead.

For your information

If you meant to open a window with [Command] and [N] but created a new folder with [Shift], [Command] and [N] by mistake, press [Command] and [Z] to undo the new folder action (you can also select the option from the Edit menu on the Finder menu bar). Reinstate the folder by repeating the command.

Working with files and folders (cont.)

Opening files

1 To open a file, say a word processor file for editing, double-click it. If it's not already running, OS X will launch the appropriate application and open the file. Selecting with a single click and pressing [Command] + [O] (for open) gets the same result. If there's no associated application for the file (when you've downloaded an item from the Internet, for example), Finder will prompt you to search through a list of likely candidates and you can select the most suitable.

2 You can also drag and drop a file onto the icon of the application that created it, either in the Dock or in the Applications window to launch the application and open the file.

3 To open multiple items, select by lassoing or Shift-clicking them and then drag and drop on the application icon. After selecting, you can also press [Command] + [O] to open them.

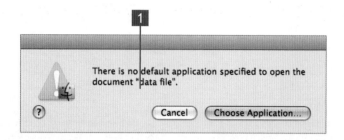

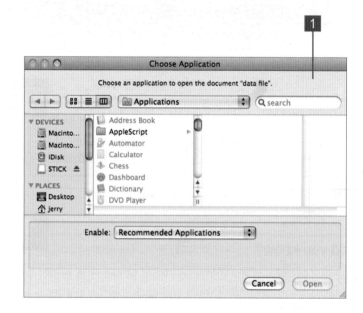

Fast file opening using filetype associations is the Mac's forte, but sometimes even that process is cumbersome – you might prefer a quick peek at a file without having to open it. Fortunately, with Quick Look (new for OS X 10.5 Leopard) you can – here's how …

Quick Look is a new tool available from the Finder toolbar. You can peek into virtually anything on your Mac… folders, text and image files – even movies!

If you have a file associated with one application that you'd prefer to open with another – you might want to open a plain text file in a word processor to apply complex formatting, for example – [Control] and click to invoke the contextual menu and then choose an application from the Open With… list. If the program that you want isn't listed, click Other… and the Choose Application will appear. Navigate to the program and select it.

Peeking with Quick Look

1 Navigate to a file whose contents you'd like to look at. You can choose a file on the Desktop or else open a Finder window.

2 Select the file and press the [Spacebar]. A preview is displayed.

3 Toggle windowed and full-screen viewing using the arrows button.

4 You can also zoom PDFs and images. For a PDF, select it and press [Command] + [=] (i.e. [Command] + [equals]) to zoom in and [Command] + [–] ([Command] + [minus]) to zoom out. To zoom an image, [Option] and click the image to zoom in and [Shift], [Option] and click to zoom out.

5 Use the resize handle to alter the size of the Quick Look window and click the close button to close Quick Look and return to the Finder.

3

Working with files and folders (cont.)

Viewing files with Preview

1 Preview is an OS X application for viewing PDFs, digital images and certain other files (such as digital faxes) without having to install or use dedicated software. Preview is located in the Applications folder. Claimed to be the fastest PDF viewer available, Preview is certainly speedy and offers many convenient tools for manipulating files. You can convert between image formats (BMP to JPEG, for example), resize, crop and rotate images, search for text in a PDF and select, copy and paste text elsewhere via the Clipboard. You can even mark PDFs with electronic 'stickies'. Preview is a true rarity in the computing world: compact, fast and capable, no fuss and a genuine delight to use.

2 Unless you install third-party applications that reassign file associations, PDFs and many other file types are associated with Preview by default. To open a document or an image with the application, double-click it. Preview will open and display the item.

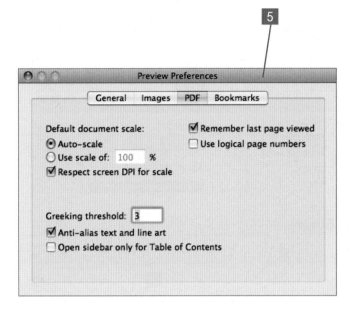

3 It's easy to use Preview to view an item that isn't associated by default. Open Preview and then select Open… from the File menu (or press [Command] + [O]). Navigate to the item and Preview will open it.

4 You can convert between file types using the Save As… option from Preview's File menu. Choose a file type from the pop-up Format menu and click the Save button.

5 Preview can be customised to suit your viewing preferences. Choose the Preferences option from the Preview menu. Other options (how PDFs are displayed, for example) can be selected from the View menu.

Working with files and folders (cont.)

Copying items

1. You can duplicate any item, including applications. Duplicate a folder and a copy is created, complete with everything that the source folder contained (including nested folders).

2. Click to select an item and choose Duplicate from the File menu or press [Command] + [D]. A duplicate is created in the same location. OS X appends 'copy' to the duplicate name.

3. Rename, drag and drop the copy as necessary.

4. Alternatively, click and drag an item while pressing the Option key. You'll see a green plus symbol over the ghosted copy. Drag to a suitable destination (the Desktop, say, or a folder) and release to make a copy. The Finder appends a number (two, if this is the first copy) to the file name.

5. You can also use the copy and paste options from the Edit menu to duplicate a folder. Click the target and select Copy from the Edit menu on the menu bar, or press [Command] + [C].

6. Navigate to the location for the duplicate folder and select Paste from the Edit menu or press [Command] + [V]. Note: OS X doesn't append the word 'copy' to the duplicate's name if you copy and paste.

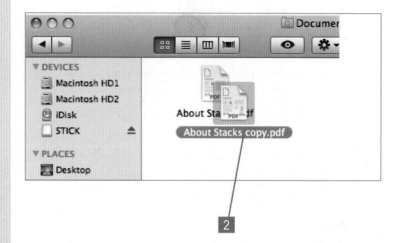

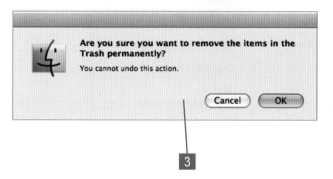

Are you sure you want to remove the items in the Trash permanently?

You cannot undo this action.

Cancel   OK

Deleting items

1 To delete an item, select it and drag and drop to the Trash on the Dock.

2 The Trash acts as a holding area for unwanted items – nothing is deleted until you select Empty Trash on the Finder menu or press [Shift], [Command] + [Backspace].

3 Empty the Trash and the Finder asks you for confirmation. You can sidestep the warning by holding down the Option key while selecting Empty Trash or press [Shift], [Option], [Command] + [Backspace] (easier than it sounds!)

4 OS X offers a secure delete option for removing sensitive files. Select Secure Empty Trash from the Finder menu and OS X writes random data over the locations on the hard drive that once stored your deleted file. This ensures that not a fragment of the original data remains.

5 You can open the Trash just like a folder window. To retrieve an item from the Trash, mouse over the Dock and click the Trash to open its window. Drag out items you want to retain.

See also

You can control the Trash from the Unix command line via Terminal to clear stubborn files that can't be deleted – turn to Chapter 9 for more on this.

Important

Unlike some other operating systems and partly because of the way in which Unix manages its file system, items emptied from the Trash are exceedingly difficult to rescue – even if you don't use the secure delete option. Be absolutely sure that you really do want to remove items before taking out the trash…

Working with files and folders (cont.)

Working with aliases

An alias is a shortcut to a file, folder or application on your Mac. Aliases use little disk space and you can create any number for an item, locating them to suit your needs for easy access to the original.

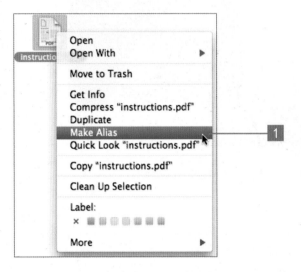

1 To create an alias click an item and press [Command] + [L] (or choose Make Alias from the File menu, or [Control] and click the item to summon a contextual menu and choose Make Alias). The shortcut is created with the word 'alias' appended to the original name. You can rename and relocate the alias – drag it to the Desktop, for example.

2 To create an alias and relocate it at the same time, [Option] + [Command] and click (i.e. hold-down the [Option] and [Command] keys while you click), drag and drop the item to your chosen destination.

3 You can easily find the original by [Control] and clicking an alias and choosing Show Original from the contextual menu.

For your information

Occasionally you'll encounter difficulties when dragging a file to the Trash ... troublesome files that, for no obvious reason, can't be trashed. The commonest of these problems is the 'file in use' error. Finder warns that a file cannot be deleted because it is in use by an application (even though you know you've closed the file). The problem is to do with a system of indicators (AKA 'flags') set by the operating system to sidestep the potential for having a file opened and edited concurrently leading to corruption and disaster. Some applications forget to clear the 'file in use' flag and the system becomes confused. If it happens and you're sure that the file is closed, exit the application and try again. Occasionally a system restart helps.

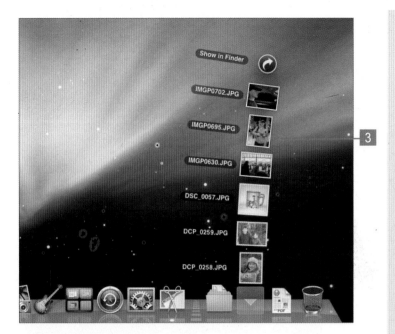

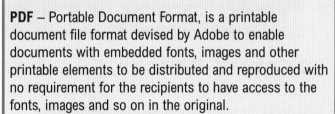

Viewing folder contents with Stacks

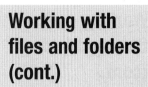

1 Stacks (new in OS X 10.5 Leopard) is the latest way to organise items for swift access. A folder of items located in the Dock will spring open with a stacking or grid effect when you click it, enabling you to see and choose exactly what you're looking for with ease.

2 OS X places default stacks for your Downloads and Documents folders in the Dock to get you started. Attachments from Mail and files from Safari and iChat are automatically saved to the downloads stack – you'll see it bouncing in the Dock when an item is added. Click the stack and the new item is at the top.

3 To create a stack select a folder (or make a new one) with the files you would like in the stack and drag and drop it to the right of the divider bar in the Dock.

3

Jargon buster

PDF – Portable Document Format, is a printable document file format devised by Adobe to enable documents with embedded fonts, images and other printable elements to be distributed and reproduced with no requirement for the recipients to have access to the fonts, images and so on in the original.

Timesaver tip

Keyboard shortcuts such as [Command] and [O] (open), [Command] and [C] and [Command] and [V] (copy and paste), and [Command] and [A] (select all) are common to almost every Mac operation – whether you're working in the Finder or in an application, you'll find that these standard keyboard shortcuts work as expected.

Working with files and folders (cont.)

4 Access the stack by clicking it. When it opens, choose an item with a single-click to open it in the Finder. If the item is a file the Finder will open a suitable application to view or manipulate it. Click the Open in Finder button to open the stack as a Finder window.

5 A stack with lots of files will open as a grid, but you can also customise stacks to set grid display as the default if you prefer. Click and hold the stack for a contextual menu and select Grid from the View As menu option.

6 Using the contextual menu you can choose other options too, such as how the contents of the stack are sorted.

Years ago, when storage space was at a premium and a floppy disk – a recordable piece of flexible plastic in a hard plastic shell with 1 Mb of space (compare with a CD at 700 Mb) was the only removable media available – archiving and compression were not only hugely popular but also super-important. Using a mathematical algorithm, it was possible to 'squeeze' a file such that the space it required for storage was reduced significantly. What's more, it was possible to gather together a number of files into one compressed archive – all the files in a folder, for example – and then retrieve one or more from the archive when required.

Although popular, compression was at best a workaround. The process is generally slow: you couldn't really compress all the files on your hard drive on the fly (a number of methods to do just that were available but none of them met with any great take-up) and so an archive was just that – a way to back up, save and possibly transmit over a network files that would otherwise require lots of space or else an enormous amount of time to send.

Weirdly, given that a terabyte of backing storage is available to users with all but the meanest of budgets, archiving and compression are still popular. Especially when sending files as email attachments, archiving saves time and resources. What's more, there are now many file formats – JPEG and MP3, for example – that use advanced archive techniques for on-the-fly compression.

The de facto standard for compression on the Mac was, for a considerable time, Stuffit, devised in 1987 by Raymond Lau, a high-school student from New York. The standard in the PC world (and, therefore, *the* standard) is the ZIP, an archiving method created by Phil Katz and used with his PKZIP utility. OS X also offers standard archivers from the Unix world, such as gzip and tar.

Occasionally, you'll come into contact with archives in one or more of these formats or else have cause to create one yourself to send as a email attachment for example. Here's how.

3

The big squeeze (cont.)

Archiving files and folders

1. Choose one or more items (files, folders, programs or a combination) to archive and click the Action button in the toolbar or [Control] and click to summon a contextual menu.

2. Select Compress... to compress the item(s) into an archive.

3. If you compress one item Finder retains the original's name and appends the .zip filename suffix. For multiple items, Finder creates an archive called Archive.zip.

4. You can rename the archive as you would any other file, though it's a good idea to retain the .zip extender (especially if you're sharing the archive with users of other operating systems).

5. Use archives when you want to send email attachments to reduce the load on resources and increase the likelihood that an email server will accept and pass on your attachment.

Open
Move to Trash
Get Info
Compress "pics"   2
Duplicate
Make Alias
Copy "pics"
Clean Up Selection
Label:
×
More   ▶

pics   pics.zip   4

For your information

Although a space saving of up 80% is possible, ZIPing certain files such as JPEGs and MP3s, which are already stored in an archive format, will not show any significant reduction in size.

nstuffit_exp_12.0.1.dmg

3

The big squeeze (cont.)

Important

Because it's primarily a PC archiving format, you can easily share ZIP archives with Microsoft Windows users.

Timesaver tip

Archives with a .sit or .sitx extender were created by the one-time Mac standard archiving software Stuffit. You can download a free expander for these archives from **www.stuffit.com**. Keep it on your Desktop – you can decompress all kinds of obscure archiving formats simply by dropping the file on the Expander icon.

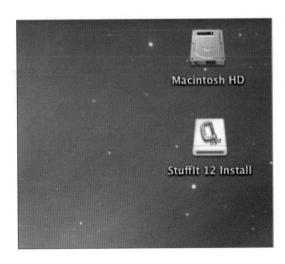

Macintosh HD

Stuffit 12 Install

Decompressing an archive

1 To retrieve the file(s) within an archive, double-click it.

2 If the archive contains multiple items, the Finder decompresses them and puts them into a folder with the same name as the archive.

3 Another type of archive you'll see occasionally is a disk image – especially if you download software from the Apple website. These images have a .dmg extender and an icon that looks like a drive.

4 To use a compressed disk image, double-click its icon. OS X will mount the image just like a drive, placing an icon on the desktop that you can open and manipulate in exactly the same way you would any other backing storage.

5 A mounted disk image must be ejected before it can be disconnected. Click the eject button in the sidebar, select Eject from the File menu, press [Command] + [E] or drag the disk to the Trash.

3

Search and retain

Use your Mac for any length of time and you'll be amazed at how quickly you amass dozens – hundreds! – of documents, images, utilities and the like downloaded from the Internet and as email attachments. OS X provides for simple and convenient file organisation, but by the time you've added your own folders and filed stuff away in them, created archives as backups and generally made a monster mish-mash of entangled files, locating any one of them can be a bit tricky, to say the least.

Fortunately, Apple has pre-empted the arduous path to file finding with a search tool called Spotlight, which makes drumming up anything quick and simple.

Searching with Spotlight

1 Spotlight is a super-fast search tool that is always available. Spotlight maintains an index of every item on your Mac and uses metadata (data that describe other data) such as creation date, file name and type, size and contents to make searches almost instant. What's more, using Spotlight, you can search for all kinds of stuff as well as files: search for dictionary definitions or transcripts from iChat sessions – you can even search for answers to simple mathematical problems by typing in an equation and having Spotlight solve it for you!

2 For a Mac-wide search click the Spotlight icon at the right of the menu bar. Type a word or phrase. Notice that Spotlight searches are dynamic: even as you type the Mac begins to display results.

3 You can click any item from the list of results to open it. Alternatively, click on Show All to open the results in a search window. Now select an item

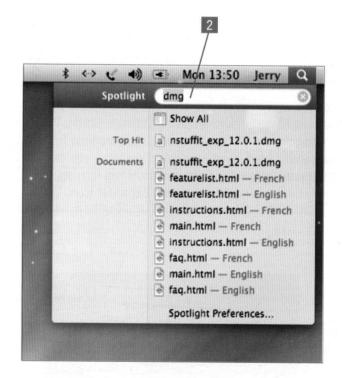

3

to view its path. You can also drag an item from the results window to the Desktop (or any other destination).

4 To find exact matches and narrow the search, enclose your search string with inverted commas like this: "Letter to Yvette" (otherwise Spotlight would return all items that matched any part of the search string: 'letter', 'to' and 'yvette').

5 For more powerful searching, Spotlight uses the Boolean operators AND, OR, NOT, – (and not) and range delimiters < (less than), > (more than) and = (equals) as well as specifiers for metadata. You can search on a number of possibilities by linking them with AND in the search field (letter AND Yvette created:>= "26.11.2007" will find all items matching the words 'letter' and 'yvette' created on or after 26.11.2007) or else filter out results you're not interested in using either NOT or <>.

Timesaver tip

Combine Quick Look (select an item and tap the spacebar) to rummage quickly through search results from Spotlight.

For your information

In the world of computing, the multiply sign is an asterisk (*) and the divide sign is a forward slash (/). For example, nine multiplied by nine would be entered into Spotlight as: 9*9 and eighty-one divided by nine would look like this: 81/9.

Search and retain (cont.)

Spotlight at full volume

1 For complete access to all of Spotlight's search functions press [Command] + [F] in the Finder to summon the utility's search window.

2 Now you can choose where to search and filter metadata attributes to supercharge your searches.

3 Choose Other from the Kind menu to select from a vast range of metadata options. You can have these included on the menu as standard by clicking the checkboxes of those you want – everything from Altitude to White balance.

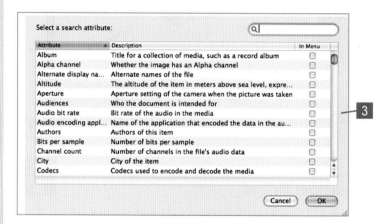

4 Use the Add and Delete checkboxes to add extra search criteria and increase the resolution of your search.

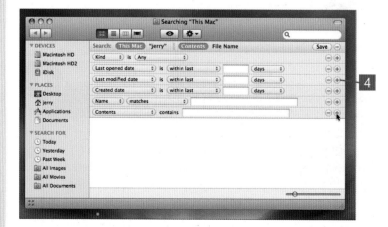

However robust a computer and its operating system, the possibility of losing or corrupting data is always there. Without doubt the Mac and OS X make for arguably the sturdiest combination available, but no system can guard against its owner inadvertently (or just plain stupidly!) throwing away some vitally important document, a cherished image or deleting a necessary support file for an application. Over the years, a number of third-party software providers have created backup applications that help to protect your data. Few, however, have been able to make a true snapshot of your machine to make anything and everything instantly restorable whatever mishap occurs. Possibly the biggest failing of these systems, is you ... that is, any time a backup requires intervention and action from a user, you can be sure that, beyond initial enthusiasm, the task is soon allowed to drift from 'Now!' to 'Some time soon ...'

Apple's research claims that less than 4% of computer users make regular backups. That's why it created Time Machine, a backup utility that ships with OS X and automates the process of making thorough and ongoing backups such that if, at any time you lose or delete an important file from your Mac, it can be restored quickly and easily – and with a fun-to-use interface.

Back up and burn

3

Backing up with Time Machine

1. Time Machine requires a non-booting external hard drive (USB or FireWire) or a partition on your existing drive to do its stuff. Mac laptop users can also back up to another Mac across an AirPort wireless network.

2. To use Time Machine click its icon in the Dock. The first task is to set up the program to use your external hard drive. Time Machine will show a list of those it considers suitable for the task. Select one and the backup process begins.

3. This first backup will probably take what seems like an age but, once that first snapshot of your Mac is complete and stored on the Time Machine drive, it's only necessary for the program to add new or amended files and you'll notice the utility becomes swift and largely invisible in operation.

4. Click the Options button and use the Add and Remove buttons to deselect drives from the backup. You can also skip the System files and other items from the backup using Time Machine's preferences (`File>Preferences`).

Back up and burn (cont.)

Recovering files

1 To retrieve a file from a Time Machine backup, open the folder that contained the item you want to recover.

2 Launch Time Machine and use the Back and Forth icons to view previous versions of the folder and its contents.

3 When you locate the item, select it and then click Restore to recover it.

Important

Don't use a disk that has important files on it as a Time Machine backup disk – there's a faint chance they'll be lost.

Nowadays, external hard drives are so cheap that they're practically given away with breakfast cereal, and so all but those on the tightest budgets can probably stretch to a device suitable for Time Machine. If you can't or prefer for some reason not to use automated backups (perhaps because you're a laptop user moving between office and home and you don't want to maintain two Time Machine drives separately), the alternative is to burn your precious stuff to an optical disk. Depending on your Mac, you can burn either CDs (with around 700 Mb capacity) or dual-layer DVDs, which offer around 7 Gb. Whichever your Mac can handle, the process of burning (i.e. writing data to the disk) is largely the same: insert a disk, drag and drop the files you want to record on to it, and then elect to burn it – simple. If you want to burn music CDs, turn now to Chapter 5.

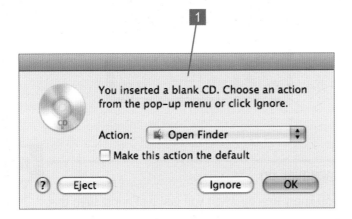

Burning optical disks

1 Insert a fresh blank optical disk into your Mac and Finder will prompt for an action: open iTunes, for example, or else ignore the disk and simply mount it on the Desktop. You can set the action you choose as the default by clicking the checkbox on the dialogue. For now click OK. The disk is mounted on the Desktop.

3

Did you know?

You can use rewritable CDs and DVDs in your Mac, but you can't erase them from the Finder. Instead, use Disk Utility (**Applications>Utilities>Disk Utility**). Launch Disk Utility, select the drive to erase in the left-hand pane, and click the Erase button. A Quick Erase deletes only the disk's catalogue (a list of the files on the disk) and takes a couple of minutes. A full burn erases the catalogue and files, and the process can take considerably longer.

Back up and burn (cont.)

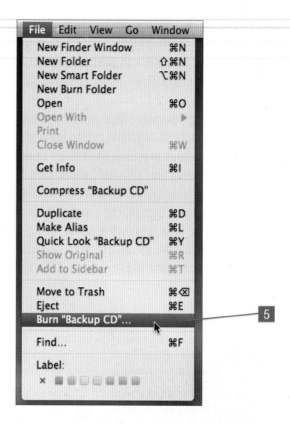

File	Edit	View	Go	Window
New Finder Window				⌘N
New Folder				⇧⌘N
New Smart Folder				⌥⌘N
New Burn Folder				
Open				⌘O
Open With				▶
Print				
Close Window				⌘W
Get Info				⌘I
Compress "Backup CD"				
Duplicate				⌘D
Make Alias				⌘L
Quick Look "Backup CD"				⌘Y
Show Original				⌘R
Add to Sidebar				⌘T
Move to Trash				⌘⌫
Eject				⌘E
Burn "Backup CD"...				5
Find...				⌘F
Label:				

2 Drag and drop the files and folders that you'd like to burn. Notice that the Finder copies aliases to the optical disk – the originals are copied when you start the burn.

3 As you drag and drop items, the space available on the disk is reduced – you can see the total number of items and the available space at the foot of the disk's window.

4 Click the disk's icon to name it and, when you're ready to burn, click Burn. The Finder will warn you if there is insufficient space for the items you've copied, at which point you can remove some and try again.

5 After burning, the disk is mounted on the Desktop. You can eject it by pressing the Eject button, select the disk and press [Command] + [E], or else choose Eject from the File menu.

Timesaver tip

If you know exactly when you last had a lost item that you want to recover, you can use the bars at the right side of the Time Machine screen to visit a specific backup date.

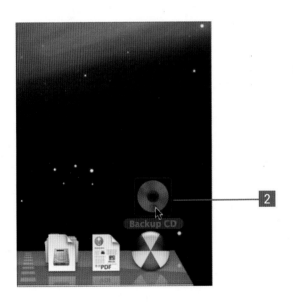

Burn folders

1 Burn folders are special folders that store items you want to write to a CD or DVD. You can use a burn folder over and over again, which makes for a convenient way to do regular backups of important files that change over time.

2 Instead of gathering them together to write, you have only to open the burn folder window, which looks just like that of a blank CD or DVD, insert a blank disk and click Burn.

3 Create a new burn folder by selecting the option from the File menu. You can name the burn folder and locate it to suit your needs.

Timesaver tip

Combine a burn with an eject by dragging your prepared but as yet unburned disk to the Trash. Finder will prompt to start the burn and eject the disk when it's finished.

The OS X applications

Introduction

The stuff of computing may be data, but you've got to have something with which to generate and manipulate the data in the first place. What set the first computers apart from their predecessors, dedicated machines solving differential equations and the like, was the potential for being turned to any task simply by issuing a new set of instructions. It's something we take for granted in the twenty-first century, but it was a revelation and a true revolution less than 50 years ago. Although you can install all kinds of third-party software – the Firefox Web browser, for example – the Mac is particularly blessed with pre-installed applications, with everything from a calculator to a DVD player. Some, such as Preview, you've already met. Others will be introduced in appropriate chapters – you'll meet Apple's Web browser, Safari, in Chapter 7. In this chapter we'll look at the best of the rest and discover how to locate, launch and use the bundled applications to good effect.

What you'll do

Learn to locate and launch applications

Switch running applications using the Dock and various shortcuts

Meet OS X's bundled suite of applications

Use Spaces, OS X's virtual Desktop

What and where?

Locating and launching applications

1. Look at the Dock: even before you install software it's bristling with applications and utilities: Dashboard, Safari, iChat, Preview, iTunes, the address book and the calendar. To launch them, all you have to do is choose one and click its icon. The bounce tells you the application is opening.

2. Now open a window on the Desktop and click Applications under Places in the Sidebar. You'll see around 30 items of software to perform all kinds of tasks, from working out simple calculations to automating repetitive tasks on your Mac, to fiddling with fonts, to capturing photo booth-like images… and much more.

3. To launch any program in the Applications folder, double-click it. As it opens, the application's icon is placed temporarily in the Dock – you'll see it bounce as the program opens. Once launched, Finder places a marker as a reminder beneath the icon in the Dock.

In principle, you could store applications more or less anywhere on your Mac. The accepted convention, however, is to locate software within the Applications folder and smaller 'helper' programs in the Utilities folder inside the Applications folder. Whenever you install third-party software, you can be sure it will be stored automatically in the Applications folder. In fact, most third-party installations involve mounting a .dmg disk image that opens automatically to reveal an icon for the application and a shortcut to your Applications folder. To install, you simply drag the one to the other – welcome to Mac software installation!

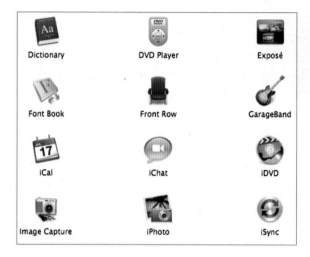

Switching and closing applications

Use the Dock to switch between applications. With several programs running at once, simply click on the one you want in the Dock.

You can also use a keyboard shortcut to switch applications. Press [Command] + [Tab] to summon a pick-list and, while continuing to hold down the [Command] key, press [Tab] (or the arrow keys) to cycle between them. Hold down the [Shift] key to cycle back through the open programs – useful if you have lots open at once.

To close an application (i.e. end it when you've finished with it), select Quit from the application's menu – that's the menu with its name located between the Apple and the File menu. [Command] + [Q] will also quit an application, or you can click and hold the application's icon in the Dock to summon a contextual menu and choose Quit. You'll be prompted to save unsaved

4

What and where? (cont.)

Startup applications

1 Setting applications to run at system startup couldn't be easier with OS X...

2 If the item you want to run at startup is in the Dock, select it with [Control] and click and, from the contextual menu, choose Open at Login.

3 Items not ordinarily in the Dock can be launched first and then accessed in the Dock to toggle Open at Login.

4 Alternatively, choose Accounts from System Preferences (`System Preferences> System>Accounts`). Click the Login Items button at the upper right of the Accounts preferences pane. Now click the Add button below the list and navigate to the application you want, clicking Add when you've selected it. (Use the Remove button to reverse the process and remove startup items.)

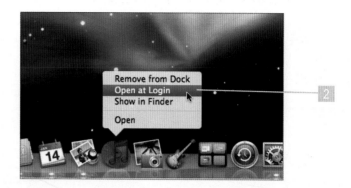

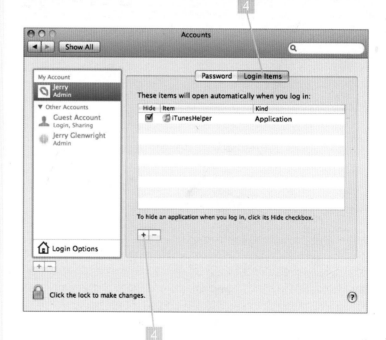

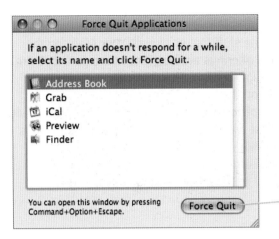

Force Quit Applications

If an application doesn't respond for a while, select its name and click Force Quit.

- Address Book
- Grab
- iCal
- Preview
- Finder

You can open this window by pressing Command+Option+Escape.

Force Quit

What and where? (cont.)

Force quit troublesome applications

1. Occasionally, and despite OS X's extremely robust structure, an application disappears into never-never land and won't respond to input from the mouse or keyboard. Try as you might, the application cannot be made to behave as advertised – sometimes even quitting won't work.

2. No problem. That robust structure of OS X means that nothing else will be affected, your other running applications will continue as normal, and the Finder provides a convenient method to rid yourself of the offending program: it's known as force quitting.

3. Select Force Quit… from the Apple menu (or press [Option], [Command] + [Escape]) to display the Force Quit Applications window.

4. Click on the unresponsive application and then click the Force Quit button. The program will end and, after a pause, you can relaunch it back to good health.

Important

You can force quit the Finder itself without having to restart the Mac. This will flush the Finder and correct untoward behaviour.

For your information

Other methods for opening programs include double-clicking an associated file (double-clicking a .txt file, for example, will open Text Edit, OS X's text editing application), [Control] and clicking a file and choosing Open With… from the contextual menu, dragging and dropping a file on to an application's icon in the Applications folder or on the Dock (which will also launch the application if it's not already running), and selecting a program icon and pressing [Command] and [O] (for 'open') or [Command] and down arrow. Finally (phew!), you can select an application from the list on the Recent Items menu option under the Apple menu.

The OS X applications 75

What and where? (cont.)

See also

As well as the stuff that ships with your Mac and the commercial offerings available from third parties, there's a mass of high-quality software available as free downloads on the Internet. OpenOffice (**www.openoffice.org**) is a superior suite of productivity software that rivals anything available anywhere and is file-compatible with Microsoft Office, while GIMP (**www.gimp.org**) is an image processor with features you'd expect to find in something with a fat price tag.

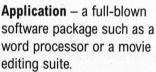

Jargon buster

Application – a full-blown software package such as a word processor or a movie editing suite.

Utility – a small, generally one-task program geared towards solving a particular problem or else manipulating the operating system in some way.

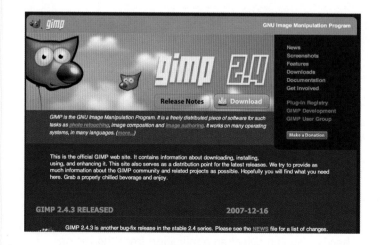

Anyone with experience of Linux will know what a boon virtual Desktops are. You can clutter up your machine's screen with all kinds of programs, open images and other stuff and then, at a click, switch to a new virtual computer with a clean Desktop, all ready to start work again, switching back at will.

Spaces is OS X's take on the virtual Desktop. You can organise up to 16 spaces and switch between them at will using a few simple key-presses. You can also customise Spaces to assign applications to particular Desktops automatically or change the hot-keys associated with the utility.

Spaces, the virtual Desktop

1. If the Spaces icon is in the Dock, click to launch it. Otherwise navigate to its icon in the Applications folder and double-click it. The utility requires some setting up the first time you run it. Click the Set Up Spaces button and check the Enable Spaces button in the Exposé & Spaces preferences pane. Close preferences.

4

What and where? (cont.)

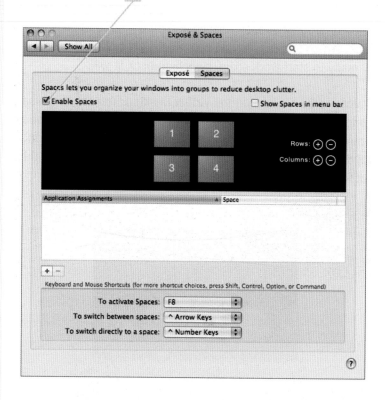

2 Now launch several applications in the normal way and press [F8] to invoke Spaces. Press the right arrow key and [Return]. You're whisked back to the Desktop, only now it's completely clear and you can launch a different set of applications. Press [F8] again, the left arrow key and [Return] and you're back to where you started.

3 With applications loaded into different Desktops you can also press [Control] and an arrow key to switch between them following the onscreen guide. Releasing [Control] and the arrow will dump you in the new space. You can also jump directly to a space by pressing the [Control] key and its number ([Control] + [4] for Space 4, for example).

4 To set an application to launch into a specific space, summon the Spaces preferences pane (`System Preferences> Exposé & Spaces`) and click the Add button in the Applications Assignments section of the pane. Navigate to the application you want

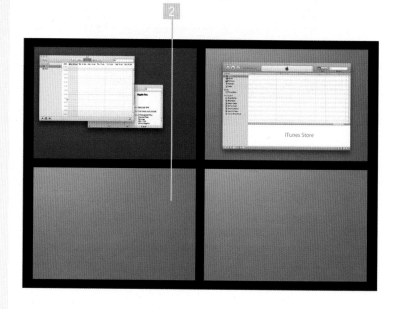

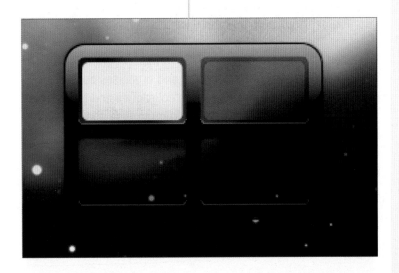

and click Add. Use the arrow keys at the far right of Applications Assignments to select a space for the program.

5 Check Show Spaces in the menu bar in the Preferences pane to add a Spaces icon to the right of the menu bar. You can use the pop-up menu that the icon displays to switch between spaces and access preferences.

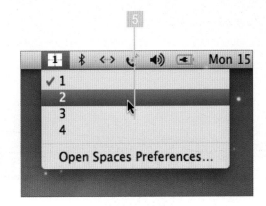

Timesaver tip

Relocate windows within your spaces by clicking and dragging to the right, left, top or bottom of the screen. Spaces will switch between the current and new space (the onscreen Spaces indicator pops up to confirm the switch) and you can drop the window into place.

Important

If Spaces doesn't respond to [F8], it probably needs to be invoked using the Exposé & Spaces pane in System Preferences. Access the pane and click the Enable Spaces checkbox.

OS X applications

Address Book

1 By default, Address Book's icon is in the Dock. To begin using the program, click the icon to launch it. The Address Book window is divided into three columns: Group, Name and cards. You can organise contacts into distinct groups (say, Family, Work and Others) or else store all your contacts together.

2 Address Book starts with two default entries: yours and Apple's. Adding more is simple. Click the Add button at the foot of the Name column and a new card appears in the cards column with the First field (i.e. first name) ready for input. Type the first name of the new contact and then press Tab to move to the next field. Continue in this way until you've completed the information for the new contact.

So now let's have a rummage in the Applications folder. You won't meet all the apps though… some are useful only when your knowledge of the system increases beyond an introductory book and are otherwise best left alone.

Designed to integrate fully with OS X's Mail program (detailed in Chapter 7), Address Book stores and organises contact details for all your friends, business colleagues and the people you buttonhole at bus stops with minimum fuss and maximum ease of use. Address Book can sync with online contacts databases such as that provided by Yahoo!, and you can even have the program display a detailed Google map for the address of any contact.

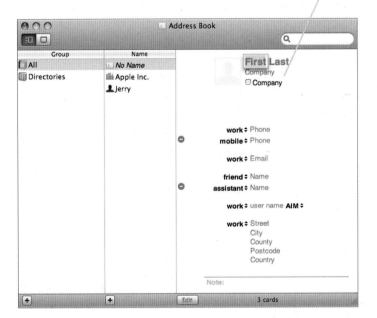

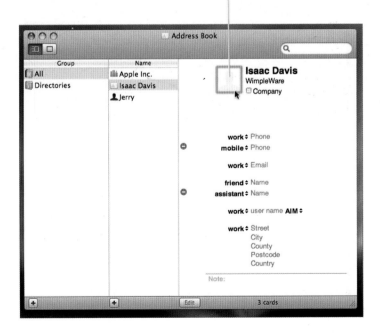

OS X applications (cont.)

Customising contacts

Contacts have different icons next to them depending on whether they're designated as personal or business contacts. Select which by clicking the Company checkbox in the cards column for a business contact. Notice that you, as the Mac's administrator, have a black silhouette as your icon.

Double-click the picture thumbnail to add an image to the contact. Use the Choose button to navigate to your pictures.

You can add effects to the image by clicking this button. Zoom the image until you're happy with its size using the slider and then click the Set button. The image is added to the contact.

To correct or change any information, click the Edit button and tab between the various fields.

OS X
applications
(cont.)

5 A green button next to a field within a card entry means that you can add further information. If there's a green button in the telephone number field, for example, you can expand the field and add further telephone numbers for work, mobile and so on.

6 You can group contacts together to organise them. Click the Add button at the foot of the Groups column and enter a name for the new group. Drag and drop contacts from the Name column to add them to a group. Contacts can be added to multiple groups, but editing the contact's details in one group will change the entry across them all.

7 To locate a contact, type all or part of a name, address, telephone number or any other associated data into the search box in the Address Book window.

Did you know?

For a detailed map of any contact's location, hold down the [Control] key while clicking the address and select Map Of... from the contextual menu.

See also

You can easily merge data from your Address Book into the Mac's email program Mail. For details see Chapter 7.

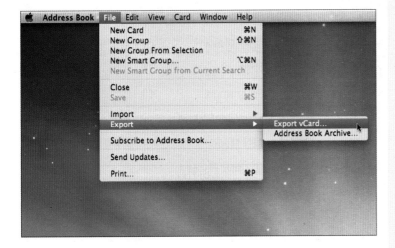

For your information

Sharing contacts between your Mac and a Windows PC is simple. Export your Windows contacts in vCards format to a pen drive or burn them to a CD. In Address Book select vCards from the Import option on the File menu and navigate to the exported cards. The process works equally well in reverse.

Jargon buster

Bundled software – the programs and utilities included free when you buy a new computer or operating system.

OS X applications (cont.)

Calculator

1. To dismiss the OS X calculator as 'simple' when you first see it is to miss out on the remarkable depth of features it offers... if only you know where to look!

2. The calculator is an ideal candidate for permanent location on the Dock (though there's also a simple calculator you can call up easily from Dashboard – see page 89). To anchor it there, navigate to the program in the Applications folder and drag it to the Dock. Now launch it.

3. At first sight, the calculator offers only the most basic arithmetic functions: add, subtract, multiply and divide. There isn't even a CE button to clear the last entry. You can use the calculator in this format for everyday problems.

4. Select Scientific from the View menu, however, and you can transform the calculator into a fully fledged scientific calculator with a complete complement of mathematical functions: pi, roots, factorials and many more.

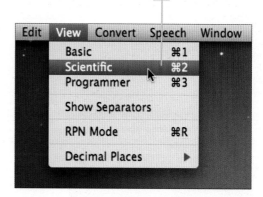

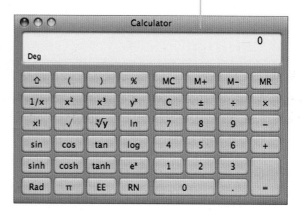

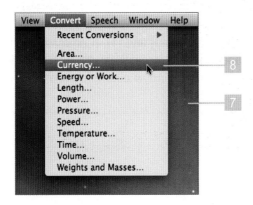

5 Novice and old-hand computer programmers alike will find the Programmer version of the calculator a joy. Moving between number bases requires no more than a click and there are bit operators and Boolean logic functions as well as a switchable 64-bit binary display – try finding that on a real-world handheld calculator!

6 To enter operands and operators into the calculator, click the buttons using a mouse or trackpad. You can also type your calculations using the number keys on your keyboard or the keypad just like a real calculator.

7 Conversions are available whichever calculator interface is currently active. Enter a figure and select the type of conversion you want from the Convert menu – everything from area to weights and masses.

8 Here's when a Mac-based calculator really comes into its own: elect to convert currency and the calculator will use the latest exchange rates updated from the Internet to ensure your conversion is accurate.

Timesaver tip

Remember: in the computer world, divide is represented with a forward slash (/) and multiply with an asterisk (*).

9 Copy a result from the calculator using [Command] + [C] and paste it into any other application (including the calculator itself) using [Command] + [V].

Press [Command] and [R] to toggle the calculator between conventional and Reverse Polish Notation entry modes – useful if you have complex calculations to perform.

Timesaver tip

Switch between basic, scientific and programmer calculators with [Command] and [1], [Command] and [2] and [Command] and [3], respectively. Alternatively, click on the green maximise window button to cycle between the modes.

Did you know?

MacBook users can access the embedded keypad by holding down the Function key (marked 'fn') to the left of the Control key.

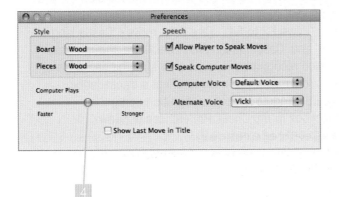

Chess

1   Unlike other operating systems, OS X ships with just one game: Chess. It's probably not what you want to while away a quiet five minutes, but if you like the game you'll certainly enjoy its Mac incarnation.

2   Launch Chess from the Applications folder. You'll see a traditional chess board and pieces in position and ready for a game. You're white, the Mac is black and you move pieces by dragging and dropping. To start playing, select a piece and move it to a new square. There's no need to be especially delicate when selecting a piece: clicking anywhere on the piece or within its square will select it.

3   Depending on the level of play and depth of the current game, the Mac will make its move within a few moments.

4   To adjust the length of time that the Mac uses to examine potential moves, select Preferences from the File menu and move the slider to the left or right.

The OS X applications 87

5 [Command] + [Z] will take back the last move and, if you're struggling, you can get a hint for your next move from the Moves menu. [Command] + [S] saves your game for posterity.

6 To start a new game press [Command] + [N]. Use the New Game dialogue to select who plays (you against another person, the computer against itself and so on) and the variant of the game they play.

Timesaver tip

If you find moving pieces with the mouse clumsy, you can speak your moves using standard coordinates like this: 'Pawn E2 to E4', 'Take back move', 'Castle king side' and 'Castle queen side'. Be aware, though, that speech recognition is, even on a Mac, hit and miss at best (or maybe you need to effect a transatlantic accent). Toggle speech recognition using the checkbox in the Chess Preferences window (`File>Preferences`).

A truly revolutionary feature of the first Mac in the early 1980s was its ability to make use of 'desk accessories', mini-applications that you summoned while using an application. Desk accessories predated multitasking desktop computers by years. You might, for example, summon a calculator while using your DTP program in order to work out dimensions for a picture box, or a thesaurus for a synonym while using a word processor. That kind of functionality is taken for granted nowadays. OS X's Dashboard application reintroduces the concept of desk accessories but shifts the idea firmly into the twenty-first century with breathtaking functionality, ease of use and a fabulous user interface.

Dashboard

1 Click the Dashboard icon or press [F12] to open it. The Desktop is dimmed and the default widgets zoom into place: a clock, calculator, weather report and so on. Widgets work intuitively: to use one – the calculator, say, click its buttons or else type input at the keyboard.

Operating within an invisible Aqua 'layer', Dashboard is made visible by selecting it from the Dock or else pressing a hot-key (by default [F12]). The program uses mini-applications known as 'widgets' to do anything and everything – you can select from those that ship with the utility, download more from the Internet and create your own as easily as clicking and dragging in some cases.

With an active connection to the Internet you can get the latest weather for virtually anywhere on Earth, check exchange rates, monitor global news and sports results in real time, get ski reports… and many, many (many!) more.

Did you know?

You can remove Dashboard from the Dock to make space for other items – it will still be available by pressing [F12].

OS X applications (cont.)

Customising widgets

Summon the widgets bar with the + button. Available widgets are shown in this bar and you can activate them by clicking (the widget is opened with a gorgeous ripple effect) or using drag and drop to position it onscreen (the widget opens with a kind of morphing action – it all adds to the user experience!).

Click the Manage Widgets... button on the widgets bar and a window appears, from which you can enable and disable widgets using checkboxes, sort them by name or date, or visit Apple's Dashboard pages on the Web to find more by clicking More Widgets.

With the widget bar revealed, remove widgets from the main display by clicking the x icon in the top left corner.

To add new widgets, download them from the Web (see elsewhere on these pages for useful sources) and double-click them on the Desktop.

Some widgets have a number of preferences that you can customise. Mouse over a widget. If an i appears in the lower right corner, click it. The widget flips over, displaying its options. Try this: mouse over the weather widget and when the i appears, click it. Now you can choose a local weather report and select between Fahrenheit and Celsius.

See also

Visit Apple's widget pages at **www.apple.com/downloads/dashboard** (or click the More Widgets button on the Manage Widgets window) or see the online Dashboard community pages at **www.dashboardwidgets.com** for thousands more downloadable widgets.

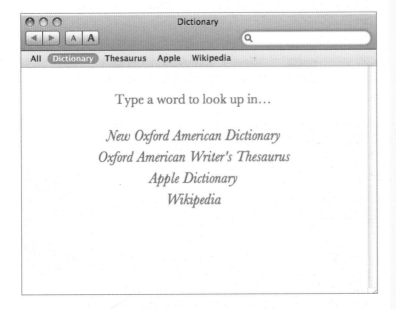

Timesaver tip

Type just the first few letters of a word to locate its definition in the Dictionary – useful if you don't know the spelling.

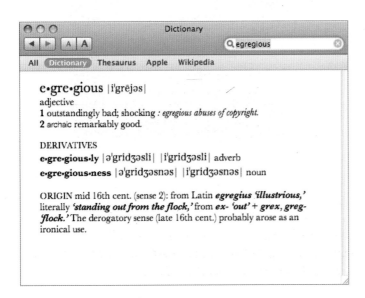

Dictionary

Stuck for a spelling? Searching for a synonym? Or looking for a pithy pop-culture definition for some modern phenomenon or other? Combining a dictionary, thesaurus, direct access to Wikipedia and the ability to add further reference sources along the way, Apple's Dictionary application has grown from a simple word-look-up tool to become a true digital library – just what Apple boss Steve Jobs set out to do with his Digital Librarian application, part of the NextStep OS, back in the 1990s. Mostly though, Dictionary simply makes for a multilingual and super-convenient way to check spellings, conjure up synonyms, conjugate verbs and check out an encyclopaedia entry for virtually any subject you care to name, and all via the comfort of the keyboard – your eyes need never leave the screen.

You can launch the Dictionary as a standalone program just as you would any other in the Applications folder, or else summon direct assistance

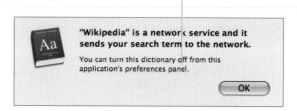

"Wikipedia" is a network service and it sends your search term to the network.

You can turn this dictionary off from this application's preferences panel.

OK

from within other applications such as TextEdit or Safari by highlighting a word, [Control] and clicking for a contextual menu and selecting **Look Up>Dictionary**.

3 Alternatively, highlight a word and press [Control], [Command] + [D] to summon a contextual panel window with the definition. Switch between the dictionary and thesaurus using the pop-up menu, or click More... to launch the Dictionary proper.

4 Dictionary will warn when it can't access Wikipedia if you don't have a network connection. Otherwise use the buttons to access the dictionary and thesaurus.

5 Dictionary is also available as a Dashboard widget – just press [F12] for Dashboard and click the widget bar button at the bottom left of the screen. From there, drag the Dictionary widget to the screen. Now when you press [F12], you have instant access to all the Dictionary's functions. Enter your word into the search box and press [Return] as usual.

For your information

When congratulated on his dictionary containing no 'foul words', Doctor Johnson replied acidly: 'I see you have been looking for them Madam'. Although it may amuse you to while away a quiet minute with the definitions for a selection of 'dirty words', you can happily restrain your kids from the same pastime by accessing the Parental Controls (System Preferences) for the Dictionary and checking the box against Hide Profanity in Dictionary. If only the playground could be similarly switched off!

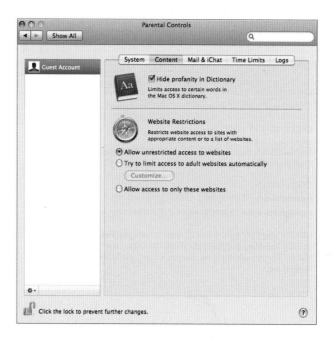

There's a whole host of other stuff in the Applications folder, some of which you can cheerfully compute for years without ever using. Some will become necessary as you use your Mac and learn more about its complexities. And beyond the Applications folder is the Utilities folder, packed with one-shot solutions to computing 'problems'.

Automator – use Automator to create workflow files that contain operations you can apply time and again to other files or applications, saving time and effort in the process.

DVD Player – insert a DVD and the Finder launches DVD player automatically to play it for you. All controls are intuitive and work just like those on a standalone (i.e. real-world) DVD player.

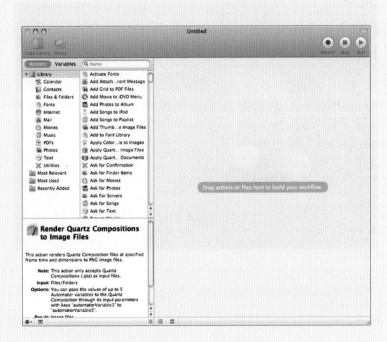

And the rest...
(cont.)

Front Row – this media browser works with the Apple remote control handset to provide convenient access to music and TV programs via iTunes Store, podcasts and more.

Font Book – this is used to install, view and organise fonts.

Image Capture – grab images from digital cameras and scanners without the need for complex third-party drivers.

iSync – synchronise the data between several Macs, an iPod and PDAs for continuity across all the devices you work with.

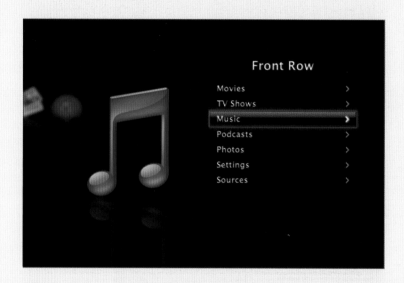

Stickies – the onscreen version of those yellow sticky pads used for scribbling notes and reminders to yourself.

TextEdit – a no-frills text editor, useful for viewing and manipulating plain text, RTF and Word documents.

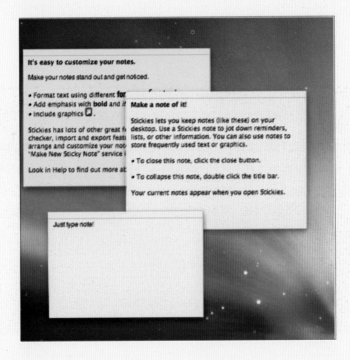

4

iLife 08

Introduction

iLife is a suite of applications bundled with new Macs (and available to buy in the guise of iLife 08) that form the cornerstone of Apple's 'digital life' philosophy. The suite comprises five applications: iPhoto, iMovie, iDVD, iWeb and GarageBand, and they're used to create, manipulate, view and publish digital material in the form of images, movie clips, music and online content. Additionally, the iApps collection features iTunes and iCal – included as part of OS X – for organising and listening to digital music files and managing personal and business events respectively.

As the iApps have evolved over the years, the user interfaces of some of them – iTunes, iPhoto, iMovie and iDVD, for example – have homogenised somewhat so that if you're comfortable using iTunes with its library and playlists, you'll be instantly at home manipulating digital pictures with iPhoto and its analogous events and albums.

What you'll do

Manage your life with iCal

Organise and manipulate your digital music collection

Create digital picture albums and share them with friends

Make, edit and manipulate digital home movies

Use iDVD to create DVDs featuring movies, slideshows and more with professional-looking menus that can be played on a computer or domestic player

Learn how to use iWeb to create fantastic web pages

Record your own songs and publish them

Get organised

Using iCal

1 By default iCal's icon lives in the Dock. To launch the program click the icon (or double-click it in the Applications folder).

2 iCal's window is organised into panes devoted to calendars, a 'mini-month' calendar for the current month (though, of course, you can display a calendar for any month and year) and, in the main pane, your scheduled events for the day (or week or month, should you so choose). The current time is represented on the events calendar by a horizontal line.

3 Events are organised into collections called 'calendars' displayed in the upper left pane and, unlike other appointments managers, you can create any number of these calendars using iCal and name them to suit yourself. When it's first launched, the application offers two default calendars: Home and Work.

Since the advent of domestic and office computers, a primary function has been to take control of your life: recording and organising your important appointments and popping up to remind you like a good and faithful servant just when you might have forgotten. Frankly, and until relatively recently, this scenario was little more than a sales pitch and a pipedream – it was easier to reach for your real-world paper organiser and jot down notes and appointments as you went along. But as computers have reached further into our daily lives, integrating with (and gradually replacing) other devices and growing ever more capable in terms of hardware and software, the potential for using a computer as a digital appointments and address book is at last a viable proposition.

iCal is OS X's versatile, adaptable, innovative and powerful calendar application. Using the program, you can record, organise, track and maintain all the social and business events in your life, calling them up at a key-stroke, setting alarms so that you're never caught out – even publish your appointments and share them with others via a .Mac account and the Web. And, combined with Address Book, the OS X contacts manager, and iSync to synchronise your information across several Macs, you have an up-to-the-minute central database of all that's required to remain organised in a convenient and integrated format.

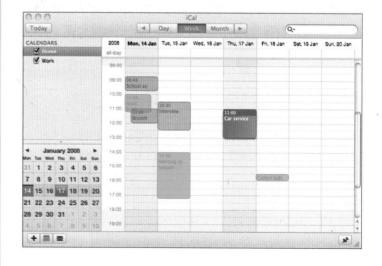

4 To view the events in a calendar, click its checkbox. To hide, them deselect the checkbox. Hold down the [Command] key as you click a checkbox to toggle all the calendars.

5 You can navigate the events in a calendar using the back and forward buttons in the toolbar. Click the Today button to return to the current day.

5

! Important

Events from different calendars scheduled at the same time are overlapped in the events display – click to bring the one you want to the front.

i For your information

iCal is also available as a Dashboard widget (press [F12] to summon Dashboard and click Manage Widgets to drag iCal from the widgets collection if it's not already live). Click in the 'today' square to reveal a further square with a mini-month calendar. Click again to reveal another square featuring a list of the day's events.

Get organised (cont.)

Creating and deleting events

1 Select a calendar from the list by clicking it, switch to day or week view using the appropriate button (both offer greater resolution when you're locating an event/time), click the time that your event begins, drag to the event end and type the details.

2 A double-click will automatically create a one-hour event.

3 Once you've created an event, you can edit it to include an alarm or set it to repeat (for a weekly game of badminton, say).

4 To remove an event, click it and press the [Delete] key or drag it to the Trash. You can also click and select Delete from the Edit menu.

Timesaver tip

Return instantly to the current day from any other date on the calendar by pressing [Command] and [T]. Alternatively, press [Shift], [Command] and [T] to go directly to a specific date.

For your information

[Control] and click an event for a contextual menu with a selection of appropriate options, including the event editor info window.

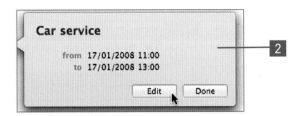

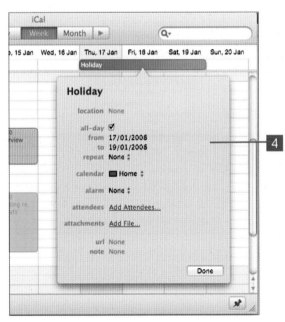

Editing an event

1. Drag and drop to move an event anywhere on the calendar. To alter the event's time span, click, hold and drag at the top or bottom of the event.

2. Double-click an event to open the event editor (a single click and [Command] + [I] works equally well). iCal displays the editor with the current settings for the event. Click Edit.

3. The editor expands to show all the options available. The event's text is highlighted at the top of the menu. Type to replace the selected information or click to add more.

4. Checking the all-day box creates an all-day event – one displayed as a coloured bar at the head of the calendar window in daily and weekly views or as a coloured bar on the appropriate day in the monthly view. Hold down [Option] as you click and drag to copy the event to other days.

5

Get organised (cont.)

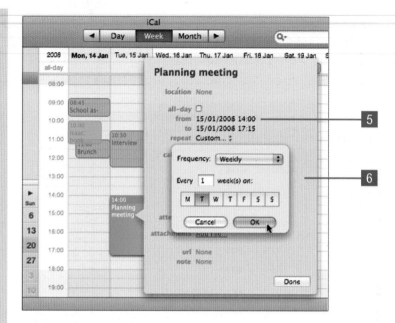

5 Using the From and To fields you can type explicit times and dates for an event. Click each field to edit.

6 A regular event can be set to repeat as often as you like by clicking the pop-up repeat menu. Choose Every day, Weekly and so on, or select Custom to further refine when the event repeats.

7 Repeating events can be set to end at a specific date using the End pop-up.

8 You can switch an event from one calendar to another using the calendar pop-up.

9 If you want to invite friends or colleagues to attend your event, click in the attendees field and type their names and email addresses, separating each with a comma. The emails of people in your Address Book are added to the list automatically as you type their names.

10 Using the notes field, you can enter extra information about your event, which will be displayed when you double-click it (or click and press [Command] + [I]).

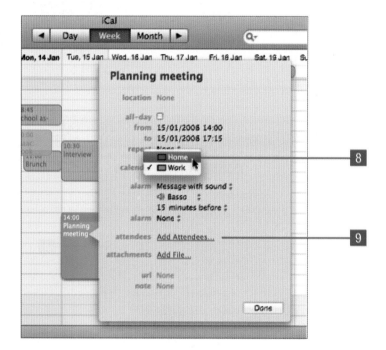

The value of an events organiser is increased exponentially if you can set alarms as reminders. iCal's alarm pop-up enables you to select a message or a sound or have the program open a file or send you an email. Better still, alarms work even when iCal isn't running.

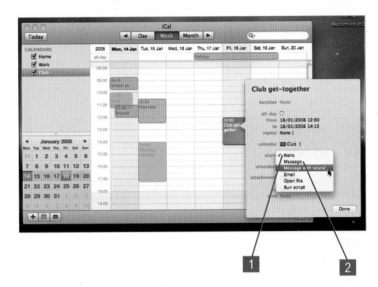

Setting an alarm

1 Summon the event editor and click Edit. Click None on the Alarms pop-up menu and choose the type of alarm you want to use.

2 Selecting Message will cause iCal to flash a dialogue on the screen with the text from the event. Click the Snooze button to set the message to reappear at any time from a minute to a week. Click the Zoom tool to launch iCal and open the event editor dialogue for the event.

3 When you've set an alarm, a further alarm menu appears in the event editor window. You can continue to add alarms by repeating the setting process.

4 If you choose to have an email sent to you as a reminder, iCal will prompt you to enter your email address into your Address Book card if it isn't already there.

5

iCal alarms (cont.)

Adding and deleting calendars

1. Events are organised into groups called calendars. iCal has two to get you started – Home and Work – but you can add more and group several together to help organise everything effectively.

2. To add a calendar, click the add button or [Control] and click in the free area of the Calendars list and select New Calendar from the contextual menu.

3. Type over the highlighted calendar to name it.

4. Choose a colour for the new calendar by [Control] and clicking it and selecting Get Info.

5. If you have a busy social life and lots of calendars to organise, iCal provides a grouping function so that you can group similar calendars together. To create a group, [Control] and click in the Calendars list and select New Group. Type over to name the group.

6. Drag and drop the calendars you want to group together and use the disclosure triangle to hide and reveal the calendars in the group.

Timesaver tip

Switch between day, week and month views using [Command] and [1], [Command] and [2] and [Command] and [3], respectively.

Did you know?

iCal is fully integrated with many other OS X applications, including unlikely candidates such as iTunes. For a tuneful alarm clock, try this: create a new event for the alarm you want to set, click the Add File pop-up menu and navigate to the iTunes track that you want to awaken to. Be sure to turn up your volume…

iCal supports To Do items, integrating To Dos that you've
created with the Mail application with those you make with iCal.
You can display lists of To Dos and organise them by priority,
date and other criteria.

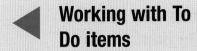

iCal To Do lists

1 To Dos are displayed in a
separate pane to the right of
the events window. You can
toggle the display of To Dos
by clicking the To Do icon in
the lower right of the iCal
window – it looks like a
pinboard pin.

2 All the To Dos you've created
with iCal (and Mail) are
displayed in the list.

3 Use the Priority pop-up menu
at the top of the list to manage
and organise your To Dos.

5

Working with To Do items (cont.)

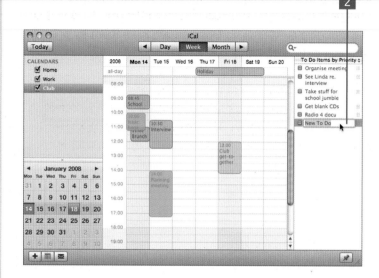

Creating, editing and deleting To Dos

1 To create a new To Do, select a calendar for the To Do and then double-click in the To Do list. You can also select New To Do from the iCal File menu.

2 A new To Do is displayed in the list highlighted in the colour of the associated calendar. Just start typing to enter your To Do information.

3 Double-click a To Do to call up an information bubble similar to the event editor window. Now you can set a priority for the To Do, reassign it to a different calendar or enter a Web page URL or further notes.

4 You can also set a due date and an alarm as a reminder. Click the due date checkbox, then click on the alarm pop-up menu and select the type of alarm you want. Choose when to be reminded and then click Done.

Timesaver tip

You can set priorities for To Dos by clicking the priority button at the right of the To Do in the list: one bar means low priority, and three bars means high priority.

For your information

A triangle next to a To Do means that it has passed its due date. Use the checkbox at the left of the To Do to indicate that it is completed.

Why stop at organising your own life? By sharing your iCal calendars online, you can keep friends and colleagues in step with your busy schedules, and have them updated automatically whenever you make changes to a local calendar. What's more, you can return the favour by subscribing to other people's calendars so that you and your friends and colleagues are perfectly synchronised. Publishing your calendars is an ideal way to share important dates for anyone who organises a club, teachers who want to maintain public schedules for assignment deadlines and so on.

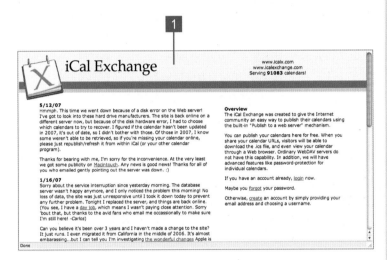

Sharing calendars

Publishing a calendar

1. To publish a calendar it's necessary to have somewhere to publish it. A .Mac account is ideal, but you can also publish to free servers such as iCal Exchange (**www.icalx.com**).

2. Open iCal and select a calendar from the Calendars list that you'd like to publish by clicking it – don't worry which calendars are checked or unchecked.

3. Select Publish… from the Calendar menu.

4. If you have a .Mac account, just select the options you want to associate with publishing the calendar – principally Publish Changes Automatically to ensure that the information in your online calendar remains current. Click Publish. A dialogue is displayed confirming that your calendar has been published successfully and showing two important URLs: the Web location for access to your calendar, and a link to the exported iCal .ics file.

5

Sharing calendars (cont.)

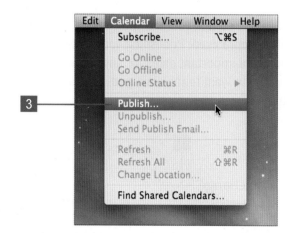

5 You can publish a calendar without a .Mac account using one of the free iCal publishing services on the Web. Choose Private Server from the Publish pop-up menu, and then type the URL for the server – the iCal Exchange server, for example – together with your name and password into the appropriate fields. Check Publish Changes Automatically, select any other options you want and click Publish.

6 Click on Your Account at iCal Exchange. Your calendar is listed under the public calendars, along with two links: one to .html (the viewable Web page for the calendar) and the other to the .ics, the subscription file. Share these links with people who want to access your calendar.

Subscribe to calendar

Calendar URL: www.icalx.com/myclubcalc

Cancel   Subscribe

5

Timesaver tip

Call up the Subscribe menu instantly by pressing [Option], [Command] and [S] from within iCal.

For your information

iCal can export a calendar as a .ics file that other iCal users can import into their iCal application and then manipulate the calendar. The .ics file can also be saved to a special page at .Mac or a free Web-based iCal publishing service enabling other people to subscribe to your calendar.

Viewing and subscribing to calendars

1 Once it's published, anyone with a computer and Internet account can view your calendar as a standard Web page by pointing their browser at the .Mac '...view with a browser' or iCal Exchange .html URLs.

2 Alternatively, your friends and colleagues with Macs can subscribe to your calendar using the .Mac '...can be subscribed at' or iCal exchange .ics URLs.

3 iCal users who view your calendar on a Web page can also click the Subscribe link at the left of the page to subscribe to the calendar.

4 What works for other iCal users works for you too. If a friend sends you an email with a calendar subscription link, click it to launch iCal and subscribe automatically.

5 Alternatively, select Subscribe... from the Calendar menu, paste the calendar's address into the Calendar URL field and click

5

Sharing
calendars (cont.)

Subscribe. iCal checks that the calendar is available and downloads it to your iCal.

6 If you want your version of the subscribed calendar to remain in sync with the original, choose a frequency from the Auto-refresh pop-up menu. Deselect the Remove checkboxes on other options to receive attachments and To Dos and to hear alarms associated with calendar events.

7 Subscription calendars are marked as such in the Calendars list.

8 To stop subscribing, select a calendar and delete it by selecting Delete from the Edit menu, or press the [Delete] key.

9 To stop sharing a calendar, select it and select Unpublish from the Calendar menu.

See also

The Web is awash with interesting, amusing, useful and just plain wacky calendars published by sporting associations, TV companies, academic establishments and complete strangers for your enjoyment. Select Find Shared Calendars from iCal's Calendar menu, or search for them using your favourite search engine. Alternatively, point your browser at **www.icalshare.com** for a huge selection to get you started.

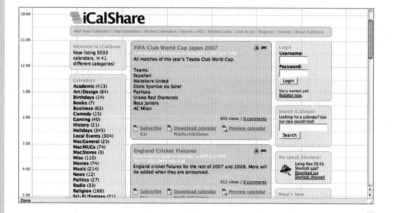

iTunes is an application that has defined the zeitgeist for a generation. Launched as a digital music jukebox in 2001, iTunes caught the public's imagination and spawned a phenomenon in digital media players, the shockwaves of which are still rippling through the industry today – in fact, many people think of Apple primarily as a digital media company rather than as a manufacturer of computers. Along with the revolutionary iMac computer and the iPod digital music player, iTunes revamped Apple's fortunes, bringing to the company a return to the cool and groovy image that it enjoyed in the early 1980s but lost with the inexorable rise of the execrable 'three-box' PC-lookalikes of the early and mid-1990s.

As well as storing and organising digital media files, iTunes doubles as an interface to the massively popular iPod media player and the iPhone, and as a shop front for Apple's iTunes Store, using which you can download music, TV shows and more.

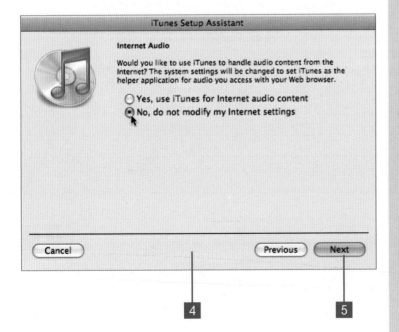

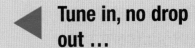

Tune in, no drop out ...

Meet iTunes

1 Launch iTunes by clicking its icon in the Dock or double-clicking in the Applications folder. Alternatively, insert a music CD into your Mac and iTunes will launch automatically.

2 At its simplest, iTunes can play and make backups of your music CDs and enable you to connect and listen to dozens of Internet-based radio stations. Explore further, and you can import ('rip') music from CDs, store and organise music tracks into playlists, burn them to your own compilation CDs, and convert between various music file formats. You can download and listen to podcasts, subscribe and have new content delivered to your Mac ready to listen to, and display the iTunes 'visualizer', hypnotic graphic effects that pulsate in time to the music you're playing. What's more, the application interfaces seamlessly with Apple's iPod media player, downloading any or all of your music

5

Tune in, no drop out ... (cont.)

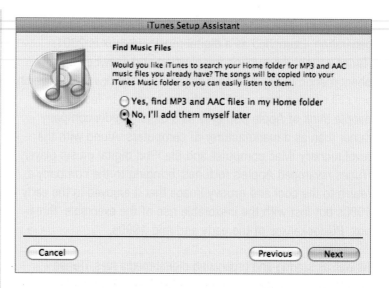

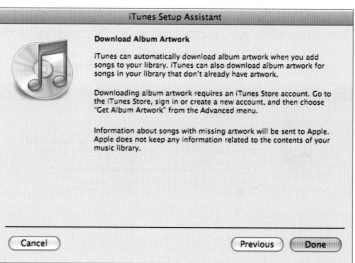

collection to your iPod and synchronising newly acquired audio files whenever you connect the player to your Mac. You can also sync Address Book and iCal data to your iPod via iTunes.

3　iTunes is available as a free download for Microsoft Windows Vista and XP as well as OS X. Updates are released regularly and distributed automatically for OS X users via Software Update.

4　The first time you launch the application, the iTunes Setup Assistant will guide you through the simple setup process (click Cancel if you have previous experience of the program).

5　Answer the assistant's questions, clicking Next as you go along. You can return to a question by clicking the Previous button.

6　You can also change iTunes settings using the application's Preferences, available from the iTunes menu (or by pressing [Command] + [,]).

Important

If in doubt when using the Setup Assistant, answer in the negative. For example, if you're unsure whether or not to use iTunes for Internet audio (there are several popular standards and audio players), select No, do not modify my Internet settings. You can toggle this option later when you're familiar with iTunes and its capabilities and the types of streaming audio content you like to listen to.

Listen to a CD

1 To play an audio CD on your Mac, insert the disk. OS X will launch iTunes and the application will prompt you to import or 'rip' the music from the CD and store it in your iTunes library. Doing so speeds up the listening process, keeps all your audio in one convenient location and lets you make playlists of favourite tracks from different CDs. Click Yes or No (hint: click yes!).

2 With a live Internet connection iTunes will access the Apple CDDB (CD database) and download and display artist and track information. If not, you'll see Track 01, Track 02... and so on in the tracklist.

3 Notice that the CD appears in the Source list under a new category: Devices. To play the CD from the first track, click the Play button. Alternatively, double-click a track in the track listing to start playing from that track. The Play button is also a pause button. Click to toggle playing and pausing.

4 Click and hold the fast-forward and rewind buttons to move to and fro in the track, or click either button once to jump forward to the next track or back to the previous track.

5 The information window shows the name of the song (or other audio content) that's playing and alternates the name of the artist with the name of the album. Also in the display is a time slider, which you can click and drag to move to and fro in the song – drag the diamond position marker. You can also click anywhere in the slider to jump to that position in the song.

6 Adjust the volume using the volume slider. Click on the speakers at either end to mute iTunes or switch to full volume.

7 Click the Eject button to eject the CD when you're done listening.

Did you know?

You can also control iTunes from the Dock: click and hold the iTunes icon for a contextual menu with options for skipping and repeating tracks, pausing and so on.

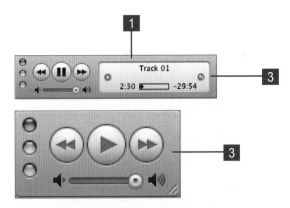

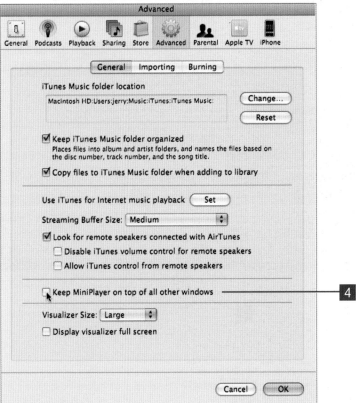

iTunes MiniPlayer

1 If the iTunes window requires more screen real estate than you're prepared or able to give it, click the resize (green traffic light) button to switch to the iTunes MiniPlayer.

2 The MiniPlayer displays only the most-needed controls.

3 Click and drag the resize corner to toggle the info display and reduce the required space further.

4 You can elect to have the MiniPlayer window remain at the front whatever else you're doing by selecting the option from iTune's Preferences (**Preferences> Advanced>Keep MiniPlayer on top of all other windows**).

5

For your information

Click the Shuffle button to toggle a random ordering of the playlist. Click the repeat button to repeat the entire playlist. Click again to repeat the current track. A third click restores single play mode.

Tune in, no drop out ... (cont.)

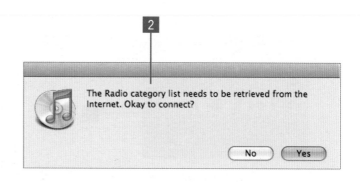

Alternative sources

1 As well as listening to music, you can use iTunes to listen to Internet radio stations and audio books, download and subscribe to podcasts, watch videos and TV and access the iTunes Store. It's all available by selecting the appropriate category under Library.

2 For example, to listen to an Internet radio station, click Radio under Library in the Source list.

3 Browse the radio genres and click the disclosure triangle to see the available stations.

4 When you find a station you'd like to hear, double-click it. Some stations offer several streaming speeds (32 kbit, 64 kbit, 128 kbit). Try the fastest speed first, but if the broadcast stutters, select a different speed until you can hear the station without interference.

1

iTunes Store

1 To buy music tracks, audio books, TV programmes and other content, click iTunes Store under Store in the Source list.

2 The iTunes Store shop window is clearly organised so that you can easily find what you're looking for. Browse the items in the store and use the tabs at the top of the window to help you navigate. You can also search for items – a track or artist name, for example – by typing it into the search field.

3 When you're ready to make a purchase, simply click the item's Buy button. You'll be prompted to sign in to your iTunes Store account or create a new one if this is your first time. If you're short of cash, visit anyway... there are many free items such as podcasts in the Store. Free items are indicated clearly.

4 After making your purchase or selecting a free item, iTunes downloads it to the Library. You can then listen to it, include it in a playlist, burn it to a disk or anything else you can do with Library items.

3

Sign In to download music from the iTunes Store
To create an Apple Account, click Create New Account.

Create New Account

If you have an Apple Account (from the iTunes Store or .Mac, for example), enter your Apple ID and password. Otherwise, if you are an AOL member, enter your AOL screen name and password.

Apple ID:

Example: steve@mac.com

Password:

Forgot Password?

☐ Remember password for purchasing

Cancel   **Buy**

Timesaver tip

Pause playback by pressing the [Spacebar]. Press again to resume playing.

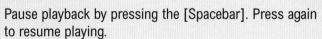

Copying (ripping) audio from CDs

You can import – or rip – audio from your CDs and store it in the iTunes library. Doing so provides speedy, convenient one-click access to all your audio and enables you to create playlists by mixing and matching tracks. You can play a playlist using iTunes or burn it to a CD and play it away from your Mac.

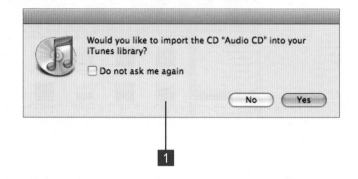

Ripping a CD

1 Insert a CD and (unless you turn off the feature in Preferences) iTunes will prompt you to import its contents into the library. Click Yes. The CD will play in the usual way but, as it does, each track is copied and stored as a digital file.

2 Alternatively, once you're playing a CD, click the Import CD button at any time to rip the CD.

3 You can view the tracks you've imported by clicking on Music in the Library section of the iTunes window Source list. The contents of the library, sorted by name, are displayed in the tracklist window.

4 Click any of the tabs in the tracklist to organise your view of the tracks. For example, if you've ripped two or three albums, by default all the tracks are displayed together in alphabetical order in the tracklist. Click on the Album tab to view tracks grouped by their respective albums. Click the same tab again to sort albums by artist or click again to sort albums by year. A third click returns you to Album view.

For your information

iTunes works with several digital file types, some of which compromise quality (slightly) in favour of smaller files or are incompatible with certain types of player. By default, iTunes rips and imports using its own AAC format (high-quality/128 kbit), but the application can also manipulate MP3 and WAV files, among others.

iTunes Store

Import digital audio files

1 As well as ripping CDs, you can import digital music files from, say, an MP3 player, a memory stick or another computer into the iTunes library.

2 Select Add to Library from the File menu and navigate to the source of the files.

3 Click to select the file or [Shift] and click for multiple selections and then click Choose.

4 iTunes imports the files into the Library. You can play them as you would any others, make playlists and burn them to CDs.

Important

Connect an iPod and it appears under Devices in the Source list. By default, iTunes syncs the Library with your iPod automatically.

Timesaver tip

[Control] and click in the tracklist tab bar to toggle all the possible columns of information associated with your tracks.

Timesaver tip

Import MP3s and other audio files by clicking on Library and dragging and dropping the files to the Source list.

Browsing, organising and backing up tracks

Given the many options for sourcing audio content within iTunes – ripping CDs, downloading from the Web and the Apple iTunes Store, importing MP3s and the like, you'll find that it's possible to amass a huge audio collection very quickly indeed. Almost without realising it, you'll have dozens of tracks – hundreds, perhaps even thousands if you're really keen. Fortunately, iTunes offers many ways to view and organise your audio collection (though it's not always obvious), and there's even a built-in backup option so you can be sure your precious library is protected from loss in the event of system failure.

Viewing tracks

1 Click on the Music category in the Library section of the Source list and you'll see a complete list of all your tracks in the tracklist pane.

2 Click the Browse icon at the bottom right of the iTunes window. The tracklist view is sorted by genre, artist and album. Click an entry in any category to further refine what's shown in the tracklist.

3 If you'd prefer to view your tracks together with their artwork, click the Album View button in the toolbar.

4 Cover Flow is Apple's groovy new viewing tool (you met it viewing the contents of Finder windows in Chapter 2) that enables you to flick through iTunes items much as you would CD jewel cases. Cover Flow is also used on the iPhone and iPod. Click the Cover Flow button to switch to the Cover Flow view.

5 Click and drag the slider to flick to and fro through your tracks. You can also use the left and right arrow keys.

With content in the Library you can create playlists to organise and view or listen to your tracks just the way you like. You can make playlists to suit events – a birthday, say – or your mood – perhaps easy listening for late evenings. You can also use playlists as convenient compilations for burning to a CD or DVD. You can make any number of playlists, using any items from the Library.

1

1

2

4

Playlists

1 To make a playlist, click the Add button in the lower left of the iTunes window and type over to name your playlist. Playlists are organised alphabetically.

2 Select a category under Library, navigate to the items you want, and then click, drag and drop them on to the playlist. iTunes doesn't actually copy items; it simply records their names in the playlist – much as you would if you jotted down tracks for a DJ to play.

3 To reorder the items within the playlist, click the ordering tab (left-hand column) and drag the items up and down in the list.

4 iTunes displays a summary of the playlist – the number of tracks, the time and the size – at the foot of the window.

5 To watch or listen to your playlist, click to select it and click the Play button.

5

Browsing, organising and backing up tracks (cont.)

Smart playlists

1. You can use Smart Playlists to add items automatically to a playlist based on rules that you've set previously. You might choose to add items from a particular artist whenever new items appear in the Library, for example. iTunes features a selection of Smart Playlists to get you started (Recently Played, Top 25 Most Played and so on).

2. Select New Smart Playlist… from the File menu (or hold down Option as you click the Add button). Use the pop-up menus to choose from the dozens of options to customise the rules for the playlist – the Limit to pop-up will limit the duration or size of the playlist, for example. Click the Add and Remove buttons at the right of the criteria pop-ups to add or remove further options.

3. Check Live Updating to ensure the playlist remains synchronised with your iTunes library. Click OK. The playlist will include Library items that match your rules, and you can play it in the normal way.

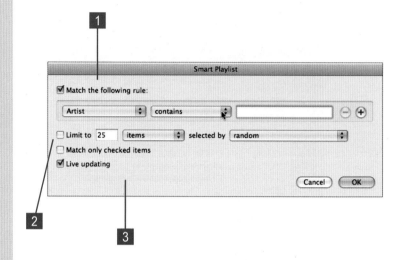

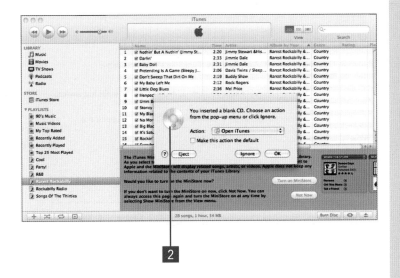

2

3   3

Burning a CD

1 iTunes is the perfect way to make compilation CDs to listen to away from your Mac.

2 Insert a blank CD, launch iTunes and select a playlist to burn. Make sure your selection will fit on a CD by checking the summary information at the bottom of the iTunes window.

3 Click the Burn Disk button at the bottom right of the window.

4 When the burn is complete, iTunes will eject the disk.

5

Browsing, organising and backing up tracks (cont.)

Backing up your iTunes library

1. Using iTunes' built-in backup function, you can create archives of your Library that can be restored easily in the event of a catastrophic system failure.

2. Select Back Up To Disk from the File menu. iTunes will prompt you for a blank disk.

3. Insert a blank optical disk. You can use a DVD if your Mac has a SuperDrive.

4. iTunes creates a backup (prompting for further disks if it runs out of space) and ejects the disk when the process is complete.

5. To restore from a backup, insert the disk. OS X launches iTunes and the application prompts you to confirm that you want to restore.

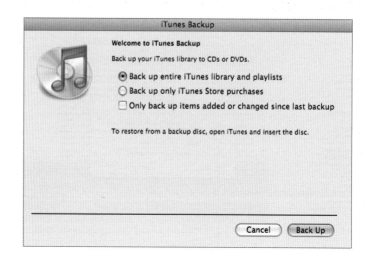

Timesaver tip

Switch between List, Album and Cover Flow views instantly using [Option], [Command] and [3], [Option], [Command] and [4] and [Option], [Command] and [5], respectively.

After almost 200 years, conventional photography – creating pictures using chemical processes – has gone the way of the vinyl record: into the realms of history. In less than 10 years, digital photography has evolved from crude, blocky images and expensive, bulky equipment fit only for geeks and the gadget-obsessed to high-quality pictures that satisfy even professional requirements and cameras that are either cheap and tiny pocketable affairs or else almost indistinguishable from the film-based professional SLRs that they've replaced. Now your processing environment is no longer the darkroom but your Mac and an image-processing, -manipulating and -publishing application, such as iPhoto, is your chemicals, enlarger and album. With a Mac, iPhoto and a digital camera, you're truly standing at the threshold of the future of photography.

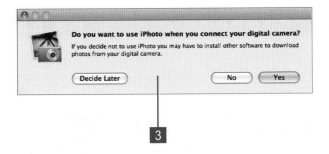

3

Picture this

Meet iPhoto

1 Anyone who's used iTunes will be instantly familiar with iPhoto. Apple's image management application imports pictures from your digital camera whenever you connect it to the Mac, organises the images into 'events', and enables you to view, edit, print, publish online and share them.

2 Once you've installed iLife 08, iPhoto's icon is placed in the Dock. Click the icon to launch the program.

3 The first time it's launched, the application will ask 'Do you want to use iPhoto when you connect your digital camera?' – click Yes.

4 Now you're ready to hook up your camera and start downloading images.

5

Picture this (cont.)

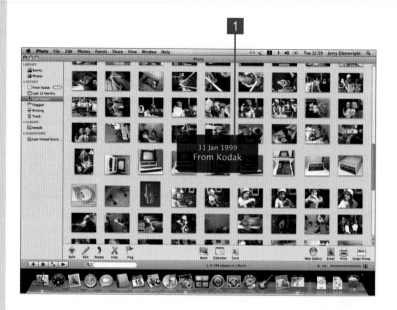

Importing images

1 iPhoto works on the assumption that, when you hook up your camera, it's to upload images based on some recent event – following a holiday, say, or a birthday party. An event is simply a convenient group for each session importing pictures. You can name events as you please and iPhoto appends the date stamp on the pictures to the event too, to further distinguish the importing session (a good reason for setting your camera's clock). With one or more events, you can create 'albums', collections of pictures analogous to iTunes' playlists.

2 To upload images to your Mac, connect your camera via a USB cable. iPhoto launches and the images in the camera are displayed as thumbnails.

For your information

If you already have pictures on your Mac that you'd like to organise and edit with iPhoto, use the Import function (**File>Import to Library** or press [Shift], [Command] and [I]). Navigate to the folder containing the pictures and click Import. Now you can work with the images just as if they'd come from your digital camera.

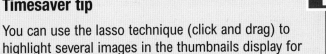

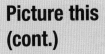

3

3 Zoom the thumbnails using the slider, and name and describe them by typing into the Event and Description fields. To upload all the images, click the Import All button, or else [Command] and click to select the images you want to import and then click Import Selected. iPhoto will prompt you to delete the images from the camera after importing them.

4 If you've bothered to set the correct time in your digital camera and your images are properly time-stamped, check the Autosplit events after importing button below the thumbnails and the application will create distinct events for each day's pictures according to their date stamps.

5 Click Last Import under Recent to display the images the newly created event contains as thumbnails.

Timesaver tip

You can use the lasso technique (click and drag) to highlight several images in the thumbnails display for importing or dragging and dropping between events and from events to albums.

Picture this (cont.)

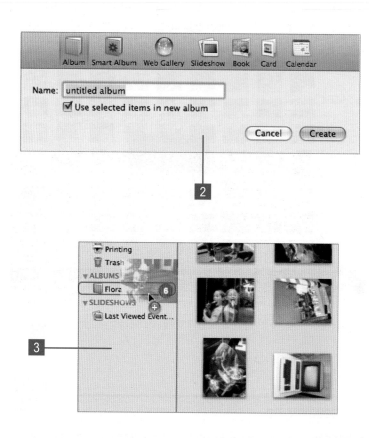

Working with albums

1 Albums work like iTunes playlists. You create an album and copy pictures to it. The pictures aren't actually copied; the album is just a visual list of those pictures you want to group together. Once you've made an album, you can reorganise, view, print, publish and share it.

2 To make a new album, click the Add button, name it and click Create. The album appears under Albums in the Source list.

3 Now click Events and drag your mouse slowly over an event to see its contents. Alternatively, double-click an event to open its contents as thumbnails in the viewing area. When you see an image you want to include in an album, drag and drop it. If you're viewing thumbnails you can also use the lasso technique (see the Timesaver Tip).

4 Click an album to view its contents (much as you would an event). And when you've made an album, it's time to start getting creative!

Important

By default, the Autosplit function works on day-sized gaps, but you can also set it to import pictures based on weekly or even eight- or two-hourly gaps using iPhoto's preferences (`iPhoto>Preferences> Events>Autosplit into Events`).

iPhoto offers a limited (when compared with dedicated image-processing software) but worthy and exceptionally useful selection of editing functions to help you improve your pictures without you having to import and export pics from iPhoto to edit them in some other application.

Cropping

1 Almost every commercial image that you see reproduced in a newspaper or magazine has been cropped before publication – trimmed so that the most interesting part of the picture is teased out. Careful cropping can turn an otherwise mundane picture into a truly eye-grabbing image. iPhoto offers a simple-to-use cropping tool with a helpful 'rule-of-thirds' grid to help you compose the cropped area of the picture.

2 First select the event or album containing the image you want to crop and then click the Edit button.

3 iPhoto switches to the edit window with the images from the event or album in a strip along the top of the editing area and the editing tools below it. Choose the image to edit. Scroll using the slider or left and right slider arrows or press the arrow keys on the keyboard.

4 Click Crop. To maintain a particular size or shape regardless of what you do with the cropping tool, check

5

Editing images (cont.)

Constrain and choose a size or shape from the pop-up menu.

5 Click and drag an edge or corner to resize the cropping box. Click anywhere within the area covered by the box to move it around the picture and home in on the section of the image you want. As you do so, a useful grid is displayed to help you define the areas of interest in the picture using the rule of thirds.

6 The area outside the crop box is dimmed to help you visualise what the cropped image will look like.

7 When you've defined the crop in the way you want it, click Apply.

8 The newly cropped image is zoomed in the viewing area. If you're happy with the result, click Done.

Jargon buster

On the wonk – deviating from the horizontal or vertical.

For your information

The rule of thirds is a compositional guideline for painters, photographers and others who create pictures. By aligning the points of interest in a picture on the intersections of a grid formed with two vertical and two horizontal lines, an image will have arguably greater tension and artistic merit.

Did you know?

The straighten function also works well in reverse, as a rotation tool, enabling you to twist a picture by large or small amounts for creative effect. Of course, you can also use the Rotation tool proper to turn an image through 90-degree steps.

Important

Editing images within iPhoto is non-destructive. iPhoto creates a list of the editing processes you've applied to an image, and returning and recovering the original image is as simple as selecting Revert to Previous (if you've just edited) or Revert to Original from the Photos menu.

Straightening

1. Unless you're claiming artistic licence, a picture that's on the wonk is just a bad version of a picture that would probably be far better if it aligned with the horizontal or vertical. A shot of Pisa's famous tower might justifiably lean to the edge of your picture, but a snap of the kids at the seaside, say, with the sea running out of one side of the image does not make for an attractive shot.

2. Correcting inadvertent leaning is simple and effective using iPhoto's Straighten function. Choose an event or album containing the picture you want to correct and then click Edit.

3. Select your picture so that it's displayed in the viewing area. Now click Straighten.

4. A grid is overlaid on the image. Drag the slider left or right until your picture aligns with a horizontal or vertical grid guide. You can drag the slider, click anywhere within it, or click the icons at each end to move the picture.

5. Notice that, in order to keep the picture square, straightening causes a small of amount of cropping.

Editing images (cont.)

Removing red-eye

1 Even in an age of super-sensitive digital cameras, flash is a necessary evil of indoor photography, and with flash comes a secondary evil: red-eye. Pets are particularly prone, people less so, but still it happens with annoying regularity. However, using iPhoto to rid an image of red-eye is simple.

2 Choose an event or album containing the picture you want to correct, click Edit and then select your picture so that it's displayed in the viewing area.

3 Zoom the image in the viewing area using the slider in the bottom right of the window so that you can see the offending eye(s) clearly. Click Red-Eye, position the cross-hairs over the eye and click to remove the red.

4 To refine the process, switch to manual using the Size pop-up and drag the slider until the circle within the cross-hairs matches the size of the pupil you're correcting. Click on the eye as before.

5 When you're satisfied, click Done.

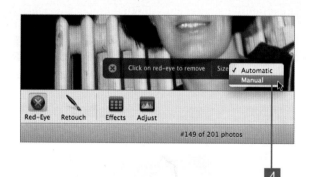

Light and dark, soft and sharp

1 Using conventional image editing software, effects such as reducing shadows and teasing out highlights involve a certain amount of expert knowledge, a combination of software tools and a delicate touch in their application. iPhoto combines all three into simple clickable functions generally applied with a slider and temporarily undone (so you can instantly appreciate the difference) by pressing the Shift key – easy!

2 The Adjust palette is the portal to making fundamental changes to light and shade, colour saturation, sharpness, noise reduction and more.

3 After clicking Edit, select the Adjust palette. The histogram at the top of the palette shows the light distribution across the image. You can tug the central slider to and fro to balance light against dark, or move the right slider gradually leftwards to alter the intensity of the light in the image. The left slider is used to intensify the dark areas. Haul the left and right sliders gently towards the centre and then tweak the middle slider for the best result.

Editing images (cont.)

4 Unlike the histogram sliders, the Exposure and Contrast controls work on all the elements of a picture. Adjusting Exposure will make everything in the picture lighter. Changing the Contrast strengthens the dark areas and intensifies the light areas. Use the Exposure and Contrast controls for general changes, and the histogram sliders for specific changes.

5 To deepen a picture's colours, tweak the Saturation slider. You can make a picture look warmer or cooler (shift the picture's overall tint towards the red or blue, respectively) using the Temperature slider. You can remove a tint (the greenish cast that comes from taking pictures under tungsten lights, for example) using the Tint tool. Use the slider or click the pipette and then click a neutral area in the picture to balance the colour reproduction.

6 The Sharpness slider is useful for correcting inadvertent soft focus, but use the function sparingly otherwise you'll have jagged edges where they're ought to be smooth.

7 Digital camera sensors work impressively well in low-light situations, but the resulting images can be prone to noise – annoying speckles in the picture. The Reduce Noise function will remove much of this.

5

Editing images (cont.)

Other tools

1 Experiment! You won't destroy an image by editing it, and you'll be amazed at how much better a picture can be made with a bit of judicious editing. A drab image can be made instantly brighter simply by clicking the Enhance button, and the Retouch function will help remove unwanted blemishes from images (use the slider to control the size of the Retouch tool and then click, or click and drag, in the image).

2 The Rotate tool turns your picture anticlockwise in 90-degree increments. The Effects palette provides access to picture effects such as sepia, black and white, colour enhance and more. Click an effect from the palette to apply it. Some are applied in stages; use the up and down arrows at the bottom of the effect to alter its intensity.

Timesaver tip

Use the Adjust Window Copy button to copy the editing steps you've made to an image and reapply them in one step to a different image using the Paste button.

Timesaver tip

Rotate a picture clockwise by pressing [Option], [Command] and [R] or [Command] and [R] to rotate anticlockwise.

For your information

Press and hold the [Shift] key while editing to compare an edited picture with the original.

Until now, a major downside of digital photography lay in sharing images with your family, friends and colleagues. You can burn a CD, of course, but that means powering up a computer, loading the disk, sitting in front of a monitor... not exactly the cosy experience that is fishing out a photo album and sitting with your feet up, cooing over pics. And it's much the same story hooking up your camera to a TV to watch a slideshow or viewing pictures on the camera's LCD screen – none of these compares with the non-powered, paper-based presentation of snaps that you can take and view anywhere. An album might be old hat, but it's survived for so long precisely because it's user-friendly. Apple understands that, although making slideshows, Web galleries and the like is a great way to view pictures, there's little to compare with prints beautifully arranged in an album. Fortunately, with iPhoto, you can have both.

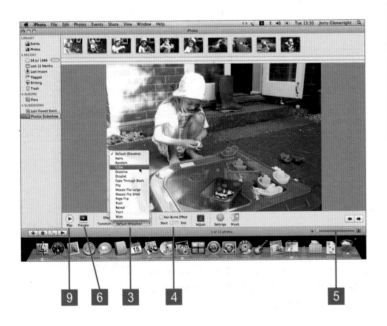

Slideshows

1 Of course, iPhoto will let you create fabulous-looking slideshows complete with all kinds of visual effects such as zooms, wipes, dissolves and the like, so you can show off your pictures at their best.

2 Select the pictures you want to include in the slideshow by clicking, [Command] and clicking or lassoing in the viewing area, and then click the Add button. Select Slideshow, name it and click Create.

3 You can apply transitional effects (dissolves, spinning cubes and so on when moving from one picture in the slideshow to the next) to a single slide or all of them in the show by selecting from the Transition menu.

4 The 'Ken Burns effect' describes the process of slowly zooming and panning a picture to bring the feeling of motion to a still image – it's a technique used heavily in documentary making where movie footage is not always available.

Sharing pictures (cont.)

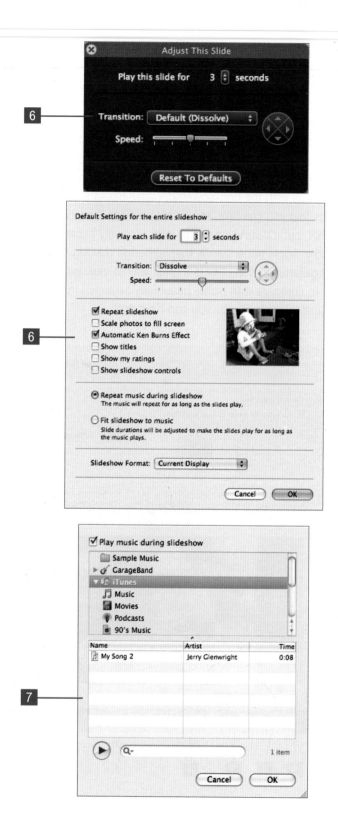

5 Check the Ken Burns Effect box and then select and use the grab hand to move the picture until the starting point for the effect is where you want it on screen. You can also use the zoom slider at the bottom right to set the level of magnification. Now click the Start/End switch to End and repeat the process, selecting the level of zoom and moving the picture so it's where you want it when the effect comes to an end.

6 Click Preview to see the effect in action. Tweak the settings if it's not quite how you want it.

7 Click the Music button to select a track from your iTunes library to play while the slideshow is running.

8 Other options – the pause between slides, for example – are available by clicking the Settings button.

9 Click the Play button to view your slideshow.

Mail Photo

Photo

Size: Small (Faster Downloading)

Photo Count: 1
Estimated Size: 63 KB ——— 3

Include: ☑ Titles   ☑ Comments

(Cancel) (Compose) ——— 4

Email

1 If, while browsing pictures, you get an overwhelming urge to share them with someone, there are fewer routes quicker and easier than email.

2 Select the pictures you want to send by clicking, [Command] and clicking or lassoing in the viewing area, and then click the Email button.

3 Use the Size pop-up menu to resize the pictures for speedier mailing – the Estimated Size field below Photo Count indicates how much data you're trying to send. Smaller files will reach their destination quicker, and it may be that your ISP limits the size of your mailbox.

4 When you're ready, click Compose. Mail opens and you can enter an email address for the recipient and a message if you like. Click Send as usual (turn to Chapter 7 for more about the Internet and using Mail) to email the pictures.

5

! Important

If you find emails bouncing back or taking an unusually long time to send, reduce the quantity or size of the pictures you're trying to email.

? Did you know?

The Ken Burns effect is named after American documentary maker Ken Burns. Apple first introduced the effect to iMovie in 2003.

Sharing pictures (cont.)

Web

1 With a .Mac account you can upload pictures and create public and private Web galleries that your friends and family can view or download pictures to their own computers for printing.

2 Select the pictures you want in the gallery by clicking, [Command] and clicking or lassoing in the viewing area, and then click the Web Gallery button. iPhoto uploads the selection direct to your .Mac account.

3 If you don't have a .Mac account, select Photo Page from the Send to iWeb option on the Share menu.

4 iWeb launches and you can select a template for the gallery.

5 Choose Publish to Folder from iWeb's File menu and select a suitable folder for the gallery.

6 Upload the folder to the space provided by your ISP for making Web pages using an FTP client (for details of uploading the data for a Website, see Meet iWeb, page 155).

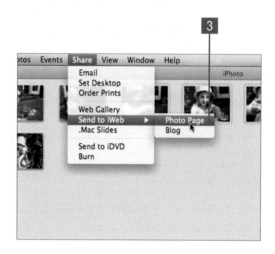

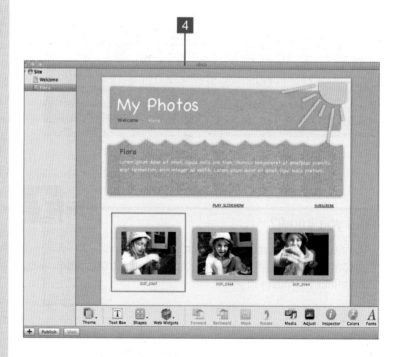

Printing

1 Click the Print button or select Print from the File menu.

2 If you have several printers, select one from the pop-up Printer menu. Use the Presets, Paper Size and Print Size pop-ups to choose a suitable output type, paper and print size.

3 Click Print and Print again.

For your information

If you'd prefer to have your digital images professionally printed, you can build them into postcards, spiral-bound calendars or even beautifully bound books and have them printed and bound by Apple.

Click the Book, Calendar or Postcard buttons and select from the various styles for the project. Follow the automated steps and a little while later, the publication will arrive in the post.

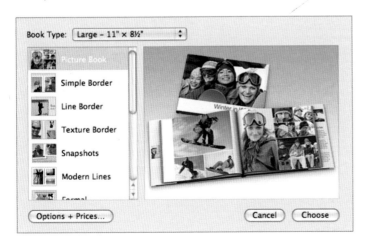

Making movies

Once upon a time, cine was thought impossibly high-tech: you needed a clockwork camera, a light meter and three minutes of 8 mm film strip that you shot, packed off for (expensive) processing and then sat for long hours with a scalpel and sticky tape, trying to edit it into a movie that didn't look like it was shot while you were under the influence of something hallucinogenic. The advent of domestic videotape cameras revolutionised home movie-making and, when camcorders went digital, the future was at last within reach. Using iMovie, iLife's digital video editing suite, you can create the kind of movies yesteryear's home directors could only dream about.

Meet iMovie

1 Double-click iMovie's icon in the Dock after installing iLife 08 to launch the application.

2 iMovie's interface is similar to iPhoto – you skim thumbnail previews of video clips imported from your video camera. Just like iPhoto, iMovie imports, organises and stores video as events – a convenient label that assumes that the video you're importing is associated with a particular date and event, such as a birthday or footage from a concert you attended.

3 As well as importing, storing, organising and previewing your clips, you can create movies by dragging and dropping sections of imported source material into a project, preview and edit to get it just right, and then share direct to your .Mac account or YouTube, export it to your iPod, iPhone or Apple TV.

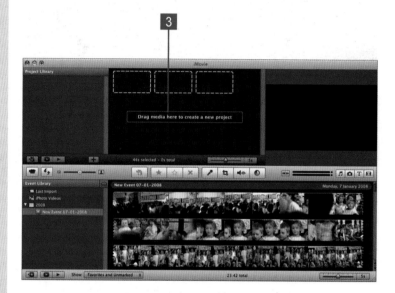

2

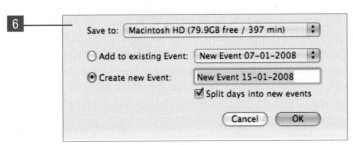

6

5

Getting started

1 Launch iMovie, hook up your camera to a suitable port on your Mac and set it to connect mode (see the manufacturer's guidelines). The Mac should recognise the camera immediately. If it doesn't, press [Command] + [I] to open the Import Window.

2 If your camcorder uses DV or HDV tapes, connecting it will launch an Import Window complete with camera controls so that you can play, rewind and fast-forward the tape in the camera. To import the entire tape, set the Mode button to Automatic and click the Import button. iMovie rewinds the tape and then imports all the video stored on it.

3 To import selections from the tape, set the Mode button to Manual and use the tape transport controls to preview and cue the video that you want to import. Be sure to import extra footage at the beginning and end of the video – you can fine-tune it later. Now click Import.

Making movies (cont.)

6

Generating Thumbnails

Processing Event: New Event 15-01-2008

Time remaining: less than a minute

4 If your camera stores video on flash cards, HD or DVD, video appears as individual clips in the Import Window. Click a clip and use the playback controls to watch it in the preview window.

5 To import all the clips, set the Mode button to Automatic and then click the Import All button. Alternatively, set the Mode button to Manual to select individual files, and then click Import Checked.

6 After clicking Import, use the pop-up Save to field to select a location for the footage and either add it to an existing event or create a new one using the appropriate dialogue options. Click OK. The footage is imported into the iMovie library and the application creates a series of thumbnails that you can skim to review what you've captured.

Did you know?

You can import video from a variety of sources as well as your camcorder. If you've used a previous version of iMovie, select Import iMovie HD Project… from the File menu. You can also import QuickTime movies direct from your hard drive or clips from video-enabled still cameras from the iPhoto video library: select Import Movies from the File menu.

Important

New and recent Macs have the processing muscle required to run iMovie, but if you've upgraded a Mac that's a few years old you might find that it doesn't quite have the necessary power. The iLife installer checks your Mac and will not install the application if your machine does not meet the minimum requirements. If it fails this check, you can take advantage of iMovie HD, a less demanding version of iMovie available as a free download from Apple.

For your information

If iMovie won't recognise your camcorder, make sure it's connected to the correct port. Cameras that record to flash, HDD or DVD connect to a USB port; cameras that record on DV or HDV tape connect via iLink to a FireWire port.

Import video into iMovie and, very quickly, you'll begin to build the perfect library and a super-convenient backup of your most precious filmed moments. You can browse and organise as easily as launching the application – no more afternoons in the dark struggling with an overheating projector or fiddling with an analogue camcorder, a sea of cables and an unresponsive television. What's more, with footage in the can, it's time to get creative, and selecting and editing clips from the library to build anything from a home short to a full cinematic feature is as easy as skimming, selecting, dragging and dropping.

Imported videos are listed in the iMovie Event Library in the lower left of the application's window. Each event appears with the name that you gave it when importing.

Reviewing events

1 To see a thumbnail filmstrip for the last footage you imported, click Last Import at the top of the library list. The thumbnails are displayed in the Event Browser at the right of the library. Move your mouse pointer over each thumbnail to skim through the footage. Choose any other event by clicking it to view its thumbnail filmstrip in the Event Browser. Events are organised by name and by year.

2 Notice the red vertical bar that moves across thumbnails as you skim: that's the playhead, which indicates where you are in the clip. Press [Spacebar] and the event plays from the location of the playhead. Press [Spacebar] again to return to skim mode. You can also click and drag anywhere in the filmstrip to select a section for playback, and then double-click at the start to view it.

3 To watch the event in full-screen mode, click Play Selected Events Full Screen. Use the [Escape] key to return to the iMovie window.

5

Did you know?

To rename an event, double-click it and type a new name. To delete it from the Event Library, select and press [Command] and [Delete] or choose Move to Trash from the File menu. You can join and split events as easily as dragging and dropping one on top of another in the Events Library, or select a frame in the Event Browser at the point you wish to split it and choose Split Event Before Selected Clip from the File menu.

Working with video (cont.)

Creating a movie

1 Click the Add button below the Project Library list, or select New Project from the File menu (or press [Command] + [N]). Double-click the new project in the Project Library and enter a name for your project.

2 Select footage to work with from the Event Library. Review and cue in the Event Browser and, when you find video you want to include in the movie, lasso it, much as you would text in a word processor or icons on the desktop. Use the grab handles at the left and right of the lasso to tweak the length of the selection.

3 Move the cursor over the selected footage. Drag and drop the video on to the project window. Build your movie by repeating the process, choosing different events, skimming and selecting footage and dragging and dropping in the project window.

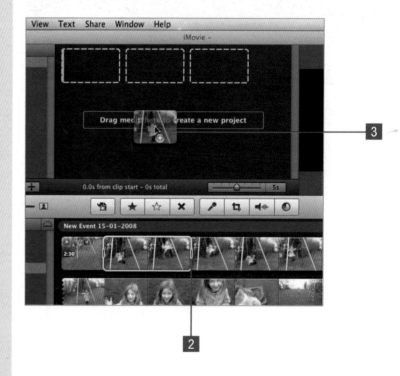

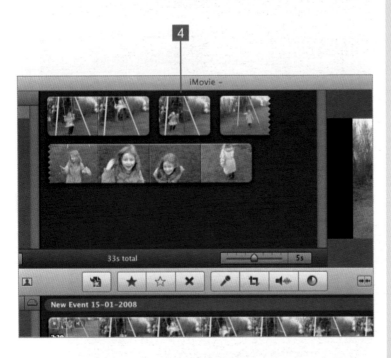

4 You can insert footage between existing clips by dragging the new selection to the point at which you want to insert it. You can also rearrange clips in the project by dragging and dropping them. To remove footage, lasso it and select Cut from the Edit menu, or press [Command] + [X] or the [Delete] key.

5 There's no need to save: iMovie tracks all your edits automatically. Quit the application and it will open exactly where you left off.

6 As you create the movie, skim the footage in the project window to preview it or position the playhead with a click and press the spacebar to watch it.

Working with video (cont.)

Going for effect

1 Using iMovie you can add titles, credits and other text to your movies and select from a variety of transitions – cross-dissolve, twirl, disintegrate and so on – for a truly professional effect.

2 Click the Titles Browser button (or press [Command] + [3]) to see the available title styles in the browser.

3 Choose a title and drag and drop it to the section of the project where you want it to appear.

4 Overtype the placeholder text and click the Show Fonts button to choose a different font.

5 Shorten or lengthen the duration of the title by clicking and dragging the blue and yellow box in the project window.

6 When you're done click the Play button in the Preview window to see the title in action. Edit if necessary, and then click Done.

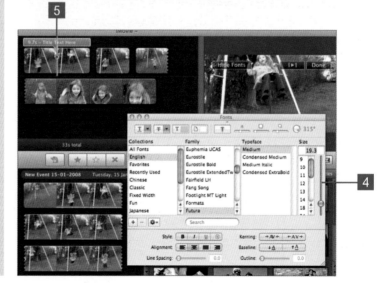

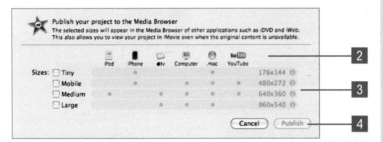

7 To add transitions to link scenes in your movie, click the Transitions Browser button (or press [Command] + [4]).

8 Mouse over a transition to preview it in action. When you've chosen one, click and drag it between the scenes that you want to link.

5

Sharing movies

1 iMovie can share movies to iTunes, your iPod and iPhone, a .Mac account and direct to YouTube. You can also export a movie to disk as a QuickTime file and burn it to a DVD.

2 Choose a destination from the Share menu. You'll be prompted for your account details if you choose YouTube.

3 Select a suitable size to share the movie – smaller is faster and more portable.

4 Click Publish to share the movie to the destination.

Timesaver tip

See and review more events in the Event Browser by toggling the Show/Hide Events List button. Skim events faster by increasing the rate of the Frames Per Thumbnail slider in the bottom right of the window.

Timesaver tip

You can print a hard copy of the thumbnails for an event by selecting Print Event from the File menu.

Jargon buster

Transition – a visual effect to link two scenes in a movie.

Burning DVDs

If your Mac has a SuperDrive you can use iDVD to burn professional-looking movie DVDs, and slideshows, presentations and music with animated backdrops of still images to blank or rewritable DVDs that can be played in standard domestic DVD players or in a computer. You can choose from iDVD's comprehensive selection of predesigned themes and drag and drop video, music and images from other iApps, such as iMovie, iTunes and GarageBand.

Meet iDVD

1. iDVD's icon is located in the Dock. Click the icon to launch the application.

2. Click Create a New Project, type a name for your new DVD into the Save As field and select a location to save the project.

3. Aspect Ratio governs the way in which your DVD is displayed. Click the Standard button if you have an old-style television (i.e. one that is vaguely square-shaped), or choose Widescreen if your TV conforms to the 16:9 standard. Click Create.

4. The main display area shows a preview of the selected theme from the list on the right. Decide how you'd like your finished DVD to look (you can customise the themes before burning) by clicking a theme in the list to watch a preview.

5. Each theme has a disclosure triangle, which provides access to further themed menus for chapters, extras and so on.

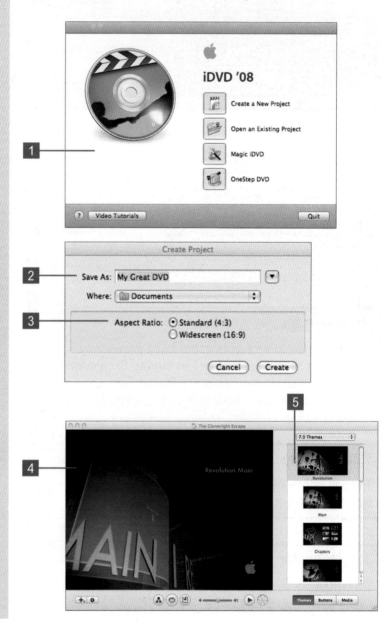

Adding content

1 When you've decided on a theme, you can begin to add video, music and other content, and customise menus and buttons.

2 iDVD works with 'Drop Zones', areas in which you add video, images, music and titles. Drop Zones are indicated by placeholders (Drop Zone 1, Drop Zone 2 and so on) in the Preview area. Click the Edit Drop Zones button, and then click the Media button to select content to fill the Drop Zones.

3 Click the Movies tab, choose a movie, and drag and drop it on a Drop Zone. The corresponding Drop Zone in the Preview area is replaced by your movie.

4 Create a Menu link to the movie by clicking the Add button and selecting Add Movie. Click the Movies tab, and drag and drop the movie to the link in the preview area. You can rename the link (and choose a different typeface, size and style) by clicking it and overtyping the default movie name.

5

For your information

You can use iDVD's built-in assistant to create DVDs until you become familiar with the application and develop confidence using its features. Select Magic DVD from the opening menu after launching the application.

Burning DVDs (cont.)

5 Each theme has default background music, which you can change as easily as clicking the Audio tab, selecting a tune you'd like to use with the theme, and dragging and dropping it on to the Preview area.

For your information

Select a link and click the Buttons icon if you'd rather use an image or animation in place of text-based movie links. Use the pop-up menu to select the type of link you'd like to include, and drag and drop one from the pane to the Preview area. Click and drag in the Preview area to position the new link. Now click the Start-Stop Motion button to preview the link.

Preview your DVD project in its finished state using iDVD's own virtual DVD player, and then burn the project direct from the application.

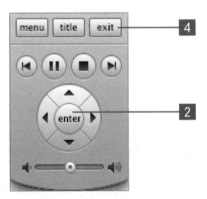

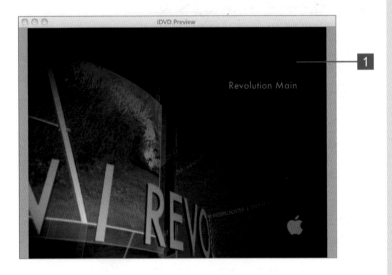

Virtual player

1 To view the DVD as it will be seen when used with a DVD player, click the Preview Playback button.

2 iDVD launches the virtual DVD player, complete with a remote control – it works just like a real-world player. Click Enter on the remote's Enter button to watch the DVD.

3 Pause, skip chapters, navigate menus or return to the DVD's title by clicking the relevant buttons on the remote control handset.

4 When you've finished watching, click Exit on the remote to return to iDVD.

5

Watch and write (cont.)

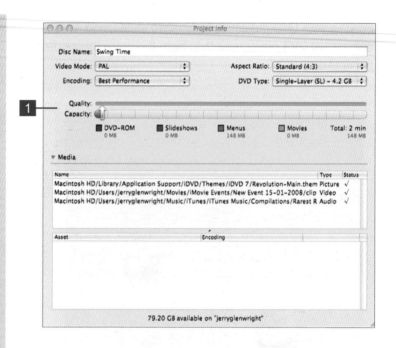

Burning

1. Before burning, select Project Info from the Project menu and choose from the various options to ensure your DVD will be suitable for the purpose intended. You can encode the DVD in the American NTSC format if you plan to send it to a friend or relative in the US. From the Encoding pop-up menu, you can trade speed against space. Best Performance is swift, but larger projects will require a more comprehensive, complex and therefore slower encoding process. Monitor the Capacity gauge and choose an encoding strategy to suit the available resources.

2. Insert a blank DVD and click the Burn button (iDVD will prompt for a disk if you're yet to insert one).

3. The application displays a progress dialogue showing the various stages of rendering and encoding before burning the disk.

4. After burning, iDVD ejects the finished DVD ready for watching in any suitable player or computer.

Errors in Project
There were errors during the project validation that have to be fixed before burning the project.

Open DVD Map   OK

Timesaver tip

Once a project has been rendered, encoded and burned, you can conveniently burn further copies by inserting another blank DVD when the burned disk is ejected.

Important

iDVD can burn single- and dual-layer DVDs, but the former will give far greater compatibility with domestic standalone players...

From nothing, the Internet – and especially the World Wide Web ('the Web' to you and me) – has become as indispensable a part of everyday life as your own living room. There are few people whose lives aren't interwoven daily with the fabric of cyberspace. We shop online, talk to our friends and make new ones, hook up with distant relatives, research school and work projects, read and publish blogs, watch movies, download podcasts, share music – truly every real-world activity has its Web counterpart. Enjoy the Web for a while and you'll start hankering to stake out your own little plot of cyberspace. The pioneers of personal Web pages had HTML coding to contend with, but, by using iWeb, iLife's website building application, putting up a Web page is as easy as selecting content, dragging it to a predesigned page theme and clicking Publish.

A place of your own

Meet iWeb

1. To launch the iWeb application, click its icon in the Dock. The application is designed to integrate perfectly with other iApps, such as iMovie, iPhoto and GarageBand (for podcasts).

2. Sign in to .Mac at the prompt if you have an account, or else click Close.

5

3. Websites are built from elements such as pictures, text, video clips, and clickable links to other parts of your site and external Web pages. iWeb's strength lies in providing attractive templates for these pages predesigned to suit all kinds of online publishing needs. To create an attractive and interactive website, all you need to do is select a template and customise it with your own content – no programming required!

4. Scroll through the various themes in the pane at the left of the Templates window. When you see a theme you like, click it to view the various publishing templates – Photos, Blog, About Me and

A place of your own (cont.)

so on – in the main part of the window. Click a template, and then click the Choose button.

5 The iWeb editing screen appears. Here you can customise the chosen template to suit your ideas and requirements.

6 The name of your site and a list of its pages is displayed in the pane on the left. The name of a page is displayed in a visitor's browser window. To change the name, double-click and type in a new name.

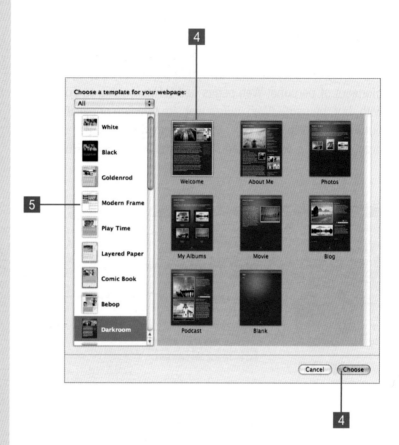

Timesaver tip

You can resize highlighted text using [Command] and [+], and [Command] and [–] ([Command] and [plus], and [Command] and [minus]) and make it bold, italic or underlined with [Command] and [B], [Command] and [I], and [Command] and [U], respectively.

Important

Making a Web page can be confusing at first – even with the simplicity of an application such as iWeb. If you make a mistake, or move or delete something you'd rather keep, just undo the last action by pressing [Command] and [Z].

For your information

It's generally considered good practice to use just one theme across all your pages – visitors to your site can be confused into thinking they've followed a link to an external page if you use different themes.

Build your page

1 Now the fun starts! Select a placeholder – text or image – on the template, and replace it with your own information. You can restyle text using the Format menu. You can also click and drag page elements to new locations.

2 To select text for editing, double-click it or click and then click again to place a cursor in the text, scrolling to select the text you want to change. The text is highlighted and you can type over it. Choose a font (**Format>Font>Show Fonts**), size (**Format> Font>Bigger/ Smaller**) and style (**Format>Font>Bold/ Italic** etc.) from the Format menu. Align the text by choosing centred, justified and so on from the **Format>Text** menu.

3 Text is contained within invisible boxes that can be relocated to suit your requirements. To tweak the location of a textbox, click and drag it. You can also position extra textboxes by clicking the Text Box icon in the toolbar at the foot of the Preview window.

5

A place of your own (cont.)

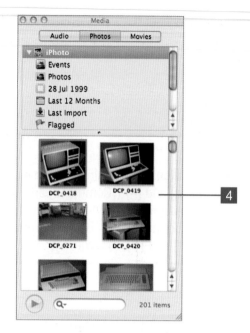

4 To replace a placeholder image with your own, click the Media icon. Navigate to the image you want and then drag and drop it on to the placeholder.

 4

5 You can resize an image by clicking to select it and using the slider. Click the Edit Mask button to alter the way the image is cropped and to determine the size of the reflection effect.

6 Add further pages by clicking the Add button at the bottom of the Pages pane and selecting a template from the Theme window (you can also select New Page from the File menu or press [Command] + [N].

7 Press [Command] + [S] to save your pages.

Important !

Be aware that choosing exotic fonts for your Web page may have unexpected results if a visitor does not have the font installed on their computer.

When your pages look just the way you want them, it's time to go live and publish them to the Web so that everyone can enjoy your handiwork.

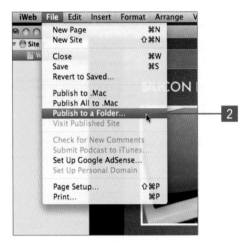

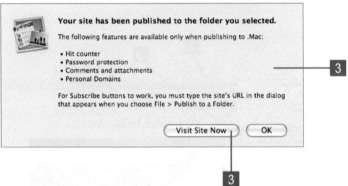

Previewing your website

1. Before publishing your website, preview it to ensure that all is working as you intended.

2. From the File menu, select Publish to a Folder... Click New Folder, enter a suitable name and then click Choose. Click Continue at the Do you really have rights permissions? dialogue (and check Don't show this again if you're happy to shoulder the burden of copyright responsibility!), and then click Continue.

3. iWeb will tell you that your website has been published to the designated folder. To preview it immediately, click Visit Site Now.

4. iWeb launches the default browser (Safari, unless you've changed the default to FireFox or some such) and you'll see the site as your visitors will see it.

5. Test links and other page elements by clicking them, but be aware that some items may not work until the site is live.

6. If all is well, it's time to get it online.

5

Going live (cont.)

Uploading with a .Mac account

1 iWeb is perfectly integrated with .Mac and designed to publish pages to your .Mac account with consummate ease.

2 Click the Publish button in the bottom left of the iWeb window (or select Publish to .Mac from the File menu). iWeb logs in to your .Mac account and uploads all the data necessary to build your website.

3 To see the site live and working, click the Visit button to pull up your index page (i.e. the first page in your website) and navigate from there.

4 Notice that the pages in the iWeb sidebar are displayed in blue when the site has been published to .Mac. Edited pages that are yet to be published appear red.

2

If you don't have a .Mac account

1 Before getting your site online, you'll need two things: online storage space for the data (provided by your ISP) and an FTP (File Transfer Protocol) client application to upload the data for your website to your storage space. FTP clients are freely available to download from a variety of freeware and shareware sources.

2 Fetch is a proven FTP client that you can try free for 15 days and buy if you like what it offers. Download it at **www.fetchsoftworks.com**.

3 Select Publish to a Folder, enter the URL for your website (provided by your ISP), click New Folder, enter a suitable name and click Choose. Click Continue at the Do you really have rights permissions? dialogue, and then click Continue. iWeb will tell you that your website has been published to the designated folder.

5

4 Launch Fetch (or your chosen FTP client), click Put and type the URL for your online storage (or follow the instructions provided by your ISP for uploading a website). Navigate to the folder published by iWeb, [Shift] and click to select its contents and Fetch will upload the data to your URL.

5 Finally, launch Safari or your browser of choice, type the URL for your Web pages, and test them for working links and other page elements.

For your information

Your .Mac website URL is:

web.mac.com/your_member_name/your_site_name

Timesaver tip

You can toggle the visibility of placeholder frames (which are invisible until you click to select) by choosing Show Layout (or pressing [Shift], [Command] and [L]) from the View menu.

GarageBand is the iLife application that transforms your Mac into a personal recording studio complete with multi-track mixer, recorder and sampled instruments. Serious musicians and budding sound engineers can use the truly immense scope and power of GarageBand to record the next top-20 hit or award-winning movie theme using the sampled loops shipped with the application, one of the many third-party plug-in packs or downloads from GarageBand users on the Web or by recording themselves and other musicians direct from life. For the rest of us, there's GarageBand's podcast studio to create podcasts that can be integrated into iWeb pages, and Magic GarageBand, a built-in wizard that will help any non-musician to put together fun music tracks to impress him- or herself, friends and family.

Music maestro

Meet GarageBand

1. GarageBand's icon is in the Dock. Click the icon to launch the application.

2. You have four options: you can open an existing music project, create a new one, launch the podcast recorder or experiment with Magic GarageBand.

3. To see the program proper, click Create New Music Project. Like real-world multi-track recorders, GarageBand records instruments, voices, drumbeats and the like as separate tracks, which are mixed together to create a song. Each track is displayed horizontally across the GarageBand window.

4. Tracks have a number of controls (from left to right): record enable (clicking the track automatically enables record); mute (to switch playback of the track on and off in the mix; the mix is the playback of all tracks in the song; a muted track is greyed in the time line display) the solo button mutes all the other tracks in the time line; the lock button copies the track to your hard drive and protects it from

5

being re-recorded or edited; locking a track eases the demand for processing power and can smooth the playback of your song.

5 At the left of a track you can see the name of the instrument that recorded the track along with a number of controls. To the right there's the mixer section, which you use to adjust panning (whether sounds come from the right or left of the stereo mix) and playback volume. Use the disclosure triangle at the right of the Tracks section to hide and reveal the mixer. To the right of the mixer is a visualisation of the recording.

6 Recordings are created with loops – individual blocks of recorded sound – placed on a time line divided into measures (numbered) and beats (vertical indicators between the measure numbers). Loops can be pre-recorded (many are shipped with GarageBand), acquired from the Web or recorded live from an instrument or voice. You can place a loop anywhere on the time line, and copy and repeat it.

Music maestro (cont.)

7

7 The playhead is the point at which the music starts to play. Click in the time line to position the playhead.

8 In the toolbar at the bottom of the editing screen, there are buttons to add a new track, toggle the loop browser and track editing window, familiar cassette-like controls for record, playback, rewind, fast-forward and so on, a digital counter (click to jump directly to measures, beats or a relative time in your song), master volume (the overall volume of the tracks in the project), track info and media browser buttons.

5

Music maestro (cont.)

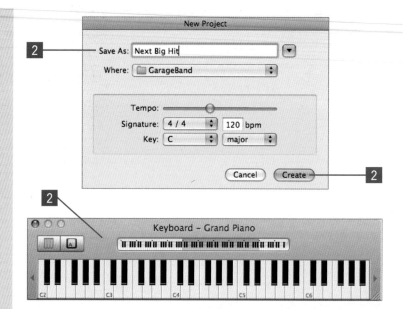

Getting started

1 No musical knowledge or previous recording experience is necessary to start using GarageBand productively right out of the box. Putting together a tune is as easy as …

2 Click Create New Music Project. Name your new project in the Save As field and then click Create. The GarageBand editing screen is displayed and there's one instrument – Grand Piano – in the tracks section. Also displayed is the virtual keyboard. You can use this to enter musical notes by clicking the piano keys, or click the Computer Key icon to switch to the Musical Typing display. Now you can enter notes by 'playing' them on your keyboard.

3 For this exercise, however, we'll use pre-recorded loops, so for now click the virtual keyboard's Close box.

4 Toggle the Track Info button and select Electric Piano from the pane on the right. Click the Track Info button again to toggle off the display.

For your information

You can add and edit 'notes' in the loops by clicking a loop and clicking on the Track Editor button (or simply double-click a loop). Click a note to select it and use the Pitch and Note Velocity controls to alter it. Click the Advanced pop-up menu for access to sustain, modulation and other exotic controls.

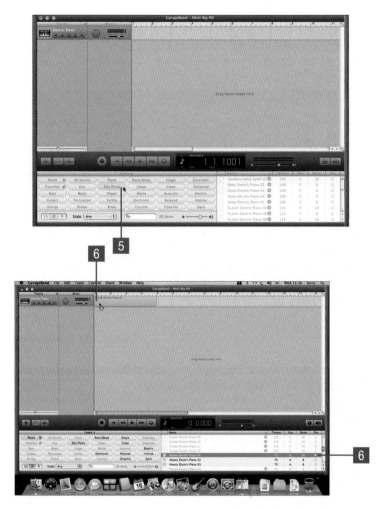

5 Click the Loop Browser toggle, click the Elec Piano tab, and then scroll the list of loops until you see Moody Electric Piano 01. Drag and drop this loop to measure 1 in the time line. Notice that the loop is one bar (four notes – we're in 4/4 time) long.

6 [Option] and click the loop and drag (hold down [Option] while clicking and dragging) it to measure 5. Now drag and drop Moody Electric Piano 03 to measure 9 and repeat it at measure 11.

7 Now press the Play button to listen to the two bars of music you've just created. Press Play again to stop the playhead. Finally, rewind the playhead to the start by clicking the Jump to beginning button.

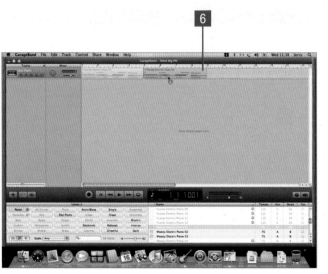

Building your song

With a basic track in place, it's time to start layering the project with extra tracks to create complete songs.

1. Click the Elec Piano tab to toggle it off, and then click the Bass tab. Drag and drop Alternative Rock Bass 04 to measure 1 below the existing track. GarageBand creates a new track for Elec Bass (you can click the Track Info button to select a different type of bass).

2. [Option] and drag the bass loop to measures 2 and 3, and then drag and drop Alternative Rock Bass 03 to measure 4. [Shift] and click all four bass loops to select them, and then [Option] and drag to measure 5.

3. Now [Shift] and click all the loops in both tracks from measures 1 to 8 and [Option] and drag them to measure 13.

4. Deselect Bass in the loop browser and click the Shaker tab. Drag, drop and [Option] and drag and drop Shaker 01 loop (two measures long) so that it plays across every measure of the song.

Building your song (cont.)

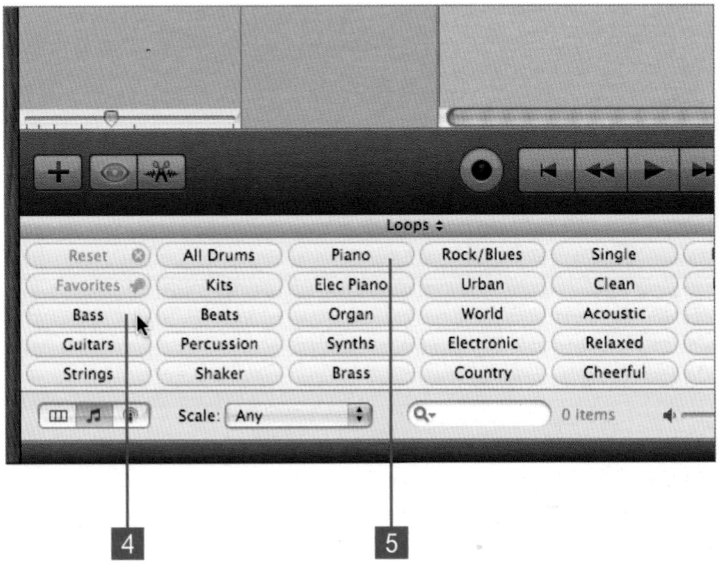

5 Ensure the playhead is at measure 1 and click Play to hear your progress so far – your tune is beginning to come together.

6 Now it's up to you. Select instruments from the loop browser and try out loops in your song, repeating them and using silence to increase musical interest. Use the backspace key to delete selected loops from the time line and [Command] and [Z] to undo if you make a mistake.

5

Building your song (cont.)

Mixing

1 The last stage in the music-making process is to mix your masterpiece – balancing the position and volume of the various tracks until they sound just right. Mixing is what teases out the best in a track.

2 Rotate a track's rotary control to pan music so that it is positioned predominately to the left or the right of the stereo mix. Panning brings life to your music, giving it a dramatic tension that attracts the ear and catches the attention. It also separates elements that might otherwise fight with each other and muddy the sound.

3 Begin with the percussion tracks (drums, followed by shakers and so on), adjusting the volume, so that there's plenty of power but without breaking up the quality of the sound. Mute all the other tracks (click the headphones button to 'solo' the track you're working with). As you bring up the volume, watch the volume indicators for left and right stereo channels so that the volume peaks at about the midway point.

2

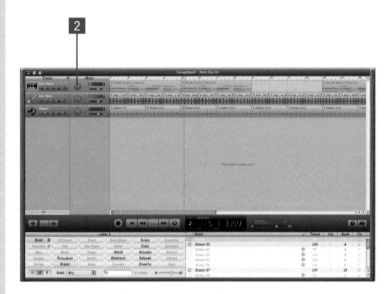

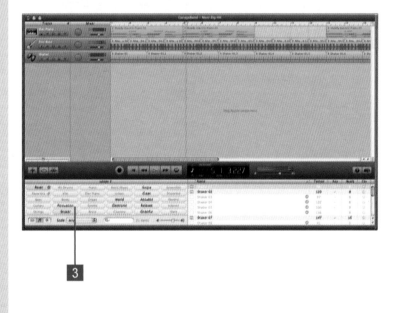

3

Building your song (cont.)

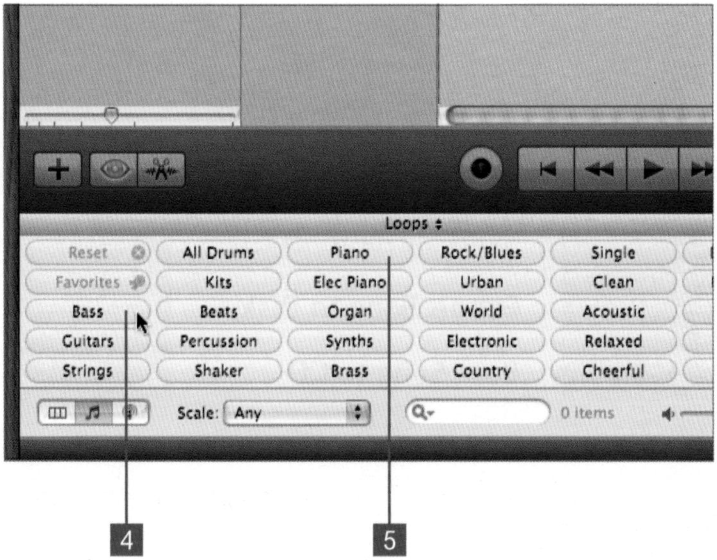

4 Now adjust the volume for the bass so that it's balanced with the drums and can be heard clearly but without being overly prominent.

5 Next, adjust the melody instruments – guitar, piano and so on – in proportion with the bass and drums, and according to your ears and what you're trying to achieve with the song.

6 Now enable all tracks and listen to your project. If some tracks seem to be competing with others, causing the sound to be muddied, pan them left and right to give the project breathing space. Try to keep the bass and drums in the centre of the mix or panned only very gently left or right of centre.

Building your song (cont.)

Sharing

1 When your project sounds as it should, it's time to let others hear it! GarageBand perfectly integrates with iApps such as iTunes, iDVD and iWeb to enable you to share your tunes, burn them to CD and publish them on the Web.

2 To export a project to your iTunes library, select Send Song to iTunes from the Share menu. Complete the various fields for artist, composer, album and so on. Select AAC encoding from the Compress Using pop-up menu. Click Share.

3 GarageBand mixes down a final take according to your track and mixing settings and saves it to the iTunes library. iTunes is launched and the song plays automatically. If further editing is required, return to GarageBand, tweak the project and Send Song... again.

4 You can also mix down a project as a standard MP3 to play on a digital music player, burn to a CD, copy to your phone for use as a ringtone or anything else you can do with MP3s.

Send your song to your iTunes library.

iTunes Playlist:	Jerry's Playlist
Artist Name:	Jumpin' Jerry
Composer Name:	JG
Album Name:	Tripping the Loop Fantastic!

☑ Compress

Compress Using:	AAC Encoder
Audio Settings:	High Quality

Ideal for music of all types. Download times
are moderate. Details: AAC, 128kbps, stereo,
optimized for music and complex audio.
Estimated Size: 0.6MB.

(Cancel) (Share)

5

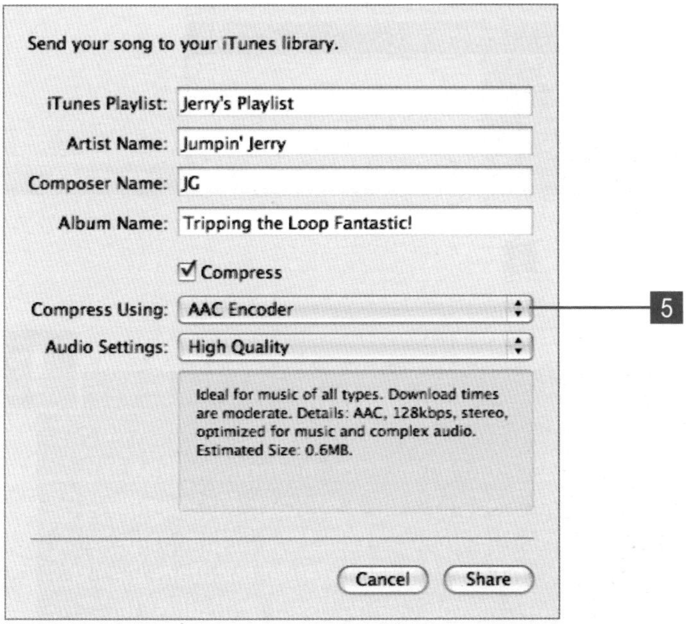

5 From the Share menu, select Export Song to Disk… Choose MP3 from the Compress Using pop-up menu.

6 To save your project at CD quality, uncheck the Compress box on the Export Song to Disk… dialogue. Select Burn Song to CD from the Share menu to burn a project direct to disk – GarageBand will prompt you for a blank disk.

5

Building your song (cont.)

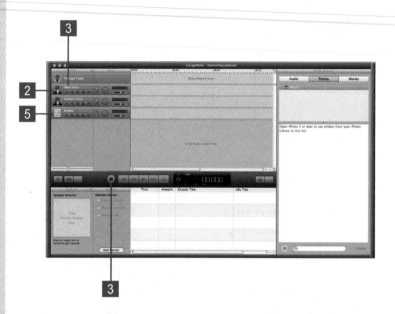

Podcasts

1 GarageBand is ideal for making podcasts – syndicated digital audio files that can be downloaded automatically and played on digital media players and computers.

2 Click Create New Podcast Episode after launching the program (or closing an existing project). The GarageBand podcast studio uses convenient tracks for male and female voices and jingles to create the podcast episode.

3 Click the track Record button to enable it for recording. When you're ready to begin recording, click the Record button in the toolbar.

4 You can record using your Mac's built-in microphone, or you can plug in a suitable external mic.

5 Mix jingles and other musical links and interludes using the jingles track.

Important

To get the best from an external microphone (line in or USB) with GarageBand – for a podcast, for example – launch System Preferences, select the Sound pane, click the Input tab and click on the external mic from the list. Position the mic as you plan to use it and adjust the input volume control while talking into the mic. You can make further volume tweaks within GarageBand using the individual track and mix controls. Now open GarageBand's Preferences from the File menu and select either System Setting (the default) or your external mic from the Audio Input pop-up menu.

Timesaver tip

To hear a loop before placing it in the time line, click to select it in the Loop Browser window.

Export your podcast to disk.

Compress Using: AAC Encoder

Audio Settings: Musical Podcast

Ideal for enhanced podcasts with voice and music. Download times are moderate. Details: AAC, 128kbps, stereo, optimized for music and complex audio. Estimated size: 0MB. ———— 7

Publish Podcast: ☑ Set artwork to recommended size for podcasts (300 x 300 pixels) when exporting

Cancel   Export

For your information

Drag images and video clips from the media browser from within the podcast studio to assign artwork to your podcast episode.

Building your song (cont.)

6 Mix down your podcast as you would a music project. Use the ducking controls to bring a voice to the fore (automatically increase volume relative to other tracks), and adjust volume and pan controls to suit.

7 You can share the podcast direct to iWeb for publishing at your .Mac account (**Share>Send Podcast to iWeb**), or export it to iTunes (**Share>Send Podcast to iTunes**) or a disk for uploading using an FTP client (**Share>Export Podcast to Disk**).

5

See also

If manipulating pre-recorded loops is beyond your musical capabilities, give Magic GarageBand a whirl (click the Magic GarageBand button after launching the application).

Customising

Introduction

Since its first incarnation, the Mac has offered fabulous potential for customising – it's a machine you can truly make your own – and it was designed that way from the outset. Even today's Macs, with their rigid Unix foundation and file structure, can be bent to your will in all manner of fab and funky ways by tweaking system settings that control everything from the mundane – font size and colour – to the Desktop picture ('wallpaper'), screensaver, toolbar and Dock. By acquiring one of the many third-party utilities, you can mess with the system in ways even Apple didn't intend. Check out TinkerTool at **www.bresink.com/osx/TinkerTool.html**.

Don't dismiss customising as a lark fit only for teenagers and geeks. There's actually nothing frivolous about making a computer your own by customising its appearance and behaviour. A machine set to operate in the way you prefer is far more likely to be enjoyed, is less likely to frustrate you with odd foibles, and is an infinitely better prospect for everyday use – especially if you have to sit in front of it for hours at a time. Some of the options for change you've probably met in other chapters without even realising you were customising the machine, but the rest – those that do little or nothing other than make the Mac a nicer environment in which to work – you'll meet here. So now, without further ado, let's start making the Mac all your own.

What you'll do

Learn about System Preferences

Change the Desktop picture

Set a screensaver

Change your login picture

Add and remove items from the toolbar

Add favourite applications to the Dock

System and software

Essentially there are two ways to customise your Mac: the System Preferences utility available from the Apple menu, and the Dock, which enables you to change settings for much of the Mac's hardware, system software and applications, and software-specific preferences usually available from the application's own menu or by pressing [Command] and [–], ([Command] and [comma]). System Preferences itself is an application that can be customised and so is much of the OS X system software, such as the Finder.

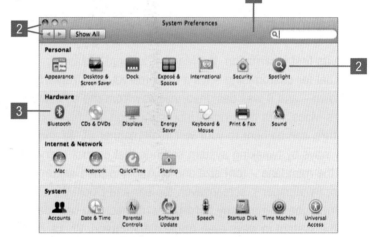

Meet System Preferences

1 The System Preferences application is a library of what are known as preferences panes – mini-modules that you can use to alter your Mac's appearances and settings. By default, System Preferences has a place in the Dock and can also be launched from the Apple menu – which means that at any time and from within any other application, you have simple and speedy access to settings.

2 Launch System Preferences by clicking its icon in the Dock. The System Preferences window is similar to the familiar Finder window. There are traffic light buttons for closing, minimising and zooming and a Spotlight search field. There are also back, forward and Show All buttons.

3 The main window is divided into four rows, each of which contains the grouped icons for preference panes that address similar functions: Personal, Hardware, Internet, and Network and System.

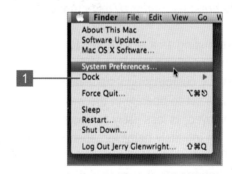

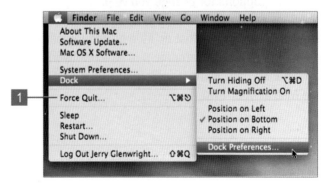

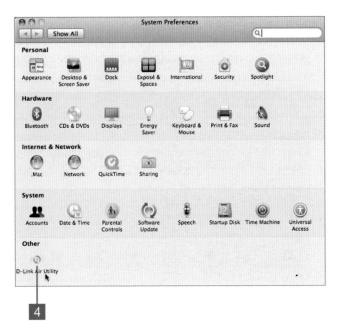

4 Some system-based third-party applications – the controls for a wireless LAN adaptor, for example – also place panes in the System Preferences window. In that case, OS X creates a fifth row at the bottom of the window called Other.

5 To access a preference pane, simply click it. The System Preferences window changes to display whatever controls are available for the chosen pane.

6 Use the System Preferences back and forward buttons to move to and fro through the panes that you've accessed in the current session, and click the Show All button while working with a pane to return to the System Preferences window proper.

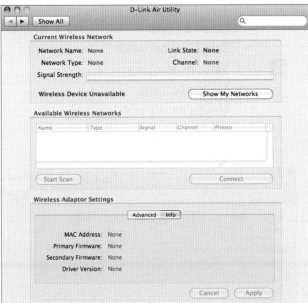

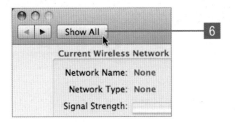

System and software (cont.)

Locate the right pane

1 The System Preferences search field enables you to find a specific pane for the settings that you want to change.

2 Click in the Search field and type, for example, 'scroll'. There is no need to press Return, as the search is dynamic. As you type, some panes are highlighted and the rest of the System Preferences window is dimmed. The highlighted panes offer access to the settings you want to change.

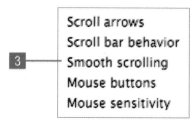

Scroll arrows
Scroll bar behavior
Smooth scrolling
Mouse buttons
Mouse sensitivity

3 The Search field also displays a drop-down list of likely results based on the characters you type. Entering the word 'scroll' produces a number of variations on the scrolling theme in the list, and there are two highlighted panes: Appearance and Keyboard & Mouse. Let's assume you want to change the location of the window scroll arrows...

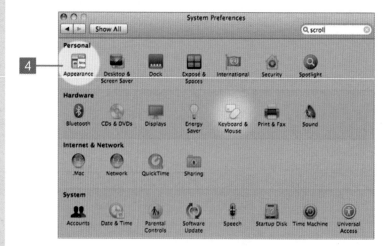

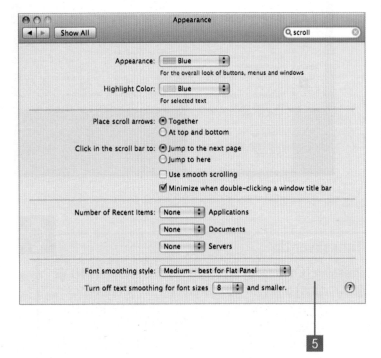

Scroll arrows   4

Scroll bar behavior

Smooth scrolling

Mouse buttons

Mouse sensitivity

6

4 Press the down arrow key to begin scrolling through the drop-down list. 'Scroll arrows' is the first option in the list, so scroll down to it and pause. Now a spotlight highlights the Appearance field, the Keyboard & Mouse field remains highlighted but less so, and the rest of the window is dimmed as before.

5 Now press [Return]. The spotlight over the Appearance pane flashes and the pane is opened to reveal options for changing the location of the scroll arrows.

6 Using simple search techniques like this, you can find the correct pane for any change that you want to make.

System and software (cont.)

Customising System Preferences

1. You can customise System Preferences itself to suit the way you like to work.

2. Although the System Preferences window is organised into categories, you can toggle an alphabetically sorted view. Select Organise Alphabetically from the View menu.

3. The View menu also gives direct access to any pane – just click it in the list on the menu.

Timesaver tip

Pressing [Command] and [[] or [Command] and []] (ie [Command] and [left square bracket] or [Command] and [right square bracket]) moves you backwards and forwards through the panes accessed in the current session, whereas [Command] and [L] highlights all of them.

Important

If you're accessing System Preferences from a standard account (i.e. one without administrator privileges), some preference panes – those that alter important system settings – won't be available to you.

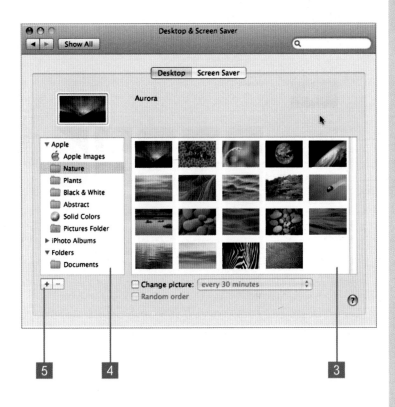

Setting Desktop wallpaper

1 The Desktop picture is simply a digital image. No fancy trickery is needed to switch to a different picture.

2 Click the System Preferences icon in the Dock and select Desktop & Screen Saver from the Personal category.

3 Once the Desktop Preferences pane is displayed, you'll see a selection of image thumbnails, any of which you can select for the Desktop. Click one and it is immediately loaded in place of the existing Desktop image. Continue in this way until you find a picture that takes your fancy.

4 To the left of the thumbnails is a media browser showing folders containing further images. Click one to display its contents as thumbnails and preview them as before.

Customising OS X (cont.)

Whatever the status of your account, you can access System Preferences and use the panes grouped under Personal to customise the look and feel of your Mac experience. The simplest changes are often the most effective, and there's little that's simpler or more effective than changing, say, the picture that is the Desktop background – otherwise known as the wallpaper. By default, OS X displays the aurora wallpaper, but there are many others on offer, and you can download more or use your own images to make wallpaper.

5 If you'd prefer to use your own picture that's currently in the Pictures folder in your Home folder for the Desktop, click to navigate to it. If your picture is somewhere else on the Mac, click the Add folder button below the list of folders, navigate to the one that contains your picture and click Choose. The folder is included in the list and you can browse its contents as before. (Delete the folder from the list using the Remove button.)

6 You can change the Desktop picture automatically – cycling through holiday images, for example.

7 Click the Change picture checkbox and use the pop-up menu to vary the countdown to change.

Important

You can apply a password to the screensaver – when your machine is left unattended, it's safe from prying eyes and meddling fingers until you return and type the password. Use `System Preferences> Personal>Security>General`.

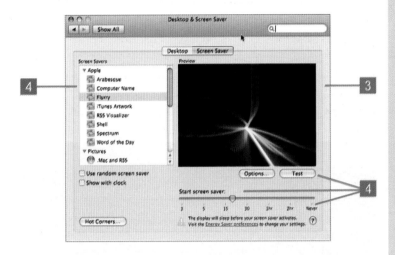

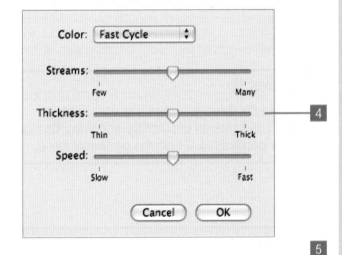

Setting and changing the screensaver

1 Screensavers date from the days of conventional CRT technology displays – those hefty old power-munching monitors with an elephant-sized footprint. Relying on a glowing phosphor coating on the inside of the screen to create the display, it was possible for a machine left unused for hours at a time to become permanently blighted with a kind of ghost image burned into the phosphor. A constantly changing screensaver sidestepped the potential for screen burn while generally providing the user with amusing flying toasters, a man moving to and fro with a lawnmower or a 'tank' of tropical fish complete with bubble noises.

2 Today's LCD screens require no saver to protect them, and even modern CRTs are resistant to screen burn, but that doesn't mean a screensaver isn't a useful or attractive proposition. The Mac has lots on offer.

3 From System Preferences, select Desktop & Screen Saver and click the Screen Saver button. The Mac defaults to the Flurry screensaver and you'll see it swishing about in the Preview window.

4 To try others, click on them in the Screen Savers list. Click the Options button to set preferences for individual screensavers. The Test button switches to a full-screen preview. Hit a key or move the mouse or trackpad to return to the Preferences pane. Use the slider to vary the time before the screensaver begins to work.

5 'Hot Corners' provide a shortcut to calling up the screensaver or inhibiting its operation – just direct the mouse pointer to a hot corner and pause for a moment. Click the Hot Corners button and select from the options there.

Important

Users of LCD screens should set their screen to dim rather than display a screensaver which, some claim, can actually shorten the lifespan of the screen's backlight. Use the System Preferences Energy Saver pane and set the period of inactivity before the screen goes to sleep.

Timesaver tip

To access the Desktop preferences pane directly, [Control] and click on the Desktop and select Change Desktop Background... from the contextual menu.

See also

Use a selection of your own pictures from an iPhoto album to create a very cool custom screensaver and choose from a number of effects – the mosaic option is really impressive! Go to **System Preferences>Desktop & Screen Saver>Pictures>Display Style>Mosaic**.

From the sublime to the… well, mundane, frankly, though if it suits you to change the themes used for features such as button appearance, highlight colour, font size and scroll arrow location, then it's all available to you from the System Preferences Personal category. You can also select a new picture for your login prompt.

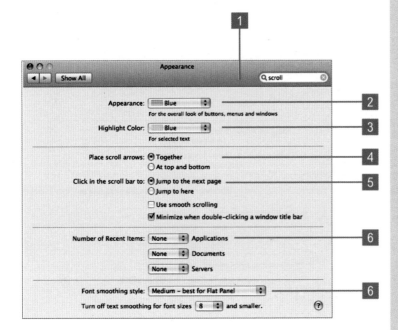

Changing faces

1. The Appearance pane gives access to the colours that your Mac uses for buttons, menus and so on.

2. Try this: click the Appearance pop-up menu on the Appearance pane and change it from Blue to Graphite. There's a slight pause, and then all the buttons and menus change to a soft grey colour.

3. You can mix and match the revised theme with the options on the Highlight Colour menu below Appearance to determine the colour that your Mac uses when you scroll over text.

4. Way back when, scroll arrows were sited at the top and bottom of a window, but the modern way of doing things is to position them together at the bottom of a window. If you prefer one location to another, make your choice using the Place scroll arrows buttons option.

Look and feel (cont.)

5 Checking the Click in the scroll bar option 'Jump to the next page' causes Finder windows and documents to scroll a screen at a time when you click in the upper or lower part of the scroll bar. The 'Jump to here' option changes the scroll bar to a proportional representation of the length of the window. Clicking a third of the way down the scroll bar when viewing a document will jump to a location a third of the way through the window's content.

6 Other options here are either obvious or best experimented with. You can select the number of recent items shown under the Apple menu's Recent Items option. You can also select from a range of font-smoothing options. Experiment, but be aware that smoothed fonts can be difficult to see in small point sizes (hence the 'Turn off... size' option).

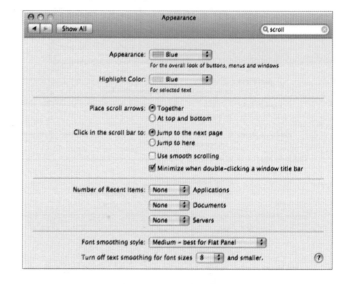

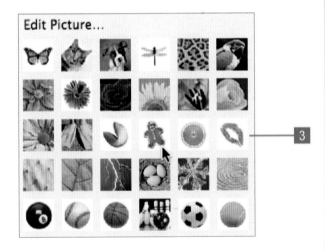

Change your login picture

1 OS X assigns a login image to all users (you may not see it if you have automatic login switched on – see Chapter 8) from a selection stored for the purpose. The choice is random – you might get a butch-looking dog or a big pink flower – but you can change the picture at any time.

2 From System Preferences, click the Accounts pane in the lower left of the System section. The current image is displayed as a thumbnail in the upper middle of the pane.

3 Mouse over the thumbnail and you'll see a disclosure triangle. Click the thumbnail and select a new image from those in the menu. Each is highlighted as you mouse over it and you can click to select.

Look and feel (cont.)

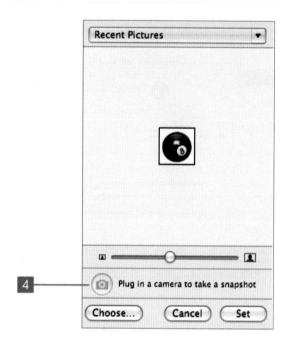

4 Alternatively, choose an image of your own – you could, for example, choose a picture of yourself. Click the thumbnail as before, but now click on Edit Picture.... Click the Choose button and navigate to the picture you want. If you have a suitable camera, you can plug it in and grab an image of yourself. Use the slider to zoom the image and then click Set.

Drag your favorite items into the toolbar...

◀ ▶	≡ ▾	🔲 ≡ ▥ ▦	✿ ▾
Back	Path	View	Action
⬆	◉	✂	⊘
Eject	Burn	Customize	Separator
☐	↔	📁	⊘
Space	Flexible Space	New Folder	Delete
🌐	ⓘ	💿	🔍
Connect	Get Info	iDisk	Search
👁			
Quick Look			

... or drag the default set into the toolbar.

◀ ▶	🔲 ≡ ▥ ▦	👁 ✿ ▾	🔍
Back	View	Quick Look Action	Search

Show [Icon Only ▾] ☐ Use Small Size   (Done)

Timesaver tip

For instant online information about the Appearance pane or any other in System Preferences, click the ? button in the lower right of the pane to summon the Apple Help Viewer.

For your information

Most of the settings you'll customise apply only to your account. If you log in with a different account or someone else logs in to your Mac with their own account, the Mac will be as it was before you customised it.

Look and feel (cont.)

6

Customising the toolbar

1 Finder windows feature a number of buttons – the 'toolbar' – for accessing Finder operations and options such as View controls, the Action and Quick Look button and so on. You can remove these buttons, add others and insert placeholder spaces to help organise them.

2 Open a Finder window ([Command] + [N]) and select Customize Toolbar from the View menu.

3 Drag and drop the buttons from the selection to the toolbar to include them.

4 Remove a button by dragging it off the toolbar and letting go – the item disappears with a puff of smoke.

5 Restore the original setting by dragging and dropping the default set.

Doctoring the Dock

The Dock is universally applauded as an efficient route to your applications and system tools, but its look and feel can provoke joy and dissatisfaction in equal measure. Some users like a visible Dock, while others prefer it hidden until required. Some reduce the Dock to little more than a few pixels' worth of colour barely visible to the naked eye, and still others like a great big storehouse of stuff that waddles on to the screen like a digital pack elephant. Whichever category you fall into, the Dock can be customised every which way to suit your preferences.

Dock: position and visibility

1 Simple changes can be made using the Dock entry on the Apple menu.

2 Choose left or right to relocate the Dock to the left or right of the Desktop.

3 Select Hiding and the Dock remains invisible until you mouse over its location (left, right or bottom of the Desktop), whereupon it pops up ready for use.

4 Magnification causes the icons in the Dock to enlarge as your mouse pointer passes over them.

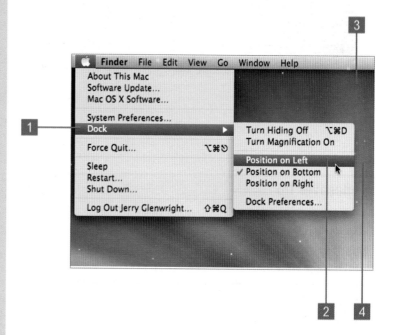

Important

Items removed from the Dock are not removed from the Mac – you're only removing the shortcut.

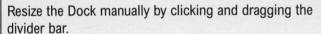

Size counts

1. Combine magnification with Dock size to reduce its impact on Desktop real estate. Select Dock Preferences from the Apple menu, or click System Preferences in the Dock and choose Dock from the Personal section of the Dock panel.

2. Use the Size and Magnification sliders until you're happy with the appearance of the Dock.

3. Using Dock Preferences, you can also animate opening applications (the bouncing icon) and change the graphic effect when an item is minimised to the Dock.

Timesaver tip

Resize the Dock manually by clicking and dragging the divider bar.

For your information

Remember that applications are stored to the left of the divider, and stacks and individual files are stored to the right.

Talk to the world

7

Introduction

Back in the 1960s when computers were emerging into the light from the hitherto closed worlds of academia, government departments and the military, a few far-sighted scientists realised that the true purpose of a general-purpose computer (i.e. one that could be programmed to perform lots of tasks rather than being dedicated to a single task) wasn't to crunch numbers that would form economic plans, search for primes or plot missile trajectories but to facilitate human communication. By linking the machines together into a network, it would be possible to share information, pool resources and bring together interested minds, with the result that the whole was exponentially more powerful than the parts.

Nowadays, people all around the world use global communications via computer in the way they'd check the time on a wristwatch – with zero fanfare and no fuss – exactly the reason why the computer is right at the heart of the much-vaunted twenty-first-century digital lifestyle.

Getting online

To get online, your Mac must be set up to connect to an ISP, either via its internal modem, Ethernet port and an external DSL modem/router or wirelessly with AirPort. Networking is fundamental to the Mac and its OS X operating system, and making a connection is simple even for the decidedly non-technical. And because the Mac uses the DHCP protocol to negotiate suitable settings automatically, it's usually only a matter of connecting the machine to your network or DSL modem/router before you can start surfing without having to change and settings.

Broadband versus dial-up

1 In the past few years, broadband has virtually replaced dial-up as a means of connecting to the Internet.

2 Broadband uses a special connection at the telephone exchange and is typically at least 10 times faster. It's also permanently connected and your online charge is contained within a monthly fee.

3 Dial-up on the other hand is charged minute by minute, just like any telephone call, and it's relatively slow and unreliable.

4 There are times, however – say, when you're away from your office or home – that the built-in modem in a Mac laptop offers the only route to getting online. It's therefore worth familiarising yourself with the use of the modem and the method for making a connection.

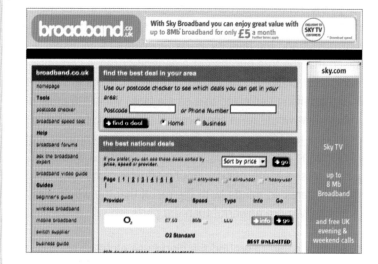

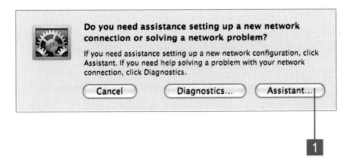

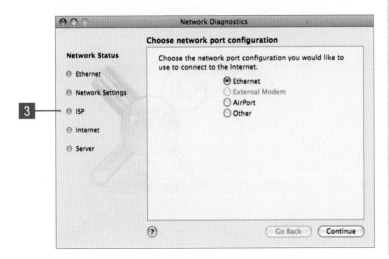

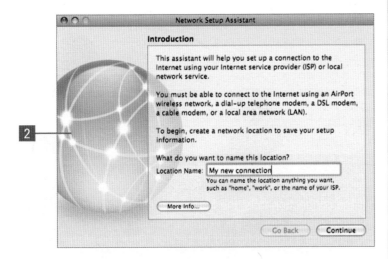

Using Network Setup Assistant

1 If you've connected your Mac to your DSL modem/router or network but you're not yet online, OS X provides a simple assistant to guide you through the process of connecting to the Internet. Launch System Preferences from the Dock, click the Network pane, click Assist Me and then click Assistant.

2 Type a suitable name for the new 'location' (i.e. the settings for your new connection) into the Location Name field and then click Continue.

3 Select an appropriate method for making the connection to the Internet from the list and click Continue.

4 If you choose dial-up, enter the Account name and password assigned by your ISP and type in the telephone number that you use to dial the service.

5 Plug your modem cable into the Mac (there's only one port that will accept the cable) and into your phone socket. Click Continue. The Mac will dial your ISP and negotiate a connection, giving you

7

confirmation when the process is complete. The settings are saved and you can begin surfing. Back on the Network pane, be sure to check Show modem status in the Menu bar for a convenient route to starting and stopping a dial-up connection.

6 Dial-up must be disconnected when you've finished and then reconnected each time you want to use it (otherwise there's the potential of you running up a huge phone bill). To disconnect, select Disconnect Internal Modem from the Modem status menu in the menu bar. To initiate a connection, plug in the modem cable and select Connect Internal Modem from the menu.

7 The other three options – DSL modem, cable and network – are used to connect your Mac to a broadband service. Choose the one that applies to you. If your ISP gave you a DSL or a cable modem for making a connection, make sure it's plugged in and switched on. If your Internet is provided by a router or computer network, make sure you're linked to it with an Ethernet cable.

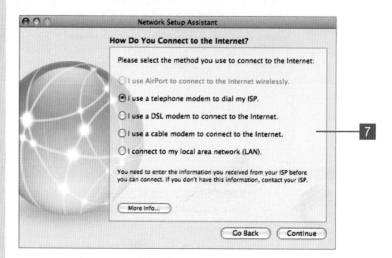

Important

If the connection fails, the Mac will prompt you for further information – the details provided by your ISP for making a connection to its service. Click the More Details button for further information about what might be required. Enter the required information and then click Continue to connect.

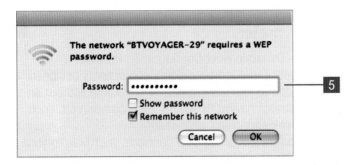

Connecting wirelessly with AirPort

1. All new Macs have a built-in AirPort card for making wireless connections to the Internet. AirPort is Apple's version of the industry standard WiFi system, which means you can happily connect to wireless DSL modems and routers from third-party manufacturers as well as Apple's own base station.

2. Click the AirPort icon in the menu extras (right-hand side) of the Menu bar.

3. Click the name of your wireless network to select it.

4. If your router is protected by WPA or WEP, you'll be prompted for the password.

5. Enter the password and the Mac will negotiate a wireless connection. You're ready to surf.

For your information

All Mac laptops ship with a built-in modem – the device used to transmit data from your computer to others via a telephone line and the Internet. A few years ago, a modem was essential to get online, but now broadband, which uses the computer's Ethernet connection or AirPort card, is the usual route.

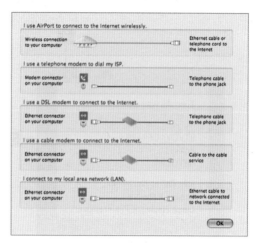

For your information

If you're at all unsure about how to connect to the Internet and what type of equipment is available to you, click the More Info... button on the Network Setup Assistant's How Do You Connect To The Internet? screen to see explanatory diagrams and details of the various methods.

Jargon buster

DHCP – Dynamic Host Configuration Protocol – essentially a method by which a computer is assigned all it needs to join a network and get online without an administrator having to specify each component, such as network addresses, individually.

DSL modem – a device that connects your Mac to your phone line to enable the computer to use a broadband Internet connection.

ISP – Internet Service Provider – the organisation that provides you with a dial-up or broadband Internet account.

Router – a device that shares a broadband connection between several computers via an Ethernet or wireless (or both) network. Routers generally incorporate a DSL modem.

WEP – Wired Equivalent Privacy – an algorithm to secure a wireless network.

WPA – WiFi Protected Access – another algorithm to secure a wireless network.

Yesterday's impossibly exotic electronic messages are today's emails, taken for granted such that the conventional methods for sending mail are in genuine danger of being entirely surpassed. Email is a primary reason for breaking your Mac out of its bubble and connecting to the Internet. You can send a message complete with images or any other type of file as an attachment to anywhere on the planet in the blink of an eye.

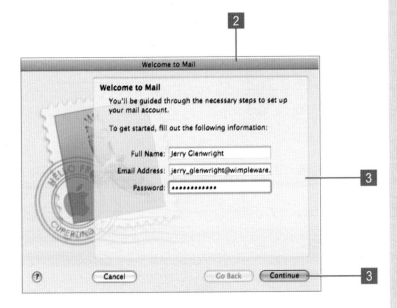

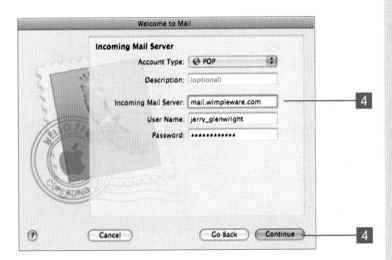

Mail: OS X's email client

1 To send and receive email you use a program called an email client. Mail is the client shipped with OS X. You'll find its icon in the Dock. Click to launch the program.

2 Before using Mail it must be set up to access your email account. The first time you launch Mail the set-up process will start automatically.

3 Enter the email address and password provided by your ISP and click Continue.

4 The name of your Incoming Mail Server is provided by your ISP. Enter it in the appropriate field and click Continue. (You can safely ignore the Description field – it's simply a reminder for you.) The Mac will attempt to establish contact with the POP server. If it fails, check that you've entered the name of the server, your account details and your password correctly and try again (a simple full stop out of place will result in failure). Click Continue.

7

Email (cont.)

5 Check and select the necessary security measures as defined by your ISP on the Incoming Mail Security page and click Continue. Don't be tempted to set these options arbitrarily in a bid to increase security, otherwise your email connection won't work.

6 Enter the name of the Outgoing Mail Server and, if authentication is required to access and use it, type your account name and password in the User Name and Password fields. Click Continue.

7 Once more, select appropriate security options as advised by your ISP and click Continue.

8 Check over the summary of your email details and click Create to complete the process.

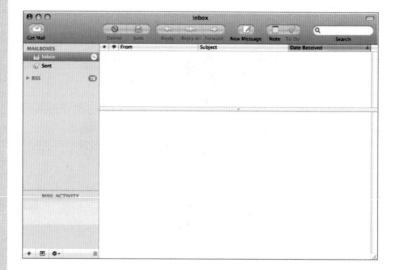

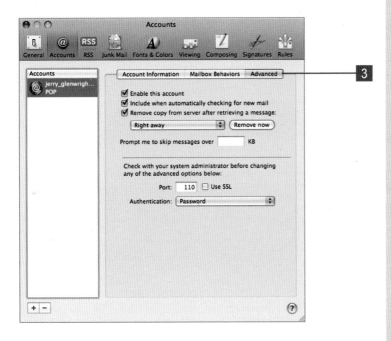

Mail preferences

1 Before using the Mail program, there are a number of preferences to enhance or otherwise streamline the experience. To access Mail's preferences, click the Mail menu and select Preferences.

2 From the General preferences window, you can choose how often to check for new emails and what alert to sound when they arrive. The Dock unread count option shows unread messages for the various mailboxes (Inbox, Junk etc.). Other options here include where downloaded attachments are stored and criteria for searching mailboxes.

3 Using Accounts preferences, you can edit your email account and add or delete extra accounts (there's no rule against having more than one email account). You can also direct the way your ISP's email servers respond to your collecting messages. Using the Advanced tab, choose which accounts are included when Mail checks for emails for you. You can also set when

7

emails are removed from the POP server. Set this option to Right away if you use different computers to access the same mail accounts, otherwise you'll receive the same emails again and again.

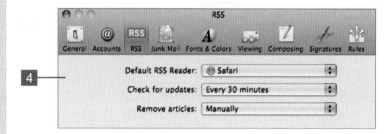

4 Using Mail, you can receive RSS feeds direct to your Mailbox. Use the RSS preferences to choose a default RSS reader, how often feeds are checked and what happens to them when they're received.

Junk email ('spam') was once a pretty serious blight in the world of email, but the increased sophistication of spam blocking means that nowadays you can easily avoid most of it. Mail keeps copies in a special junk mail folder, which you can check periodically to be sure you haven't missed an important email.

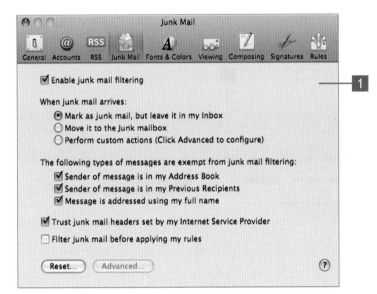

Dealing with spam

1. Use the Junk mail preferences to select what happens to messages that Mail considers junk. On the Junk Mail pane, make sure the Enable junk mail filtering option is checked to switch on the function.

2. You can choose to leave the messages that Mail considers junk mail in your inbox but shaded brown. In this special training mode, you can see the messages that Mail thinks are junk and delete them, thereby adding to the program's database of junk mail filtering rules (click the Not Junk button if the program makes a mistake with an item that isn't junk).

3. Alternatively, you can have Mail send junk emails direct to the Junk mailbox – click the appropriate button when you've made a choice.

4. Unless you have any special requirements, leave the rest of the options set to the Mail defaults. Once trained, the program's spam filtering is effective and doesn't require a great deal of intervention.

7

Email (cont.)

Adding a signature

1 If you want to add a sign-off message ('signature') to your outgoing emails, click to select the Signatures, pane.

2 Select an account from the left column for the signature (the default is to apply the signature to all emails), and then click the Add button to add a new signature.

3 Type over the default name (Signature #1) to rename it, and then click and drag in the right column to edit and enter your signature. [Command] + [A] selects all the text. You can create a signature with fancy fonts and styling and paste it into place if you'd prefer. For the technically minded, there's the possibility of adding HTML to the signature to provide further styling.

4 You can also paste an image into the signature, but beware: a large image could take a long time to send, even on a fast broadband connection.

5 When you've created a signature, drag and drop it to the account that you want to use it with.

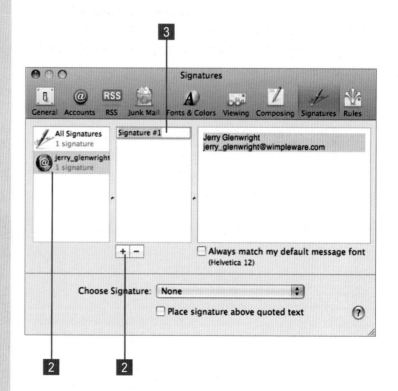

By default, Mail will check your mail server for new emails every five minutes and sound an alert to signal when a new message is waiting for you.

You can also direct the program to check for emails immediately by clicking the Get Mail button.

New messages are stored in the Inbox and appear in the message list. To read a message, click it in the message list. The message is displayed in the window below the message list. A double-click will open the message in a new window.

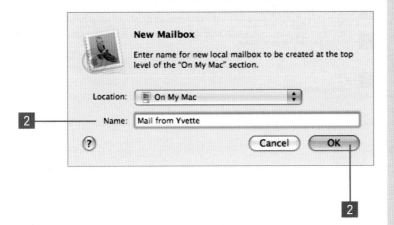

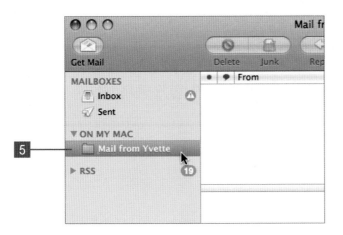

Receiving, deleting and organising emails

1. When you've read an email, you can leave it where it is in the Inbox, click Delete to send it to the Trash or archive it to another mailbox.

2. For example, let's say you converse via email regularly with your buddy Yvette, who lives in New Zealand. Your Inbox would soon be cluttered with her emails, but you don't want to delete them. Click the Add button at the foot of the mailboxes column and select New Mailbox... Type a name for the mailbox, say 'Mail from Yvette', and click OK. A new heading appears on the Mailboxes list named On My Mac, which contains your new mailbox. Click the disclosure triangle to view its contents.

3. Drag and drop messages from Yvette to the new mailbox.

4. Using the Action button, you can rename, delete or archive disused mailboxes.

Email (cont.)

Sending an email

1 To send a new email, click New Message.

2 Type the name of the recipient in the To field. As you enter characters, Mail searches for matching contacts in your Address Book. Press [Return] if a match is found; otherwise type the address manually.

3 Use the [Tab] key to move between fields. Type a subject line and then [Tab] again to enter your message. Mail checks your spelling as you type and uses a red underline to query suspect words (use `Preferences> Composing>Check Spelling>Never` to switch off this feature).

4 Use the Photo Browser button to select and include images from your iPhoto albums and the Photo Booth application.

5 Using the Show Stationery button, you can select from a wide range of styles for your email. Click to select one and then use the scroll bars and mouse to select and type over the example text and add your own message.

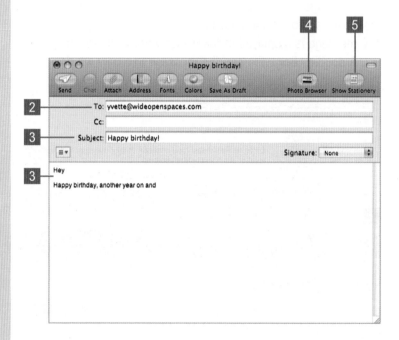

Timesaver tip

Press [Shift], [Command] and [N] to cause Mail to check for emails immediately.

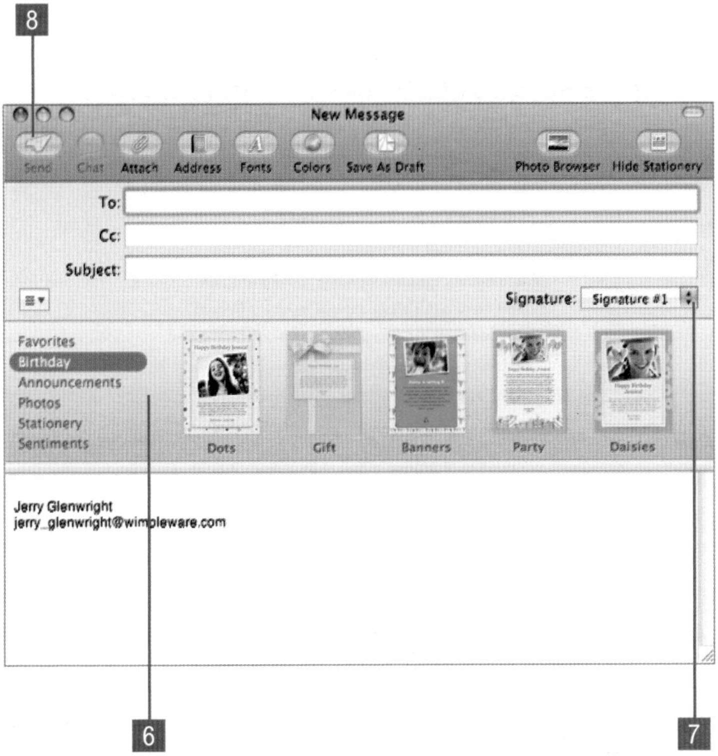

6 The Customize button provides further options for message windows, including a bcc (blind carbon copy) field.

7 If you've created a number of signatures, you can choose one from the pop-up menu.

8 When you're ready, click Send. When the email has been sent, a copy will be stored automatically in the Sent mailbox.

7

Email (cont.)

Replying to an email

1 Click to select an email from the message list, or double-click to open it in a new window.

2 Click the Reply button. Mail opens a reply message window with the To and Subject fields already completed (the Subject field is a repeat of the original with 'Re:' appended as prefix).

3 By default, the body of the original email is quoted within the reply. You can turn off this feature in Mail Preferences (go to **Preferences> Composing> Responding**, and then uncheck 'Quote the text of the original message').

4 Type your message and click Send.

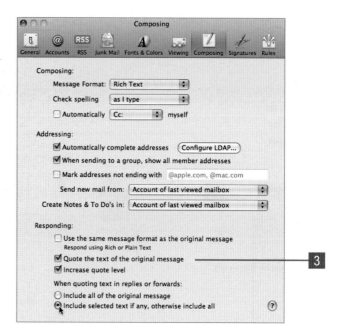

Did you know?

You can create smart mailboxes to filter emails according to your rules. Click the Add mailbox button and select New Smart Mailbox, and then choose from the options in the Smart Mailbox configuration window.

Although email was intended to be a low-bandwidth, text-only service, it's possible to send files – documents, pictures and so on – as 'attachments' to your emails.

Most ISPs set a size limit for attachments, so that beyond an individual file size of, say, 8–10 Mb, it's better to use some other method of transmitting files – FTP for example.

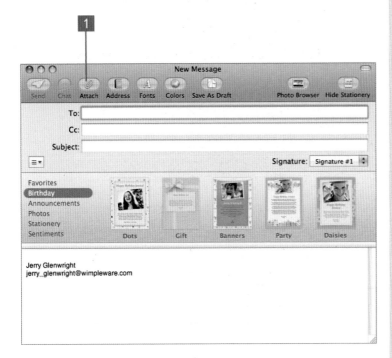

Working with attachments

1. To send an attachment using Mail, click the Attach button and navigate to the file(s) you want to attach. Select a file. You can make multiple selections by [Shift] and clicking.

2. If you're sending the email to a Microsoft Windows user, check the Send Windows-Friendly Attachments box. Click Choose File to attach the files.

3. Delete an attachment by clicking to select it and pressing the [Delete] key.

4. If you receive an email with attachments, drag them from the body of the email to the Desktop or a Finder window to save them. Alternatively, use the disclosure triangle in the email header to view a list of attachments. Drag them from the list, or click the Save button and navigate to a suitable location to save them.

7

Email (cont.)

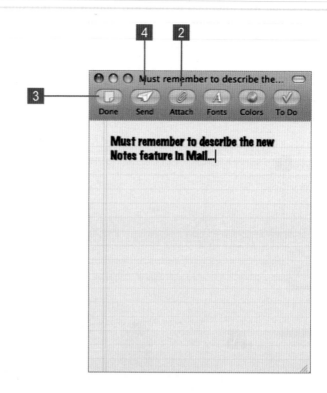

Using Notes

1. New to Mail for OS X 10.5 Leopard is a useful Note feature that neatly does away with the old trick of sending emails to yourself as reminders.

2. Click the Note button to open a new note and start typing. Add attachments by clicking the Attach button in the Notes toolbar and then navigate to the attachment. You can drag and drop pictures, graphics and other items just as you would with an email.

3. Click Done to save the note under Reminders in the mailboxes column.

4. You can also click Send to convert the note to an email. The first line of the note becomes the Subject.

Jargon buster

IMAP – Internet Message Access Protocol, used to access email messages from the Web.

POP – Post Office Protocol, a system by which emails are retrieved from remote servers (i.e. you connect to your ISP's POP server and collect your email).

RSS – Really Simple Syndication, a format for distributing frequently updated Web content such as news headlines, podcasts and blogs.

SMTP – Simple Mail Transfer Protocol – the email-sending counterpart to POP.

To Dos

1. Click the To Do button on the Note window toolbar or select text from an email and click the To Do button to create an instant alarm for a task or event. To Dos link automatically with iCal and, because they're also linked with the original note or email, you can access them remotely.

2. Click the To Do options button and select a Date Due. Check the box and click on the date to change the default.

3. You can set an alarm to accompany your reminder by clicking the Alarm button. Use the pop-up menus to select the type of alarm and when it's sent. Click on the time field to enter a new time. You can set a number of alarms for any given To Do – just click another alarm button.

For your information

The Mail Reminders folder behaves just like a mailbox, which means that you can access it and retrieve your notes remotely via an IMAP mail service such as .Mac.

Timesaver tip

You can drag and drop files from a Finder window or the Desktop directly to an email message window.

Surf the Web

Despite being less than 20 years old, the World Wide Web ('the Web' to you and me) has become such a part of our everyday experience that it's difficult to imagine life without it. Anything and everything you can think of (and probably a lot you can't!) has a Web page devoted to it. You can shop online, indulge your hobbies with likeminded people, acquire academic qualifications via distance learning courses, watch movies, listen to radio, download music – frankly, it'd be easier to list what you can't do. When CERN contractor Tim Berners-Lee crafted what would become the World Wide Web out of an interlinked system of HTML 'pages' because he'd glimpsed the future in Apple's linking HyperCard stacks application, little did he know that, in the first decade of the twenty-first century, there'd be hardly an entity on the planet without some kind of presence on the Web. There's a lot of rubbish out there too, of course, but to sidestep the Web is to reject the digital version of the Delphic oracle – yes, it often speaks in riddles, but when you get the good stuff it's well worth having.

Surfing Safari

1 The Mac is blessed with a truly excellent browser called Safari. Despite a shaky start, consistent updates and new versions have resulted in a competent, robust, speedy and intuitive browser that is a joy to use.

2 There was a joke at Mac owners' expense that did the geek rounds at the end of the 1990s and went something like this: on the Web no one knows you're using a Mac. With the latest version of Safari, this has become the case, because every server you access will work just as expected, plus you'll get all the security, speed and other benefits of using a Mac-based browser.

3 Safari is in the Dock by default. Click its icon to launch the program.

4 After only a few minutes of using a browser, you'll soon be at home with Safari. There's the familiar address bar, back and forward buttons, page refresh, scroll bars and window for Web content.

5 To use it, just enter a URL and start surfing.

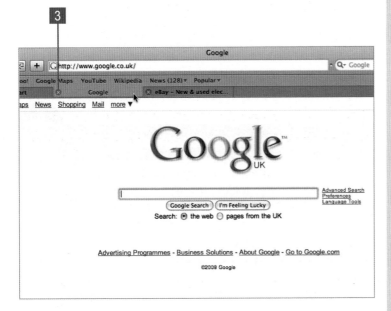

Tab browsing

1 Using Safari you can have several pages open at once, each represented by a tab on the toolbar, rather than opening a new window. This saves on screen real estate and makes for an altogether more streamlined browsing experience.

2 From the View menu, select Show Tab Bar or press [Shift]. [Command] + [T]. [Command] and click links to open a page as a tab.

3 Switch between open pages by clicking tabs below the toolbar. Close a tab by clicking its Close (X) button.

Did you know?

You can drag a Safari tab into the Dock to create a link to the page. Click the link and Safari launches and opens the page.

Surf the Web (cont.)

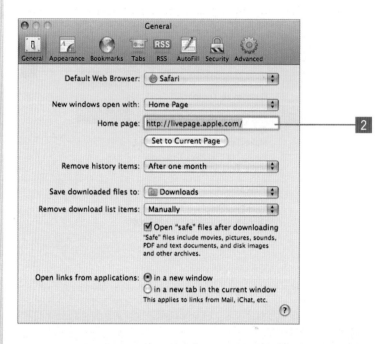

Setting your home page

1 A home page is the website that Safari opens automatically when it's launched. By default, the home page is Apple's own website.

2 To change your home page, select Preferences from the Safari menu (or press [Command] + [,]), select the General preferences, and type or paste a new URL into the Home page field.

3 If you select Empty Page from the pop-up New windows open with menu, Safari starts with a blank page. The Same Page option is the last website you looked at before closing the program, and Bookmarks is your saved list of URLs for favourite Web pages.

4 If you select Empty page or Bookmarks, Safari won't try to access the Web when it's launched – useful if you're using a modem and are yet to connect.

For your information

To sidestep the potential for running out of space on the Bookmarks bar, use folders for related bookmarks (**Bookmarks>Show All Bookmarks** followed by the Add button). The folder will appear as a pop-up menu on the Bookmarks bar.

Timesaver tip

Select multiple pages to open as tabs by opening your bookmarks (click the Open Book button in the toolbar), [Shift] and click the bookmarks you want to open and then press the spacebar.

Even in plain English, URLs can be difficult to remember – especially once you stir a few forward slashes and tildes (~) into the mix. Bookmarks obviate the need to remember. You can save the URL for any site you visit as a bookmark, naming and organising your bookmarks to suit yourself and returning to the associated Web pages with a simple click.

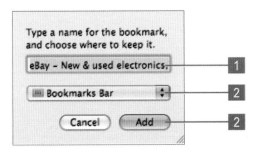

While surfing, you can also mark a page for SnapBack – the Safari feature that enables you to switch instantly back to a page you visited previously. Press [Option], [Command] and [K] (or select Mark Page for SnapBack from the History menu) to mark a page for SnapBack. Return to the page from wherever you are by pressing [Option], [Command] and [P] (which will also wing you back to the first page you viewed if you haven't marked anything for SnapBack), or use the SnapBack button in the address field.

Working with bookmarks

1 To bookmark the current page, click the Add button or press [Command] + [D]. Type a name that means something to you (or accept the default culled from the page itself) and use the pop-up Create In menu to select a location for the bookmark.

2 Store bookmarks on the Bookmark menu or, if the page is a special favourite, on the Bookmarks Bar for easy access. Click Add to complete the process.

3 Use the Show All Bookmarks option on the Bookmarks menu to view all your saved bookmarks in a browser window. You can drag and drop to organise them, and use the Add button in the Collections column to create one or more folders to store them.

4 Bookmark groups of live tabbed Web pages by selecting Add Bookmark For These Tabs from the Bookmarks menu.

7

Surf the Web (cont.)

Working with RSS

1 Really Simple Syndication (RSS) is a protocol for publishing and distributing regularly updated Web data in what are called 'feeds'. RSS is used by news services, television channels, radio stations and the like to stream headline data to interested people. When you see something you want to pursue further, click the RSS feed.

2 Safari supports RSS and displays the RSS button in the address bar when you browse a Web page with an RSS feed. Click the icon to view the content.

3 You can also save your favourite RSS feeds to the Bookmarks Bar, where they'll update automatically every 30 minutes (change the frequency by accessing the pop-up menu at `Safari>Preferences> RSS> Check For Updates`).

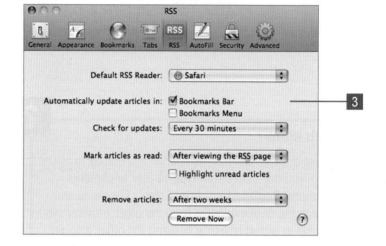

218

3 **2** **3**

strings&ie=UTF-8&o‹ ^ | Q▾ ukulele strings | ⊗

Recent Searches
ukulele strings
builders merchants
typewriter repair

Clear Recent Searches

Sign in

ch

Results **1 - 10** of about **115,000** for ukulele strings. **(0.10 seconds)**

Sponsored Links   Sponsored Links

Google search field

1 Safari features a built-in Google search field, which means you don't need to visit the Google website to use its Internet search facilities.

2 Use the search field as you would the search field in a Finder window. Enter your search and press Return. The results are displayed in the browser window.

3 Click the X to clear the search field, and use the disclosure triangle to the right of the magnifying glass to access previous searches.

Timesaver tip

Combine the Google search field with the SnapBack feature to return instantly to the search results after viewing a page.

7

Surf the Web (cont.)

Web page widgets

1. In OS X 10.5 Leopard, Safari sports a brand new button in the toolbar. Mouse over it and you'll see Open this page in Dashboard...

2. You can save a 'clip' from a Web page as a Dashboard widget (see Chapter 4 for a guide to using Dashboard) and it will update automatically as the page is updated – sporting results, say, updated content on blog sites or a database of software downloads.

3. Navigate to the page you want to capture as a widget. Click the Open This Page In Dashboard button and, when the page dims, move the white triangle to the part of the page you want to clip.

4. Click to select and then use the adjustment circles on the edges of the rectangle to tune the selection. Now click Add and Dashboard will open and display your newly created widget.

5. Use the i button to choose a theme for the new widget. Now, whenever you press [F12], the widget will be displayed alongside any others you have selected to open in Dashboard.

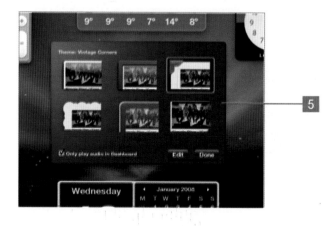

And if that wasn't enough ...

1 Being such a slim, efficient, sexy application, Safari is packed with features. Here's a few more of the most notable ...

2 Rid your browsing experience of annoying pop-ups forever by ensuring the Block Pop-Up Windows is checked in the File menu (press [Shift], [Command] + [K] to toggle the feature).

3 Use Reopen Last Closed Window to revisit the last page you looked at if you closed it inadvertently. Reopen All Windows From The Last Session will open all the windowed and tabbed pages that were live when you last quit Safari.

4 Organise tabs in the Tab bar by dragging and dropping them.

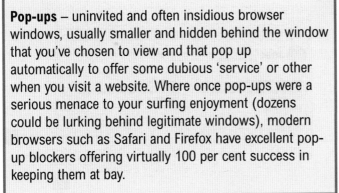

Jargon buster

Pop-ups – uninvited and often insidious browser windows, usually smaller and hidden behind the window that you've chosen to view and that pop up automatically to offer some dubious 'service' or other when you visit a website. Where once pop-ups were a serious menace to your surfing enjoyment (dozens could be lurking behind legitimate windows), modern browsers such as Safari and Firefox have excellent pop-up blockers offering virtually 100 per cent success in keeping them at bay.

Important

A Web clip widget cannot be saved as such, so if you close it by clicking its Close (X) button you'll have to return to the original page and recapture the widget.

.Mac, your world online

.Mac is an online service from Apple that you can use as an extension to your Mac to store, share and back up files via iDisk, enjoy a Web-based email account that syncs with Mail on your own machine, put up a website of your own, make a gallery of pictures and video clips, and publish your address book and calendar, synchronising with other Macs at a click. The service seamlessly integrates with iLife applications and, once registered, you can access your .Mac account from anywhere and allow other computer users (on whatever platform) to share your files.

Other features include Back to My Mac, which lets you control your Mac remotely from any other Mac (running OS X 10.5 Leopard) using a virtual Desktop in the Finder. You can use the remote Mac exactly as you would if you were sitting at it to access files and launch applications. .Mac is a commercial service – you pay a monthly subscription – but you can register and try it for free for 60 days before making a commitment.

Register for .Mac

1 Launch System Preferences and click the .Mac pane under Internet & Network.

2 On the .Mac Preferences pane, click the Learn More button and, when the .Mac Web page is displayed, click the Free Trial button.

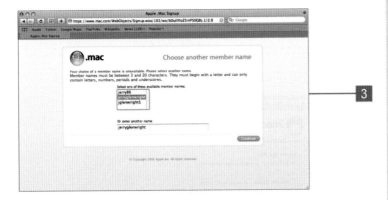

3 Complete the registration (encrypted), check Terms & Conditions and click Continue.

4 Note your account settings and then return to the .Mac preferences pane. Enter your member name and password and click Sign In.

5 Once you're signed into .Mac, the Preferences pane changes to display tabs for setting preferences for the various .Mac features: Sync, iDisk and Back to My Mac. Click the tabs to access the preferences options.

.Mac, your world online (cont.)

Using .iDisk

1 Principal among .Mac's many features is iDisk, 10Gb of secure online storage space (50Mb in the trial version) that you can use to back up data, store and share files such as pictures and music, and host a website or photo gallery. iDisk is available from wherever you are, so long as you have access to the Internet, and you can sync your online iDisk with a copy on your hard drive to keep up to date automatically.

2 Using iDisk is as simple as signing in to .Mac and then clicking the iDisk icon under Devices in the sidebar. iDisk contains similar folders to those in the Home folder on your Mac – use them to store appropriate data.

3 Check out iWeb in Chapter 5 to learn how to host a website via iDisk and .Mac.

4 The iDisk Software folder contains Backup, an application that can be set to archive copies of your important files automatically.

You can use Back to My Mac (BtMM) to access your Mac remotely if each machine has an Internet connection and is running OS X 10.5 Leopard. BtMM Macs appear under Shared in the sidebar.

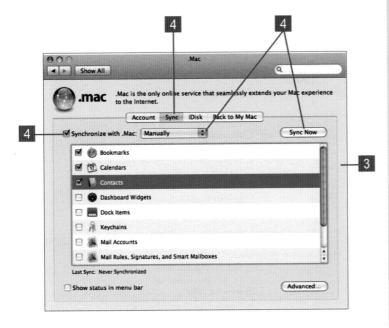

Timesaver tip

To sync iDisk manually, select it in the Sidebar and then select Sync Now from the Action button in the toolbar.

Did you know?

Copying iDisk to your Mac lets you access it even without an Internet connection, syncing the next time you connect. To save space, only aliases are stored for the Software, Library and Backup folders.

Back to My Mac and Sync

1 To toggle Back to My Mac, launch System Preferences, select the .Mac pane, click the Back to My Mac tab and click the Start button. To access a remote Mac, select it from the Sidebar. The remote machine's Desktop appears in a window on your Mac.

2 The Sync function synchronises your iCal, Address Book, Mail accounts, Safari bookmarks, Dashboard widgets, System Preferences and more with .Mac and other Macs with access to the Internet. Syncing is the perfect way to keep desktop and laptop Macs in step.

3 From the .Mac Preferences pane, click the Sync tab, click the Synchronization checkbox and select a syncing strategy from the pop-up menu: Automatically syncs whenever your data changes, Every Hour... syncs after the selected period, and Manually syncs when you initiate the process by clicking the Sync Now button.

7

Instant messaging with iChat

iChat is OS X's instant messaging program. You can engage in instant text, audio and video chats, apply funky effects and backdrops to your video chat, and share files, iPhoto galleries, movies and presentations with a buddy across the Internet using the iChat Theater function.

Setting up iChat

1. iChat uses your .Mac account settings so you can get online and start chatting right away.

2. iChat's icon is in the Dock. Click to launch it. Once live, iChat watches for connections from your buddies and tells them that you're available.

3. Before using iChat you must set it up. Launch the program, select Preferences from the File menu, click the Accounts button and then click the Add button to add your account. Choose .Mac from the pop-up menu and enter your member name and password.

4. If you don't have a .Mac account, you can get a free AOL Instant Messenger account by visiting **http://dashboard.aim.com** and clicking the Get a Screen Name link. Back on the iChat Accounts pane select AIM Account from the Account Type pop-up and enter your AIM screen name and password.

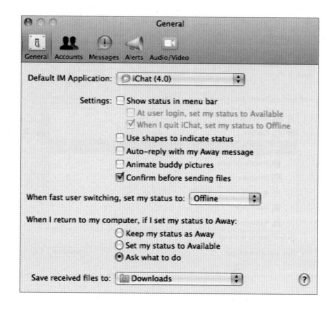

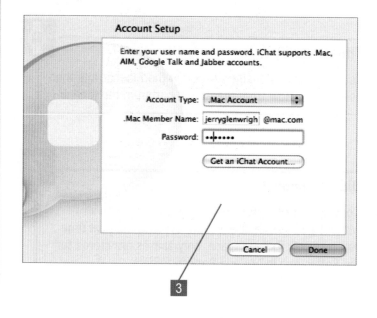

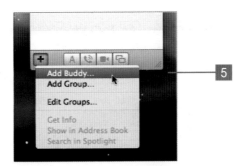

5 Add iChat buddies by selecting .Mac (or AIM) Buddy List from the Window menu. Click Add Buddy from the list and enter the buddy's details into the appropriate fields. If the buddy appears in your Address Book, click the disclosure triangle to the right of the Last Name field and select the person from the Address Book browser.

7

Timesaver tip

Initiate an iChat Theater session by dragging and dropping a file on the Video Chat window.

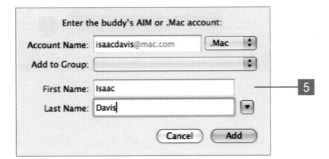

5

Instant messaging with iChat (cont.)

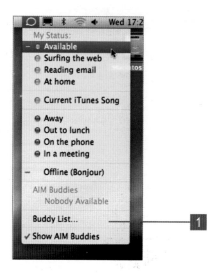

Messaging and audio iChats

1. From the Buddy List (`iChat>Window>.Mac/A IM Buddy List`), double-click the person you want to message.

2. Enter your message in the field at the foot of the Chat window and press Return.

3. Repeat the process to reply when your buddy responds.

4. With a microphone, you can talk to your buddies over the Internet. If your Mac has a built-in microphone, you can use that, otherwise almost any cheap mic will work fine.

5. Buddies with a phone icon by their name in the Buddy List also have a mic. Select a mic-equipped buddy and then click the Start Audio Chat button in the toolbar at the foot of the Buddy List to start a conversation (or just click on the phone icon).

6. iChat displays a window when you receive an invitation to chat. Click to expand it, enter your message in the text field and then click Accept. The window expands again and you can continue to chat.

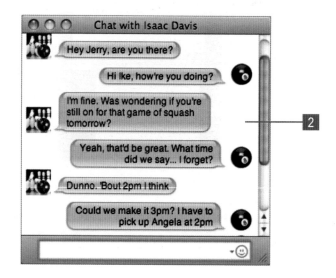

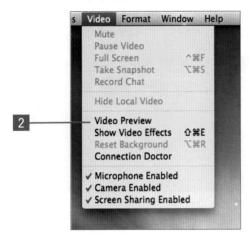

Video chats

1. Connect an appropriate camera (see Important box, page 230) to your Mac. By default, iChat launches when a compatible camera is connected.

2. Click the camera next to your name in the Buddy List, or select Video Preview from the Video menu to see a preview window of what you'll transmit to buddies. Adjust the camera angle until you're happy with the way you look. Try talking too: audio volume is indicated in the bar at the foot of the preview window.

3. Select a buddy from the list and click the Start Video Chat button in the toolbar or click the camera next to a buddy's name.

4. On the Chat window, click the Mute button to freeze and mute your video and audio (useful if you want to sneeze or scratch!). Click the Full Screen button to toggle a full screen display. Clicking the Add button will let you add another chat buddy to the conversation.

Timesaver tip

From iChat's General Preferences tab, select Show status in menu bar, and then you can initiate a chat without having to launch the program first.

Instant messaging with iChat (cont.)

5 You can apply special Photo Booth-like effects to your video output by clicking the Effects button. Use the left and right arrow buttons on the Video Effects window to cycle through the available effects and apply one by clicking to select it. You can restore normal service by clicking the Original thumbnail.

6 If you want to get really funky, scroll through the effects until the backdrops come into view. Select a backdrop and your chat buddy will see you on the beach, in the sea – even in front of the Eiffel Tower!

Important

To use video conferencing, you'll need an iSight or compatible camera – a camcorder with an iLink port or a FireWire-equipped webcam will probably work too and, as a bonus, you can use the camcorder's built-in mic for audio conferencing.

Did you know?

With just one mic or camera, you can engage in one-way audio and video chats while maintaining a two-way text messaging session.

For your information

You can also use Apple's Bonjour protocol to iChat with Mac users on a local network. Check Use Bonjour Instant Messaging on iChat's Accounts Preference pane.

File	Edit	View	Buddies	Video	F(
New Chat...					⌘N
Go to Chat Room...					⌘R
Open...					⌘O
Recent Items					▶
Share a File With iChat Theater...					
Share iPhoto With iChat Theater...					
Close Window					⌘W
Close Chat					⇧⌘W
Save a Copy As...					⌘S
Page Setup...					⇧⌘P
Print...					⌘P

2

**iChat Theater is ready to begin.
Invite a buddy to a video chat.**

iChat Theater begins when your buddy accepts the
chat.

(Cancel iChat Theater)

Sharing files with iChat Theater

1 Using iChat Theater, you can share files, iPhoto galleries and more with video chat buddies. File sharing works like the Quick Look feature in a Finder window, and any file that can be viewed with Quick Look will work with iChat Theater.

7

2 Choose either Share a File With iChat Theater or Share iPhoto With iChat Theater from iChat's File menu.

3 Navigate to the file or iPhoto event that you want to share.

4 Select a buddy and start a video chat.

5 The shared file will appear in the Video Chat window and also as a Quick Look preview. Manipulate the Quick Look just as you would when using Quick Look in the Finder, and the preview will be echoed on the Video Chat screen.

The alternatives

OS X used to be shipped with a copy of Microsoft's Internet Explorer browser ready installed in case you preferred it to Safari or you were forced to use it because some Web features were unsupported in earlier versions of Apple's own browser. Those days are gone, and the native Apple application is the only one you'll get these days with OS X. Internet Explorer hasn't gone away, however, and you can still download a copy, free, from Microsoft. Other alternatives are available too, one of which, Firefox, we'll take a closer look at here.

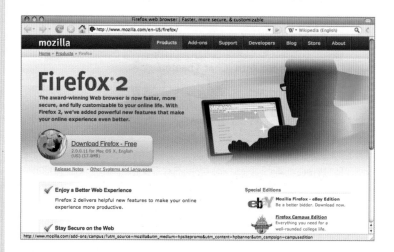

Mozilla Firefox®

Originally named Phoenix and created as a standalone offshoot of the grandfather of all Web browsers, Mozilla, at the time of writing (early 2008) Firefox is the world's second-most popular Web browser – quite a feat for an open source free download, especially given the number of commercial competitors.

Firefox's popularity is well deserved. The intuitive, attractive and feature-rich browser was designed, according to its developers, to 'just surf the web [and provide] the best possible browsing experience to the widest possible set of people'. Use it and you'll quickly agree that they've achieved their goal (and then some).

So why should you use it? Firefox is widely regarded as being one of the most secure browsers available. Machines running Firefox are typically less likely to become infected with nasties such as spyware, and the program has built-in anti-phishing and other security measures to protect you while you're online. Firefox is widely compatible with the websites you'll visit too. What's more, there are thousands of downloadable third-party add-ons available to bring new features to the browser and enable you to customise it to suit the way you like to surf.

See also

Camino is a Web browser from the developers of Firefox but, rather than supporting many OS platforms, Camino is available only for the Mac and is designed to take full advantage of all the features that make Apple's computer the superior choice for your desktop or laptop. Camino is super-fast, and its keyboard shortcuts and navigational tools are finely tuned to Mac users. Check it out at **www.caminobrowser.org**. Seamonkey is an integrated all-in-one suite of Internet software that includes a Web browser, Usenet and email clients, an IRC chat application and an HTML editor. The development community releases regular updates to ensure the suite keeps pace with Internet developments. Check out the project at **www.seamonkey-project.org**.

The alternatives (cont.)

Grab a copy

1 Firefox is available as a free download. Visit **www.mozilla.com/en-US firefox** and click the Download Firefox Free button. The program is downloaded to your computer as a mountable .dmg file.

2 Drag Firefox from the .dmg to your Applications folder and, from there, to the Dock.

3 To launch the program, click its icon in the Dock. You're ready to start surfing.

7

The alternatives (cont.)

The Firefox interface

1. Like Safari, the Firefox user interface will be recognisable to anyone with even passing familiarity with other browsers.

2. Back, forward, reload and stop buttons are all in the usual place to the left of the address field. Pages with RSS feeds are indicated to the right of the URL. Click the button to subscribe to the feed.

3. Tabbed browsing, inline spell-checking (as you type), dynamic searching and an integrated download manager are all leading lights in the line-up of features, while the browser, as was intended from the outset, remains slim and avoids being bloated with unnecessary features that few people will use.

4. Use Firefox's preferences (**File>Preferences**) to customise the program to suit yourself.

5. Don't miss the Firefox add-ons at **http://addons.mozilla.org/en-US/firefox** to increase the scope of the browser to your specifications.

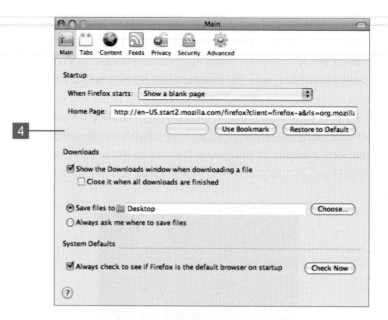

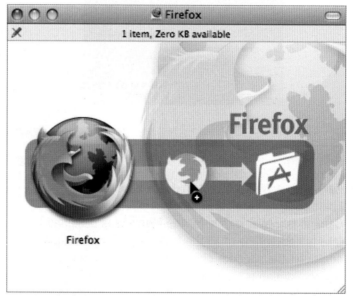

Jargon buster

Phishing – the process of pretending to be a trustworthy entity (such as your bank) in order to acquire sensitive information, such as your account details, password and PIN.

Fifty million downloads is some kind of testament to the ongoing popularity of the **Thunderbird** free mail and news client project. A sibling to Firefox, Thunderbird is a simple and yet fully realised alternative to OS X's Mail program and can be used to organise and read RSS feeds and Usenet news postings as well as your email. The program is open source and available for free download from the Mozilla Foundation, the organisation behind Firefox.

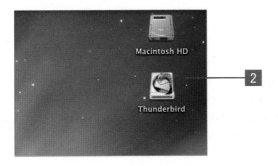

A Mail alternative

First, catch your bird ...

1. Point your browser at **www.mozilla.com/en-US/thunderbird** and click the Download Thunderbird button to download the application to your Mac.

2. Double-click the .dmg file to mount it and click on Accept if you agree to the conditions for installation. Drag the application from the .dmg to your Applications folder and from there to the Dock. Launch the program by clicking its icon in the Dock. You're now ready to set up Thunderbird as your email client.

7

A Mail alternative (cont.)

Take wing

1. One of Thunderbird's great strengths is its ability to seamlessly adopt the settings you've already created for some other email client. First step to using the program is to import Preferences, Mail Account settings and data from your Address Book. Click Continue.

2. To work with email, and to access newsgroups and RSS feeds, you must set up the program with your account details. Thunderbird can divine much of this information from your existing client, but you might need to enter details such as the URLs for your ISP's POP and SMTP servers, together with a password if required. You can also set up, the program to access a .Mac account for syncing emails.

3. Once Thunderbird is set up, it will access your various servers and you can begin to use the program.

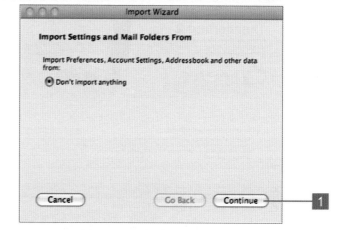

4

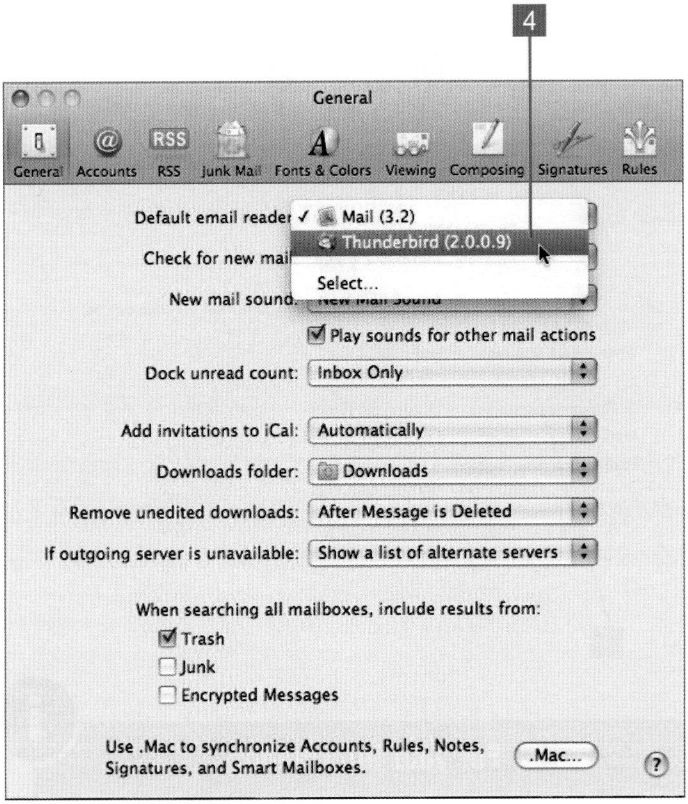

4 There is, however, just one more step – making Thunderbird the default email client, otherwise clicking a contact link on a Web page will cause OS X to open Mail rather than the newly installed Thunderbird.

5 Open Mail and select Preferences from the Mail menu. Click on the General pane and choose Thunderbird from the pop-up Default email reader list (it's the first option in the pane). Close Preferences and quit Mail. Thunderbird is now set as the default email client.

7

A Mail alternative (cont.)

Preen your inbox

1. First, ensure that the junk filtering controls are switched on. Select the Privacy pane from Preferences (**Thunderbird> Preferences>Privacy**) and click the Junk tab. Check all the options and choose between moving Junk mail to the junk folder or deleting junk immediately. Click the E-mail Scams tab and check the Tell Me… option.

2. Now select Account Settings from the Tools menu and click on Junk Settings in the Accounts column. Ensure Enable adaptive junk mail controls for this account is checked.

3. To set a message as junk or not junk, select it and press [J] or [Shift] + [J], respectively (you can also use the junk icon in the toolbar and the **Mark>junk**, **Mark>not junk** options on the Message menu).

Thunderbird's adaptive spam filtering is arguably its best feature. The program uses a mathematical system called Bayesian Filtering, and to get the most from its ability to reject junk mail you must train it – typically over several hundred emails before it's finely honed. But don't worry: your only input during this phase is to click Junk or Not junk when you receive an email.

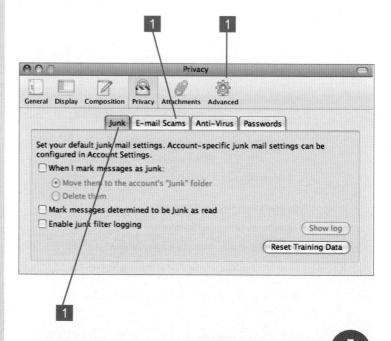

For your information

Usenet is the news network that's one of the subordinate networks that make up the Internet. There's actually very little news … instead, Usenet plays host to thousands of electronic bulletin boards where users can read and post messages to one another. However, problems with spam and trolls (users who make gleefully deliberate inflammatory postings to invite 'flame' responses) have led to many aficionados migrating to moderated Web-based forums. To access Usenet with a newsreader client program, your ISP must offer Usenet as part of its online package (you can also read and write Usenet postings via the Web at Google Groups).

Nest building

1 Principal among Thunderbird's features is its extensibility – the ability to accept add-ons, just like its sibling Firefox. You can use the program as is, at its simplest, or you can download all kinds of interesting and useful extras to customise it just the way you want it.

2 You can browse for add-ons at **https://addons.mozilla.org/en-US/thunderbird** – click the Favourite Add-ons link to see a selection recommended by Mozilla, or choose from the categories on the menu at the left of the page, selecting and downloading those that appeal.

3 Installation is generally a matter of following the instructions delivered with the download, but usually you open the Thunderbird Tools menu, select Add-ons, click the Install button and then navigate to the downloaded file.

Important

No filter is infallible, so it's wise to have Thunderbird move what it believes are junk emails to the Junk folder rather than delete them. Periodically, you can have a quick look through the Junk folder and delete as necessary.

Jargon buster

Bayesian filtering – named after the eighteenth-century British cleric and amateur mathematician Reverend Thomas Bayes, whose paper on probability theory published after his death guaranteed him a special place in the study of chance.

Networking and security

Introduction

You may be the owner and only user of your Mac, but it certainly wasn't designed that way. OS X and its Unix foundation form an unrivalled multi-user system: secure, swift and able. In Chapter 7 you learned how to connect your Mac to the global network that is the Internet, and what's good for the globe is equally good in your home. A local network using the Mac's Ethernet port and a cheap hub will enable you to share files, share a printer, play network games and more.

Even if you are your Mac's sole user and have no other computers, it can be exceedingly useful to create extra accounts on your Mac – so that you can access the machine as an administrator to effect some system wizardry, for example. If you share your machine with your partner and children, you will be amazed and delighted at how OS X keeps everyone's files safe, secure and decidedly separate. What's more, with features such as Parental Control and Simple Finder, you can cheerfully allow access to your Mac, safe in the knowledge that when you log in it'll be just as you left it.

What you'll do

Create a simple two-Mac network

Connect your Mac to an Ethernet network

Learn about network security

Create new user accounts

Networking your Mac

Your Mac is designed to connect and communicate in a fuss-free way with other computers via standard Ethernet and wireless networking protocols and to hook up easily with other devices such as mobile phones and PDAs using the Bluetooth wireless protocol. Even just a few years ago a home network would've been thought a very exotic beast, but in these days of always-on broadband and computers in every room, networking is an indispensable route to sharing data, printers and the Internet. Fortunately, setting up is a relatively painless affair even for the hardened technophobe.

A simple two-Mac network

1   The simplest way to link two Macs – say, your MacBook and an iMac – is to connect them via their Ethernet ports with a single Ethernet cable – you don't even need to use a so-called 'crossover' cable (i.e. one that has its send and receive lines crossed to enable data transfer), because newer Macs are sufficiently sophisticated to realise what's happening and to route the data accordingly.

2   Connecting two Macs in this way will enable them to swap data at high speed, play a network game and essentially anything else that can be achieved by linking your machine to any network.

3   Link the Macs with the cable and start them. Launch System Preferences and select the Network pane.

4   Click Ethernet from the list on the left and make sure Using DHCP is showing on the pop-up Configure menu. Click Apply. Repeat the procedure for the second Mac.

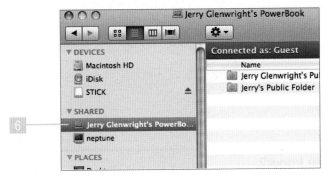

Networking your Mac (cont.)

5 Launch System Preferences and select the Sharing pane from Internet & Network. Choose the services you want – file sharing, printer sharing and so on – from the list on the left. Repeat on the second Mac if you want sharing in both directions. Make sure the Allow access for: All users is checked.

6 That's it! You've created a two-Mac network. If the other Mac is shared, it will appear under Shared in the sidebar. Click it to view what's available.

8

AirPort: no more wires

1. If your Mac has an AirPort or AirPort Extreme card, or if you buy one and install it, you can connect wirelessly to other wireless-enabled computers or to a base station (which does much the same job as an Ethernet hub). AirPort is Apple's take on the WiFi standards 802.11b and 802.11g (slower and faster throughput, respectively). AirPort equipment can happily interconnect with third-party wireless equipment that conforms to the WiFi protocol.

2. To join an AirPort network, click the AirPort icon in the menu extras section of the Menu bar and select the network you want to join.

3. Enter a password if appropriate.

4. You can create a simple computer-to-computer network (similar to the two-Mac Ethernet network) to share files with other AirPort-equipped Macs.

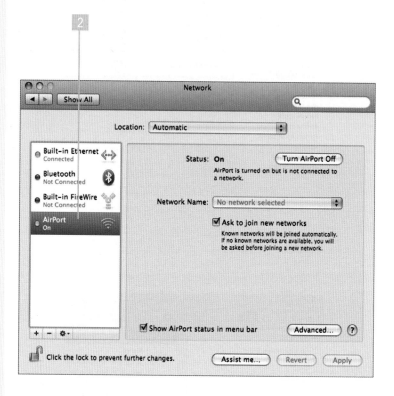

Did you know?

In earlier versions of OS X, mounted servers appeared as volumes on the Desktop. If that's where you prefer to see your servers (or for fast access alongside your Mac's own volumes), select Preferences from the Finder menu, click the General pane and check the Connected Servers in the Show these items on the Desktop list.

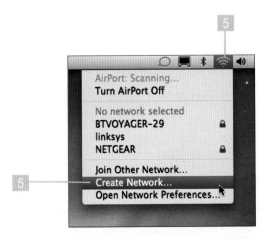

Create a Computer-to-Computer network.

Enter the name of the Computer-to-Computer network you want to create.

Name: Jerry Glenwright's Computer

Channel: Automatic (11)

☑ Require Password

The password must be entered as exactly 5 ASCII characters or 10 hex digits.

Password: ••••••••••••

Verify:

Security: 40-bit WEP (more compatible)

Cancel   OK

5 Select Create Network from the AirPort menu on the Menu bar (click the AirPort icon at the right of the menu bar).

6 Check Require Password if you want to secure the network, enter the password, verify it and click OK.

7 Select from the options in the Sharing pane of System Preferences to share your Mac. Your network is ready and other AirPort-equipped Macs can connect.

8

For your information

Recent Macs use a protocol called Auto Medium-Dependent Interface Crossover (Auto-MDIX) to ensure data are routed correctly if you link them with an ordinary Ethernet cable rather than a crossover cable.

Your Mac's unique MAC address

Data transmitted wirelessly are vulnerable. Using much the same equipment you use for legitimate networking, it's possible to intercept and view transmissions. Fortunately, a number of counter-measures are available. Data can be encrypted using the encryption protocol WEP and a password. Some wireless networks use association control, a method by which only those computers whose unique MAC (Media Access Control) addresses are made known to the base station before allowing a connection.

If a MAC address is required for you to join a network, you can find it on the Network pane of System Preferences. Click AirPort in the list on the left of the Network pane, and then click the Advanced button to view the address. It will look something like this: 00:50:e9:23:a0:c2

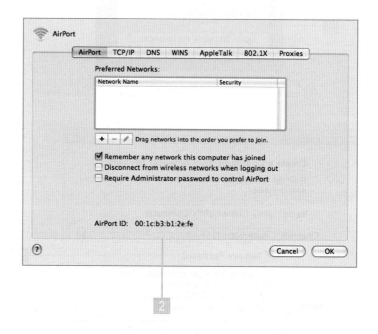

See also

You can also use often cheaper third-party USB wireless adaptors with your Mac (such as those from D-Link), but check that the manufacturer offers OS X drivers before making your purchase.

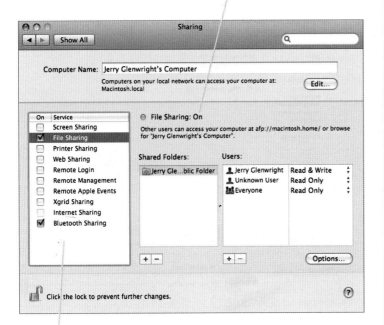

Sharing files

For Macs to connect to each other, at least one of them must have file sharing turned on.

Select the Sharing pane from System Preferences and choose from the sharing options in the list at the left of the window.

If OS X warns you that your Mac's energy saver options are set to sleep after a period of inactivity, decide whether to adjust or inhibit energy saving if other computers are to connect to your machine. Click Open Energy Saver... from the warning dialogue to alter the settings.

If you select File Sharing, click the Options button to decide what can be shared.

To share files with a PC, check Share files and folders using SMB.

Select the account(s) you want to share (check one or more boxes in the list), and enter passwords for the accounts.

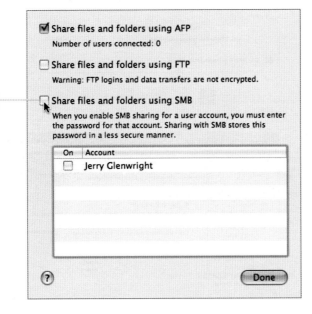

Networking your Mac (cont.)

Sharing a printer or an Internet connection

1. To share a printer, click Share Printer in the list at the left of the Share pane in System Preferences.

2. Choose one or more printers to share from the list of connected printers and click the checkbox(es).

3. To share an Internet connection, click the option on the System Preferences Share pane and then choose your Internet connection from the pop-up Share your connection from list and the network to share the connection over from the To computers using list.

4. To secure Internet sharing over AirPort, click the AirPort options button and then check Enable encryption (using WEP). Enter a password and verify according to the instructions in the dialogue and click OK.

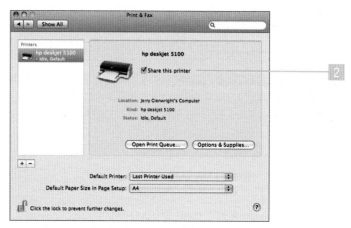

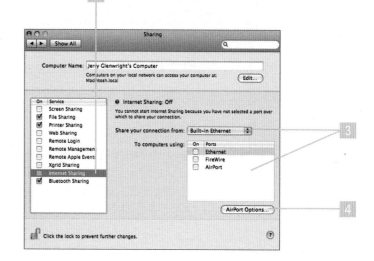

Bluetooth is a technology for communicating wirelessly with devices such as computers, mobile phones, digital cameras, PDAs, printers and more. With a range of around 10 metres, Bluetooth poses no threat of interference and requires no licence or fee – you simply set up the devices to communicate and merrily exchange data – you can even share an Internet connection via Bluetooth. Although individual devices require their own set-up routines, the procedures are broadly similar and OS X has a Bluetooth Setup Assistant to simplify the process.

Connecting via Bluetooth

Mac Bluetooth

1. Open the Bluetooth pane from the Hardware section of System Preferences.

2. Ensure that the Bluetooth Power and Discoverable boxes are checked, and then click Set Up New Device to launch the Bluetooth Setup Assistant.

3. Click Continue, and then select the device you want to connect to... say, a mobile phone.

8

Connecting via Bluetooth (cont.)

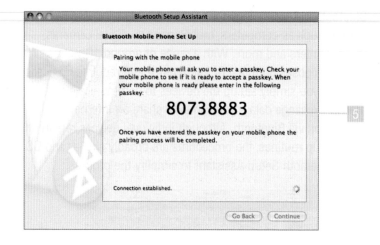

Follow the manufacturer's instructions to ensure your phone's Bluetooth is switched on and the device is set to discoverable.

Click Continue and your Mac will search for your mobile phone. Click Continue again when it's found. Continue again and enter the passcode into your mobile phone when it's displayed. The devices will be paired and you can begin to share data.

Uncheck the Access the Internet with your phone's connection box if you'd prefer not to use your phone for Internet access. Click Quit to complete the process.

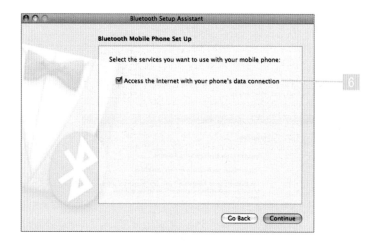

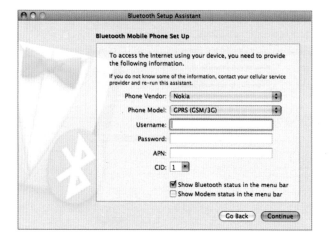

Pairing and browsing with Bluetooth

Click the Bluetooth symbol in the menu bar to begin working with the paired device.

To browse a phone, for example, select Browse. The Browsing window is displayed.

The phone will ask you to confirm that you want to connect with your Mac. Accept the connection.

Accessible folders on your phone will be displayed in the Browse window. Navigate them as you would folders on your Mac using the Back button to move back through the folders. To retrieve items, click and drag them to the Desktop or a folder.

You can also drag and drop files from your Mac into the Browser window to send them to the paired device. Use the Get and Send buttons if you prefer to navigate using standard Finder windows.

Important

To maintain security, it's a good idea to turn off Bluetooth on devices such as mobile phones when the technology isn't actually being used for data transfer.

Sharing OS X

You don't need to network your Mac for others to use it. You can simply log out and let someone else log into a different account. In doing so, OS X will create an entirely separate working environment for the other user, keeping your files and all your settings private. The other user(s) can customise the Desktop, change preferences for the Dock, Dashboard and any other application, and generally set up the Mac the way they like it. However, when you next log in the Mac will be exactly as you left it.

The Guest account

1. New in OS X 10.5 Leopard is a Guest Account that can host temporary access to your Mac.

2. For example, if your friend wants to check their email or place a last-minute bid in an online auction, you'd hardly expect to create a new user account for a few minutes of access. Do you simply step aside and allow your friend to use your account? That's a possibility, but anyone who uses your account has complete control over all your precious files and settings. A malicious act of digital vandalism is probably the last thing on your friend's mind, but it's easy to make an inadvertent key-press or mouse-click and lose data in the process. Accessing the Internet brings a whole host of other potential problems too.

3. The solution is the Guest Account, a separate account that provides a clean Desktop and 'new-user' system settings for anyone who logs in using it. When they log out, everything they did is entirely

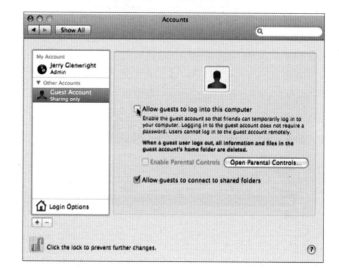

erased, so that the account is ready for the next user (handwashing is optional).

4. To set up the Guest Account, launch System Preferences, select the Accounts pane in the lower left of the System section, and click the lock to enable you to change settings. You'll be asked for an authentication: type your password (the one you entered when installing OS X).

5. Click the Guest Account in the list on the left. Now check the box Allow guests to log in to this computer.

6. Check the Parental Controls box if you want to limit access to certain applications and Internet access and to set up time restrictions. You can read more about using Parental Controls on page 262.

7. Use the Guest Account from the login window. If a list of users is displayed, click Guest. There's no password for the account. If the login window shows only the name and password prompt, simply type 'guest' for the username and press Return.

8

Sharing OS X
(cont.)

Adding user accounts

1 Launch System Preferences and select the Accounts pane in the lower left of the System section.

2 The list at the left shows the existing users. There will be at least two: yours, created when you installed OS X 10.5 Leopard, and the Guest Account (see page 252 for details of switching on and setting up the Guest Account). Click the Add button to create a new account.

3 Select Standard from the New Account pop-up menu. Alternatively, you can give the new user Administrator rights, create a sharing-only account, or create an account with Parental Controls imposed.

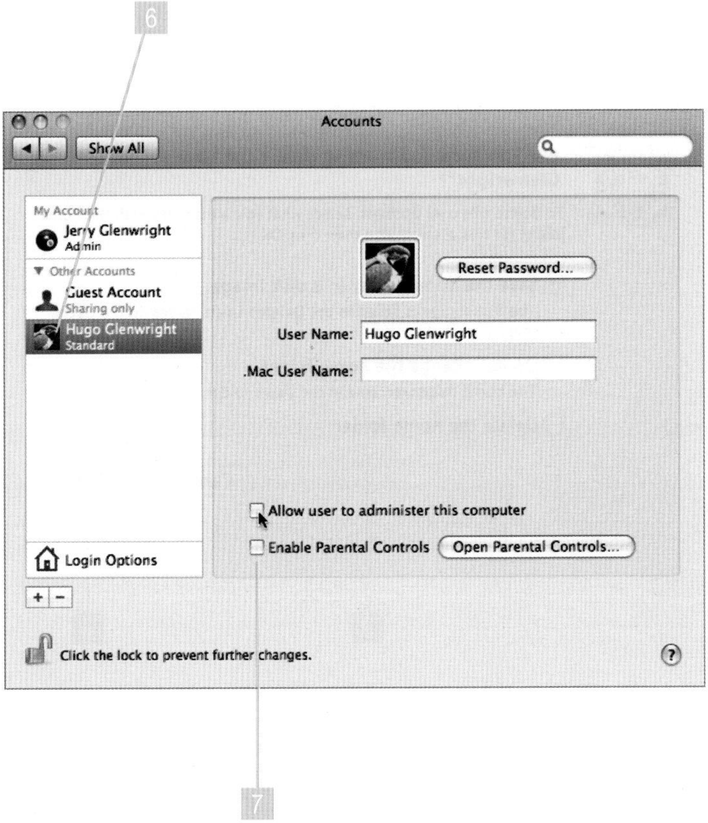

4. Complete the Name and Short Name fields (the latter is created automatically as a contraction of the name unless you type in this field). Enter a password and repeat it in the Verify field. Type a password hint if you're generally forgetful.

5. FileVault protection encrypts the Home folder. Use it with care, because files will be inaccessible if you forget your password.

6. Click the Create Account button to add the new user. If the automatic login feature is switched on, you'll be prompted to retain it or provide a login window for yourself and other users. Back at the Accounts pane, click the login picture to select something suitable from the thumbnail images.

7. You can use the checkboxes to transform a standard user into an administrator or to impose Parental Control settings.

Sharing OS X (cont.)

Deleting a user

1. You can delete redundant user accounts to reclaim file space. Alternatively, you can retain the deleted user's Home folder as it is or as an image that can be accessed to retrieve data.

2. From the Accounts pane (`System Preferences> Accounts`), select the user to delete from the list at the left and click the Remove button. OS X will prompt you for confirmation and ask you to choose what should happen to the user's files.

3. To reclaim the file space, click the Delete the home folder button. Alternatively, retain the Home folder or create an image of it.

4. Click OK to delete the user.

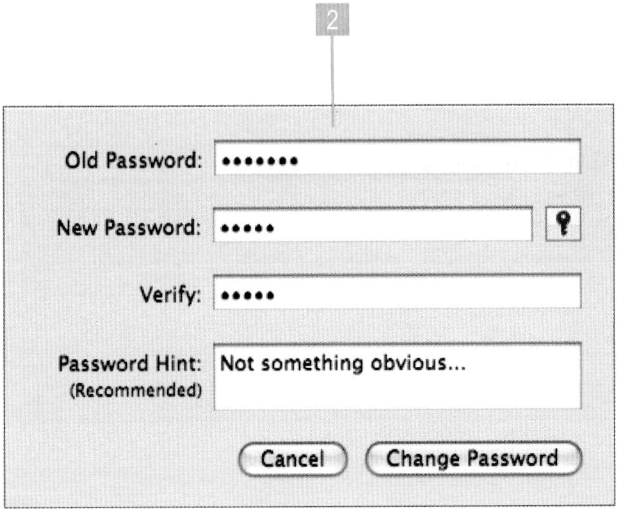

2

Old Password: •••••••

New Password: ••••• 🔑

Verify: •••••

Password Hint: Not something obvious...
(Recommended)

(Cancel) (Change Password)

Changing a password

1 To change the password for your account, select the Accounts pane from System Preferences, click the Password tab and click Change Password.

2 Before proceeding, you'll need to type the existing password (to stop a fraudulent change that would lock you out of the machine). Then type the new password and type it again into the Verify field.

3 Passwords should contain a mixture of letters, numbers and non-alphanumeric characters to prevent unscrupulous people from guessing it – the trade-off is that you're more likely to forget a password that isn't your birth date or your dog's name!

8

Sharing OS X (cont.)

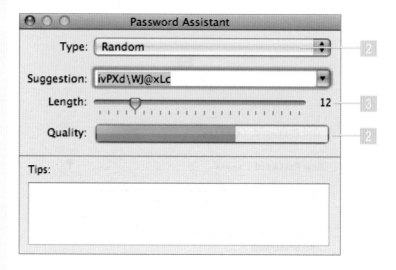

Password Assistant

1. Use Password Assistant to help you select a secure password. Click the key to the left of the New Password field on the Account Preferences pane to launch the assistant.

2. Select the type of password from the pop-up Type menu. The Quality bar will show you how unlikely the password is to be guessed or cracked.

3. Experiment with the various options until you find a password you like. Surprisingly, some of the 'memorable' passwords offer excellent security, especially if you increase the number of characters just slightly using the Length slider.

4. Click the Password Assistant close box and click Change Password.

Important

Bear in mind that, although a random password will probably provide the greatest level of security, it's difficult to remember ... in which case, you'll be tempted to write it down, thereby compromising security.

Did you know?

If you forget the master password (the one you created when you installed OS X), you can recover the system and reset the password by booting with the install disk (hold down the [C] key after restarting with the OS X DVD inserted) and choosing Reset Password from the installer Utilities menu.

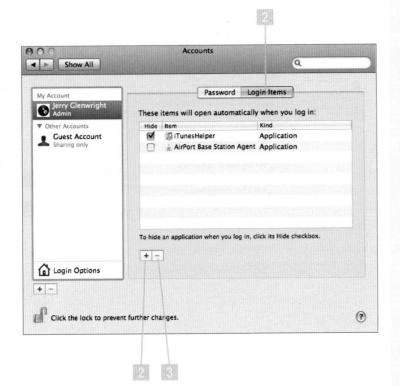

Starting applications at login

Set your favourite applications to launch automatically when you log in.

Select the Login Items tab from the Accounts pane (**Systems Preferences> Accounts**) and click the Add button to add applications.

Use the Remove button to stop application launches at login.

Sharing OS X (cont.)

Sidestepping login with fast switching

1. OS X offers fast user switching to sidestep the tedium of logging in and out in order to access the Mac via another account. You can switch to a different account by selecting it from the menu bar.

2. Click on Login Options in the user list of the Accounts pane (`System Preferences> Accounts`). Check the box Enable fast user switching. OS X then issues a dire warning about trusting other users.

3. Use the pop-up View as menu to select what to display in the Menu bar.

4. Back on the Desktop, the list of accounts is displayed on the right of the Menu bar. To switch accounts, select the one you want. You'll be prompted for a password if one is required. OS X spins the Desktop like a cube, bringing the new account into play.

5. You can also get access to a Login Window and Account Preferences from the menu.

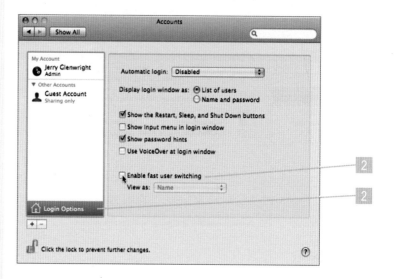

Remember that, when different users access the same Mac, it is as though they are actually accessing entirely different machines. To swap data, a picture, say, you can't simply leave it on the Desktop and hope the other user will be able to see it. Instead, you have to access a user's Public folder.

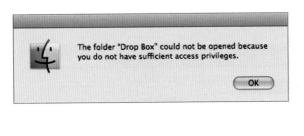

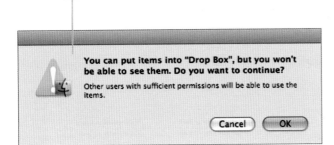

Sharing OS X (cont.)

Sharing files with Public folder

1. Open a Finder window and click on the Startup disk in the Devices list. Double-click the Users folder to open it. This is where the Home folders for each account are stored.

2. Double-click the folder of the user you want to share files with. Notice the no entry symbols next to the majority of folders – you cannot see their contents, even if you have administrator status.

3. You can double-click the Public folder to open it. Drag and drop the file(s) you want to share to the Public folder.

4. Alternatively, dragging and dropping to the Drop Box inside the Public folder will stop anyone (including you, once it's deposited) from seeing the file. The Drop Box is like a letter box: you can put items in, but you can't see what's there or take anything out.

Parental Controls

You can impose comprehensive restrictions on the way kids and any other account holders use your Mac, limiting certain applications and Internet access (independent of the browser and email client), setting time limits (including a 'bedtime') and much more. What's more, OS X keeps a log of your kids' activity – which websites they accessed, the applications they used and who they chatted to – which you can view at any time.

Parental Controls are set individually for each account. Select the Parental Controls pane from System Preferences, click on a user in the list and click Enable Parental Controls.

Click each tab in turn to customise what a user can and cannot do. On the System tab, for example, check Use Simple Finder to remove much of the complexity of the Desktop for children and novice users. Checking Only allow selected applications will provide access to the list of applications, from

Timesaver tip

You can also access Parental Controls from the System Preferences Accounts pane and via the Fast user switching menu on the Menu bar (**Account Preferences>Open Parental Controls**)

which you can add and remove suitable programs.

4 Check Hide profanity in Dictionary from the Content tab to hide naughty words. You can also limit access to adult websites and allow access only to those websites listed explicitly (use the Add and Remove buttons to add further websites or remove existing sites).

5 Using the Mail and iChat tab, you can restrict communications, while the Time Limits tab is the perfect way to ensure your kids don't spend all their free time staring at a computer screen. The logs tab provides access to the various logs gathered over a set period.

6 You can also administer Parental Controls from a remote Mac via a network if you have an administrator's account and password on the target machine.

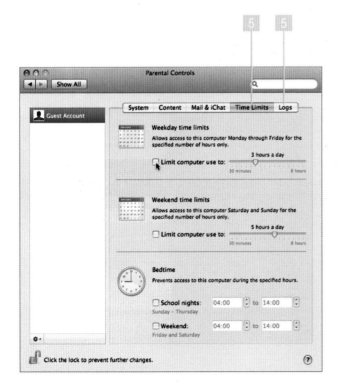

A voyage of discovery with Darwin

Introduction

Back when computers filled rooms and were attended by men and women with lab coats and hushed tones, the operating system Unix was gradually currying favour among the cognoscenti. Built from the ashes of Multics (an attempt by several manufacturers to create a hardware-independent operating system to resolve the endless incompatibilities then prevalent), Unix was a bare-bones operating system that offered many unique features, including security, novel file and peripheral organisation, and the all-important platform-independent portability.

Unix was developed in 1969 by Ken Thompson and Dennis Ritchie working at AT&T's US Bell Laboratories. In 1974, and while on a year's sabbatical at the University of California at Berkeley, Thompson introduced faculty and students to Unix. Such was its popularity that, by 1978, the university had made available its own version, known as Berkeley Software Distribution (BSD). Over time, BSD evolved and was adapted into a variety of other Unix flavours until, in 1999, a portion of it was partnered with elements of Rhapsody, the Unix-like operating system from erstwhile Apple boss Steve Jobs' company NeXT, to create Darwin, Apple's Unix replacement for the Apple operating system. Confused? See the time line on the next page.

What you'll do

Meet Darwin and log in using the Terminal application

Learn about shells

Master simple Unix commands to view, navigate and manipulate files and folders

Learn about the powerful master account 'root'

Gain temporary root status to use advanced commands

Use your new-found power over the machine – carefully – to achieve the otherwise impossible

Time line ▶

1969 – Ken Thompson and Dennis Ritchie create platform-independent operating system Unix to address the incompatibilities and inefficiencies of existing operating systems.

1974 – Thompson begins a sabbatical year teaching at the University of California at Berkeley and introduces faculty and students to his operating system.

1978 – Such is the system's popularity that the university releases its own version, called BSD.

1996 – Apple acquires original co-founder Steve Jobs' company NeXT (he'd left Apple in 1985 following a boardroom power struggle) and, with it, Jobs himself and NeXTSTEP, his company's widely respected Unix-like operating system.

1999 – Elements of BSD and NeXTSTEP (AKA 'Rhapsody') are woven together to create Darwin, the Unix replacement for the long-lived but tired Apple operating system.

For your information

Given a paucity of raw computing power, early operating systems such as Unix were necessarily text-based. That is, you typed a command on the keyboard (such as 'ls -l') and received a text response (in the previous case a verbose directory listing, i.e. a list of what's in a folder). As power increased, programmers were able to create graphic front-ends (a point-and-click interface between you and the dreary text-based operating system) to ease the learning curve and make the computing experience wholly more intuitive.

The usual way to interact with Unix is via commands typed on the keyboard (the command line). Darwin is no exception. An application called Terminal runs as a window on the Desktop and provides a command line interface to Darwin. You navigate to Terminal, double-click it to open, and start typing commands. Although you're working in a window within Aqua, Darwin (and the Mac) responds just as if you were sitting at an old-school terminal in a computer lab somewhere, interacting with Unix.

Meet Darwin

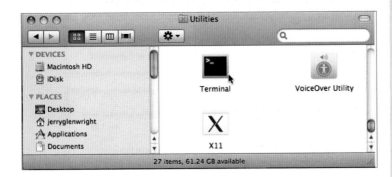

Launch Terminal

1 On the Desktop, press [Command] + [N] to open a window, click on Applications and then double-click the Utilities folder from the list.

2 Navigate to the Terminal application and double-click to open it.

3 Terminal will open and, after a few seconds while the application initialises and examines your system, you'll be presented with your very own 80×24 (that's characters by lines) window on the retro world of command line computing.

9

Meet Darwin (cont.)

What it all means

1 The Title bar shows the name of the application, Terminal, together with 'bash' and '80×24'. bash (Bourne Again SHell) is the name of the command line interface ('shell' in Unix parlance) currently running and 80×24 specifies the characters wide by lines deep of the virtual Terminal.

2 You'll also see a system message from Darwin to tell you when you last logged in. Previously, Unix users connected to a host computer via a remote terminal (teletype), and the nomenclature continues to this day. If this is your first login of the day with Darwin, then the word 'console' will follow the date and time to show that you have previously been logged in to the computer via your usual interface, Aqua, sitting at the machine. Subsequent logins will show **ttys000** as

2 ┐   1 ┐ 1 ┐ 1 ┐

```
Terminal — bash — 80×24
Last login: Thu Jan 17 10:02:44 on console
Jerry-Glenwrights-MacBook:~ jerryglenwright$ ▌
```

Timesaver tip

Think that you'll use Darwin often? Click and drag the Terminal application to the Dock. Now when you want a command line, you have one-click access to Terminal.

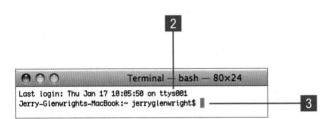

though you are logging in remotely from a terminal. It's also entirely possible to open multiple windows (multiple virtual terminals) to log in and manipulate Darwin; these will appear as `ttys001`, `ttys002` and so on. Switch between them by pressing the [Command] key and the number of the virtual terminal, e.g. [Command] + [1].

Important

Unix users each have an account on the computer with certain privileges attached: reading and deleting files, running various programs and so on. As well as your own account (which, despite the machine belonging to you, will have limited privileges), there's also an account called root. This is the master account with privileges to do anything and everything, including – Heaven forbid! – deleting the operating system and initialising the hard drive. By default, the Darwin root account is disabled. However, you can temporarily switch to root with the `sudo` command (a contraction of Unixese 'superuser do'), which gives you complete (but momentary) power over the machine. More later on page 287.

3 This is the prompt, a reminder of where you are currently in the directory hierarchy (the path). There's the name of your computer (i.e. the localhost in Darwinese), and the tilde (~) denotes your home directory. Later, when you learn how to navigate to other folders, the prompt will show a path other than the home directory. The $ symbol indicates that you're using the bash shell (yes, Unix can be impossibly obscure!).

9

Meet Darwin (cont.)

First steps

1 Go on, type something! Try: 'hello'. Hmm ... not very useful but no harm done either, right? bash tells you in essence: '"hello"? Sorry don't know that command' (i.e. it's not found). You can't actually damage anything by typing into the shell unless, ironically, you know exactly what you're doing, in which case you can wreak absolute havoc.

2 Now try a command that the shell can understand. Type:
pwd
and press [Return].

3 **pwd** means print working directory and Darwin responds with the path to your current directory (the working directory) in the file system – in this case, your Home directory (just like when you open a window on the Desktop).

4 Now type:
1s
and press [Return] and Darwin displays a list of the files and folders in your Home folder.

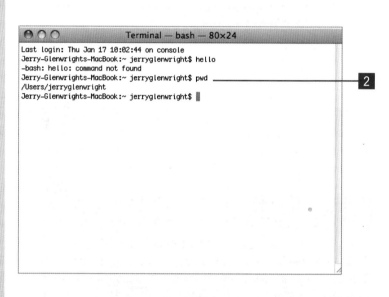

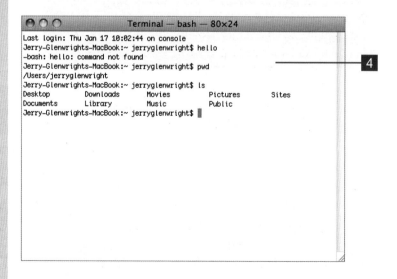

```
● ● ●                Terminal — bash — 80×24
Last login: Thu Jan 17 10:02:44 on console
Jerry-Glenwrights-MacBook:~ jerryglenwright$ hello
-bash: hello: command not found
Jerry-Glenwrights-MacBook:~ jerryglenwright$ pwd
/Users/jerryglenwright
Jerry-Glenwrights-MacBook:~ jerryglenwright$ ls
Desktop        Downloads      Movies        Pictures      Sites
Documents      Library        Music         Public
Jerry-Glenwrights-MacBook:~ jerryglenwright$ ls -l
total 0
drwx------+  4 jerryglenwright  staff    136 19 Dec 15:19 Desktop
drwx------+ 16 jerryglenwright  staff    544 15 Jan 13:00 Documents
drwx------+  4 jerryglenwright  staff    136 17 Nov 15:21 Downloads
drwx------+ 35 jerryglenwright  staff   1190 17 Dec 18:14 Library
drwx------+  3 jerryglenwright  staff    102 17 Nov 15:21 Movies
drwx------+  6 jerryglenwright  staff    204  2 Jan 17:00 Music
drwx------+  6 jerryglenwright  staff    204 19 Dec 15:20 Pictures
drwxr-xr-x+  5 jerryglenwright  staff    170 17 Nov 15:21 Public
drwxr-xr-x+  7 jerryglenwright  staff    238 15 Jan 19:59 Sites
Jerry-Glenwrights-MacBook:~ jerryglenwright$ █
```

6

Meet Darwin (cont.)

9

5 By adding a switch (AKA flag) to the **ls** command like this:
— **ls -l** —
you can modify or expand on the way the basic command behaves.

6 Using the **-l** switch, the list of files and folders now includes a time and date stamp, information on location, read, write and delete permissions and so on.

7 Congratulations! You've communicated with Darwin and, using it, you can manipulate the system far beyond what's possible with Aqua and wield enormous power over your Mac. Sounds frankly terrifying, but there are times – emptying the Trash when it contains a troublesome protected file that can't be deleted, for example – when Darwin, via the Terminal, is truly indispensable.

For your information

In much the same way that computers have different GUIs available to them (Apple's Aqua and Microsoft's Windows are but two), a Unix machine has a number of command line interfaces (CLIs) available. In Unix parlance, each is known as a 'shell' and offers greater efficiency for particular tasks. The default Darwin shell is bash, but there are others available and they can be changed using Terminal's preferences. For example, the shell csh is the standard Unix C programming language shell and is regarded as easy to learn and suited to beginners. You'll learn how to change shells and program csh later in this chapter.

Did you know?

When is an Aqua folder not a folder? When it's a Darwin directory! Folders and directories are the same thing; they just have different names in Aqua and Darwin.

Where now?

So now you've had a chance to meet Darwin and try some commands, what can be usefully achieved by getting your hands dirty? After all, isn't Apple the company that brought GUIs to the masses? Didn't it spend megabucks and hours putting together first Apple OS and then Aqua precisely so that you don't have to learn all this mumbo-jumbo computer command stuff?

Absolutely, but in terms of power the simple fact is that Darwin takes over where Aqua ends. Think of it this way: you can probably get a car from A to B by driving very slowly and steering from the back seat, but to shift up a gear and build speed – to drive efficiently and effectively, in other words – you'd need to scramble into the front seat to reach the pedals and the gearstick. That's Aqua and Darwin. The former's fine when all you want to do is steer a course through your applications (and that, in fairness, may be all that you ever want to do – and, if so, no problem!), but for the speed freaks, or even the slow-laners who find themselves stuck for one reason or another and who cannot progress using the Finder, Darwin is on hand.

Using arguments

1. Earlier in this book you learned that the Mac's file system is like the root system of a tree. You're currently in one of its lowest reaches. Type:
   `ls ..`
   and press [Return].

2. You've given the `ls` command an argument that modifies its behaviour and gives it something to work on. In this case, the argument causes `ls` to display the contents of the directory one level above your Home directory (the Users directory).

3. '.' and '..' (dot and double-dot) have special meanings in Unix. Dot represents the current directory (when you type `ls` on its own, the dot is implied) and double-dot is the directory above it in the directory tree.

4. Now type:
   `ls Pictures ls /`
   and press [Return] after each command.

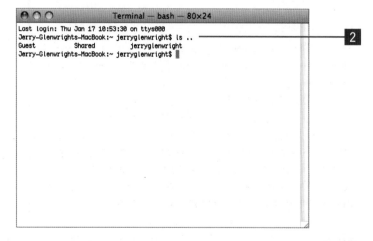

Timesaver tip

Use the up arrow key to scroll back through commands that you've typed. Press [Return] when the one you want to use reappears. The down arrow key moves forward through commands.

```
000          Terminal — bash — 80×24
Jerry-Glenwrights-MacBook:~ jerryglenwright$ ls Pictures
Photo Booth      iChat Icons     iPhoto Library
Jerry-Glenwrights-MacBook:~ jerryglenwright$ ls /
Applications         Volumes            mach_kernel.ctfsys
Desktop DB           bin                net
Desktop DF           cores              private
Library              dev                sbin
Network              etc                tmp
System               home               usr
Users                mach_kernel        var
Jerry-Glenwrights-MacBook:~ jerryglenwright$ ▊
```

4

5 Darwin responds with contents of the Pictures folder in your Home folder and a list of the standard directories and files (plus any others you've created while using your Mac) in the root directory, respectively. If you opened a window on the Desktop and clicked on your hard drive in the upper left of the window, you'd see much the same thing.

6 Using a pathname as an argument to `ls` makes it possible to view the contents of directories other than the one you're in (so long as you have permission to do so … you can't, for example, look into the Home folder of another user – more on that later).

9

For your information

The Darwin file system, like all Unix file systems (it's called a 'file' system because everything – directories, files, peripherals such as printers and disk drives and so on – is treated and manipulated as though it is a file), is structured rather like the roots of a tree (yes, once again, but this time in Darwinese!). At the ground level is the root directory (delineated as '/'), from which all others extend downwards. Branching from root are a number of standard Unix directories ('subdirectories') such as **/usr**, **/etc**, **/dev** and **/user** and, beyond that, user Home directories that contain the subdirectories and files you're familiar with. The route between directories is called the pathname, and this specifies each subdirectory separated by a / symbol (e.g. /jerryglenwright/Documents/brillbook.doc).

Moving on

Navigating the file system

1. In your Home folder, type:
   cd documents
   and press [Return]. Notice that the pathname in the prompt has changed to reflect your new position in the directory structure. The **pwd** command will verify your new location.

2. Here's an example of a wormhole type
   cd /
   followed by
   pwd.
   You're now at root level and a quick **ls** will show you the contents of the root directory. You can return to root from anywhere in the directory structure at any time by specifying **/** as the argument to **cd**.

3. From root, type:
   cd library/preferences
   followed by
   ls -al
   then
   cd /
   (i.e. back to root), and then
   cd ~
   (instant wormhole back to your Home folder) and so on, up and down the directory hierarchy.

4. Remember that double-dot will take you up one level from wherever you are currently, and you can also use multiple double-dots so that **cd ../..** will take you back two levels in the file system.

After logging in to Darwin, you're in your Home folder, a space in the directory system that is allocated to your use. Under Darwin, your Home folder contains a number of standard subdirectories – Documents, Music, Movies and so on – created automatically for your convenience, and you can navigate between them easily using the **cd** command (change directory) along with a pathname. Think of moving between directories like moving between underground stations. The stations may be adjacent, or there may be a path between them and by traversing the path you reach the destination. However, because you're now playing in geekworld, there are wormholes – shortcuts – available between certain locations and they'll be noted as we progress through this chapter.

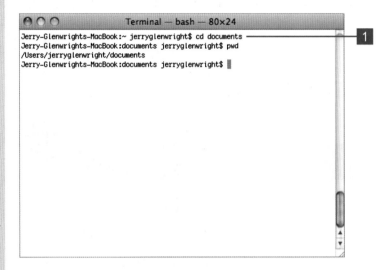

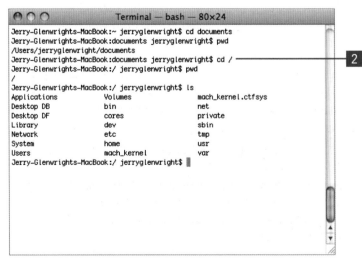

```
000                    Terminal — bash — 80×24
-rw-rw-r--   1 root   admin      60 17 Nov 15:16 com.apple.CoreRAIDServer.cfdb
-rw-r--r--   1 root   admin     460 17 Nov 15:18 com.apple.HIToolbox.plist
-rw-r--r--   1 503   admin     118 16 Jan 22:00 com.apple.SoftwareUpdate.plist
-rw-r--r--@  1 503   admin     460 16 Jan 22:07 com.apple.TimeMachine.plist
-rw-r--r--   1 root   admin    3100 10 Oct 05:48 com.apple.alf.plist
-rw-r--r--   1 root   admin    2204 17 Jan 10:01 com.apple.audio.DeviceSettings.pli
st
-rw-r--r--   1 root   admin    2003 17 Jan 10:01 com.apple.audio.SystemSettings.pli
st
-rw-rw-r--   1 root   admin    1669 25 Sep 03:03 com.apple.dockfixup.plist
-rw-rw-r--   1 root   admin    3047 24 Sep 03:27 com.apple.headerdoc.exampletoctepl
ate.html
-rw-r--r--   1 root   wheel     759 19 Dec 15:17 com.apple.iLife08.plist
-rw-r--r--   1 root   admin     124 17 Jan 10:02 com.apple.loginwindow.plist
-rw-r--r--   1 root   admin     253 17 Nov 15:06 com.apple.pcast_integration.plist
-rw-r--r--   1 root   admin     254 17 Jan 10:53 com.apple.preferences.accounts.pli
st
-rw-r--r--   1 502   admin      60 17 Jan 09:58 com.apple.preferences.sharing.plis
t
-rw-r--r--   1 root   admin     353 17 Nov 15:16 com.apple.security.systemidentitie
s.plist
-rw-r--r--   1 root   admin     469 24 Sep 06:09 com.apple.xgrid.agent.plist
-rw-rw-r--   1 root   admin     344 24 Sep 06:09 com.apple.xgrid.controller.plist
Jerry-Glenwrights-MacBook:preferences jerryglenwright$ ▌
```

2

```
000                    Terminal — bash — 80×24
Jerry-Glenwrights-MacBook:~ jerryglenwright$ cd /private/var/root
-bash: cd: /private/var/root: Permission denied
Jerry-Glenwrights-MacBook:~ jerryglenwright$ ▌
```

6

7

Moving on (cont.)

9

5 You know that the tilde (~) represents your Home directory and that using it with **cd** will return you there from wherever you are, but you can also use the tilde to reach other user's Home directories by specifying their username like this: **cd ~yvette**

6 OK, so navigating directories is relatively simple once you get a fix on the structure and feel comfortable returning to the root level or your Home directory at any time. Given the tree-like structure of Unix, you ought to be able to reach any directory from wherever you are in the system, right? Try this: **cd private/ var/root**

7 What happens? Darwin will not allow you to switch directories to root's directory because it's private – you do not have permission to visit. You'll learn more about the Unix permission system, page 282.

Timesaver tip

Tired of typing? Use the Tab key to complete part-typed pathnames automatically.

Did you know?

Stuck? You can get quick help at any time from the command line by typing **man** (short for manual, i.e. the online manual) and a subject so that, for example, **man cal** will bring up a page detailing the use of the cal(endar) command. Use the arrow keys to scroll through the available information and the [Q] key to quit and return to the shell.

Managing directories

As well as Darwin's default directories, you can create new directories, and rename and delete existing directories to suit your needs.

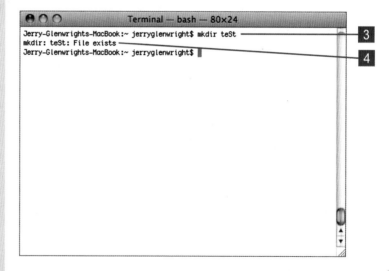

Creating a directory

1 The command **mkdir** (make directory) is used to create a new directory. In your Home folder, type:
mkdir test
to create a new directory.

2 Type:
ls –al
to verify that the new directory exists.

3 Now type:
mkdir teSt
and press [Return].

4 Darwin tells you that the directory already exists. Unless your Mac's hard drive has been formatted specifically for the Unix file system (which, in an off-the-shelf single-user computer for domestic or small business use, is highly unlikely), Darwin is not case-sensitive.

5 Unlike Darwin, 'standard' Unix *is* case-sensitive and test and test would be treated as separate entities – having both within one directory would be entirely feasible.

6 You can create directories outside the current directory by specifying a pathname so that
mkdir documents/ chapters
will create the directory chapters in your documents directory.

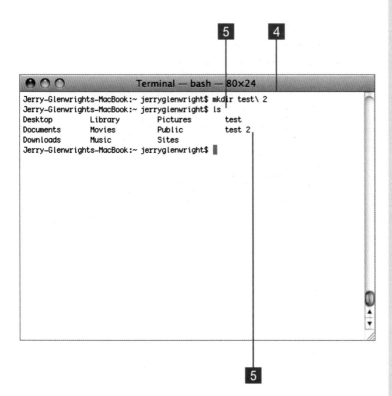

```
● ○ ○              Terminal — bash — 80×24
Jerry-Glenwrights-MacBook:~ jerryglenwright$ mkdir test\ 2
Jerry-Glenwrights-MacBook:~ jerryglenwright$ ls
Desktop        Library        Pictures       test
Documents      Movies         Public         test 2
Downloads      Music          Sites
Jerry-Glenwrights-MacBook:~ jerryglenwright$ █
```

What's in a name?

1 Darwin directory and filenames cannot contain spaces and certain other protected characters, such as the oblique pathname delimiter (/).

2 Type:
mkdir test 2
(note the space between test and 2). Press [Return].

3 All appears well, but Darwin warns you that test already exists. If you type:
ls -al
for a directory listing, you'll see that both 'test' and '2' were supplied as separate arguments to the **mkdir** command and you now have a directory called 2.

4 There is a workaround. Try this:
mkdir test\ 2
and press [Return].

5 **ls** will verify that you now have a directory called test 2.

6 The backslash tells Darwin to ignore the meaning of the next character. Unix calls this 'escaping the next character'. In this instance, therefore, the space is not a separator between arguments but part of the directory name.

9

Managing directories (cont.)

Renaming directories

1 You can rename files and directories easily using the move command **mv**.

2 In your Home folder, type:
mv test test\ 3
and press [Return].

3 **ls** confirms that test has been renamed test 3.

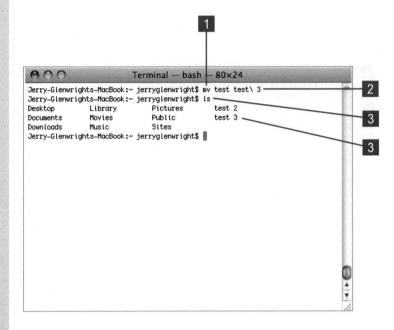

```
Jerry-Glenwrights-MacBook:~ jerryglenwright$ mv test test\ 3
Jerry-Glenwrights-MacBook:~ jerryglenwright$ ls
Desktop        Library        Pictures       test 2
Documents      Movies         Public         test 3
Downloads      Music          Sites
Jerry-Glenwrights-MacBook:~ jerryglenwright$
```

```
  ● ● ○              Terminal — bash — 80×24
Jerry-Glenwrights-MacBook:~ jerryglenwright$ mv test\ 3 documents
Jerry-Glenwrights-MacBook:~ jerryglenwright$ ls
Desktop        Downloads      Movies         Pictures       Sites
Documents      Library        Music          Public         test 2
Jerry-Glenwrights-MacBook:~ jerryglenwright$ mv documents/test\ 3 test\ 3
Jerry-Glenwrights-MacBook:~ jerryglenwright$ ls
Desktop        Library        Pictures       test 2
Documents      Movies         Public         test 3
Downloads      Music          Sites
Jerry-Glenwrights-MacBook:~ jerryglenwright$ ▌
```

2

3

Moving directories

1 Subdirectories can be moved at will using the **mv** command – you can even rename a directory as you move it.

2 At the command line, type:
mv test\ 3 documents
to relocate the test 3 directory in your Home folder to your Documents folder. The directory, and its contents if it had any, are relocated.

3 You can specify paths with the **mv** command so that
mv documents/test\ 3 test\ 3
will return test 3 from the Documents directory back to your Home directory.

4 Remember that dot (.) specifies the current directory so that
mv documents/movies .
has the same effect as step 3 but fewer keystrokes.

5 Combine the moving and renaming operations by providing a new name along with the path:
mv test\ 3 documents/ test4

6 And back again:
mv documents/test4 test4

9

For your information

Although Darwin is not case-sensitive (i.e. you can't have two files or directories with the same name differentiated on capital letters, such as Movies and movies, in the same location), if you want a directory or file to have a capital letter, you must specify it when creating or renaming directories and files.

Managing directories (cont.)

Deleting a directory

1 The **rmdir** (remove directories) command is used to delete one or more directories.

2 At the prompt, type:
mkdir trashme
to create a test directory called trashme.

3 Verify its existence with **ls**.

4 Delete it by typing:
rmdir trashme.

5 Try this:
cd trashme
and
mkdir alsotrash.
Now
cd ~
and
rmdir trashme.

6 Darwin warns 'Directory not empty' and won't delete it.

7 You can, of course, delete lots of directories at the same time simply by specifying them on the command line:
rmdir trash trash2 old\ documents mydocs
and so on.

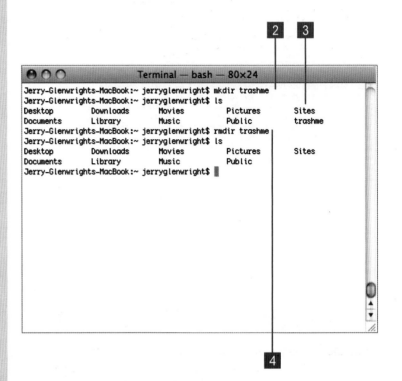

```
Terminal — bash — 80×24
Jerry-Glenwrights-MacBook:~ jerryglenwright$ mkdir trashme
Jerry-Glenwrights-MacBook:~ jerryglenwright$ ls
Desktop      Downloads    Movies       Pictures     Sites
Documents    Library      Music        Public       trashme
Jerry-Glenwrights-MacBook:~ jerryglenwright$ rmdir trashme
Jerry-Glenwrights-MacBook:~ jerryglenwright$ ls
Desktop      Downloads    Movies       Pictures     Sites
Documents    Library      Music        Public
Jerry-Glenwrights-MacBook:~ jerryglenwright$
```

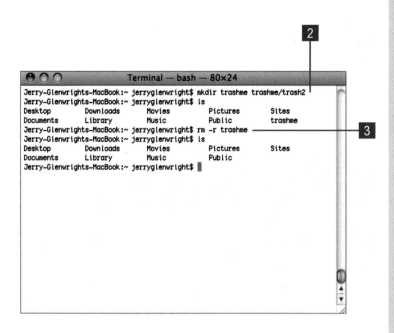

```
000                 Terminal — bash — 80×24
Jerry-Glenwrights-MacBook:~ jerryglenwright$ mkdir trashme trashme/trash2
Jerry-Glenwrights-MacBook:~ jerryglenwright$ ls
Desktop      Downloads    Movies       Pictures     Sites
Documents    Library      Music        Public       trashme
Jerry-Glenwrights-MacBook:~ jerryglenwright$ rm -r trashme
Jerry-Glenwrights-MacBook:~ jerryglenwright$ ls
Desktop      Downloads    Movies       Pictures     Sites
Documents    Library      Music        Public
Jerry-Glenwrights-MacBook:~ jerryglenwright$ █
```

Deleting file hierarchies

1 How to delete entire directory structures (Unix: 'file hierarchies') without laboriously emptying each directory first?

2 Type:

`mkdir trashme trashme/trash2`

to create the directory trashme containing the directory trash2.

3 Now enter:
`rm -r trashme`
and press [Return].

4 **`ls -l`** confirms that trashme has been removed.

5 **`rm`** is the remove command used to delete files, but you can also use it to delete directories by using the **`-d`** flag. In the example above, you used the **`-r`** flag (recursive), which will attempt to remove a file hierarchy (**`-r`** implies **`-d`**), subject to access permissions.

9

Did you know?

Use the **`-i`** flag with the **`mv`** command and Darwin will ask for confirmation before it replaces identically named files within a directory. Press [Y] to confirm.

Timesaver tip

Use **`cd -`** (i.e. the **`cd`** command and a hyphen separated by a space) to switch to the last working directory. Repeat the command to switch back again.

The permission system

The file mode column

1 Type:
```
cd ~
```
so that your Home directory is the working directory.

2 Type:
```
ls -al
```
and press [Return].

3 By now you're familiar with the list of files and folders returned in response to the `ls` command, but other than the directory entries and the time and date stamps, what do all the letters and numbers mean?

4 Reading left to right on a directory entry line, the first 10 characters comprise the file mode column and specify file type and associated permissions related to the entry.

5 The first character in the column – a hyphen or the letter d or l – denotes whether the directory entry is a file (hyphen), directory (d) or symbolic link (l).

Given the tree-like structure of the Unix file system, you might imagine that it's entirely possible to reach any branch from any other branch, manipulating files and directories at will. In fact, Unix maintains a robust permissions system with boundaries for all users (other than root), protecting your stuff from access and stopping you from probing where you shouldn't.

When it's created, your account on the computer has permissions associated with it that enable you to create and manipulate files and folders. Even though you might be the only user (i.e. the computer is yours and only you use it), these permissions will be limited in order to protect the machine from mishaps – you can't, for example, destroy the OS X system files. This status under Aqua is continued and extended in Darwin, which provides even greater control of your actions while, at the same time, enabling you to scurry freely anywhere and everywhere if you know what you're doing.

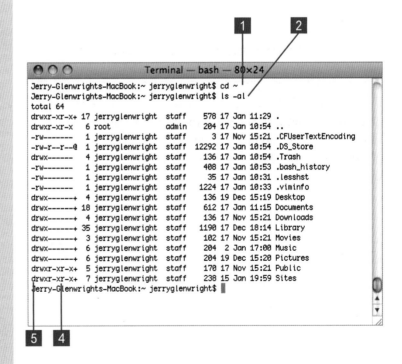

Beyond personal permissions, you will automatically belong to a group (staff, wheel, etc.) that facilitates file and resource sharing. In Darwin, a third category of user called others exists, comprising everyone else on the system who is not you and who doesn't belong to your group.

The consensus is that the Unix permission system is complex and not easily understood or manipulated by new users. For example, Unix gurus use an obscure octal number system for assigning and changing permissions at a stroke. Don't be put off! The system is complex, but you can learn to manipulate it such that all basic operations are within reach without too much effort. Learning it is essential if you want to move and delete troublesome files and directories and to protect your own with greater security than the defaults offer.

The permission system (cont.)

Read, write and execute

1 Now we come to the permissions proper. Following the file type, the next nine characters, which probably contain a mixture of letters and hyphens, list the permissions associated with the file or directory. Here's how it works: the block of nine comprises three blocks of three, and each block shows the permissions enjoyed by the user, the group and others (i.e. everyone else on the system), respectively.

2 Taking the first block of three, an r means that the user has 'read' permission. That is, if the entry is a file, you can, literally, read it. If it's a directory, you can list its contents using, say, the `ls` command. A hyphen in this first position that means that you do not have read permission. Next there's a w or a hyphen. The w gives 'write' permission and means that you can modify the file (or, if it's a directory, move or create new entries within it). A hyphen means that there is no write permission. In the third position, an x gives execute permission – you can run the file if it's an application or make it the working directory using **cd** and list the contents together with each entry's attributes if it's a directory.

3 The next group of three repeats these permissions but for the user's group, and the final block of three shows permissions for all other users of the computer.

4 Easy, right? Read, write and execute or else no permission (**rwx** or '-') for user, group and everyone else on the system for each file, folder and link.

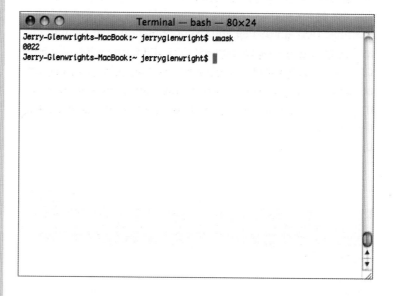

For your information

Find out what permissions are given by default to your newly created files and folders by using the **umask** command. Type **umask** and press [Return]. If umask returns 22, then your files and directories can be read but not written to; 77 means you have neither read nor write permissions.

Although the permissions system is far-reaching and rigid, Darwin provides several commands so that you can manipulate permissions, change the ownership of files and directories, and even change groups.

Of course, a file permissions system would be pretty useless if those without permission were able to use commands to change their access to files, and therefore much of what can be done requires at least administrator status and some actions require that you have root status. In a bid to protect the system from your inadvertent prodding, the root account is turned off by default, but you can use the **sudo** command mentioned on page 269 to acquire root status temporarily – its use is noted where required.

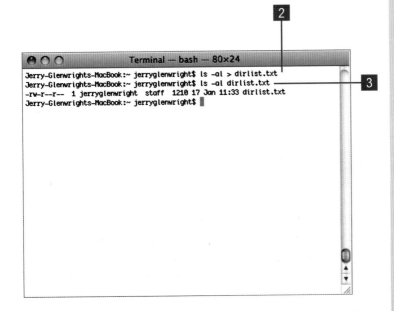

Timesaver tip

You can create a dummy file to practise using the touch command. Type: **touch junkfile.txt** to create an empty file called junkfile.txt in the working directory.

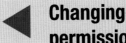

Changing permissions

Changing file permissions

1. The **chmod** (change mode) command is used to revise file and directory permissions. The command is typed together with information detailing the class of user and the permissions you're changing.

2. At the command line, type:
   ls -al > dirlist.txt
   to create a text file called dirlist.txt, which contains a long listing of the directory contents (you'll meet the indirection command '>' on page 269). This will give you a newly created junk file of text with which to experiment.

3. Now type:
   ls -al dirlist.txt
   to see all the permissions associated with your new file. Notice that the first character in the file mode column is a hyphen – in other words, you're looking at a file.

4. To use **chmod** you specify the user class (**ugoa** – user, group, others or all) and permission (**rwx**) together with a + or – to turn permission on or off so that, for example,
   chmod go+w code.html
   will give write (modify) permission to 'group' and 'others' for the file code.html.

9

Changing permissions (cont.)

chmod o-rw privatefile
will remove read and edit permissions for others for privatefile.

4 Let's change the permissions of dirlist.txt so that any system user can read and write to your file. Type:
chmod a+w dirlist.txt
and press [Return].

5 Once again type:
ls -al dirlist.txt
to confirm that permission has changed for others. You can see a w in the others group where previously there was a hyphen (scroll back through the Terminal window to compare).

6 Specify an **-R** flag (that's a capital R: the flags are case-sensitive) with the **chmod** command to cause it to work recursively – permission is changed for the item and everything in its hierarchy. For example,
chmod -R go-rwx privatedir
removes read, write and execute permission to your group and other users for the directory privatedir as well as everything in it.

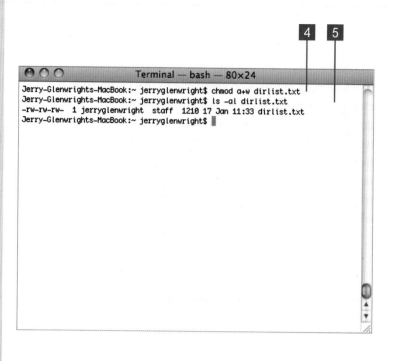

```
Terminal — bash — 80×24
Jerry-Glenwrights-MacBook:~ jerryglenwright$ chmod a+w dirlist.txt
Jerry-Glenwrights-MacBook:~ jerryglenwright$ ls -al dirlist.txt
-rw-rw-rw-  1 jerryglenwright  staff  1210 17 Jan 11:33 dirlist.txt
Jerry-Glenwrights-MacBook:~ jerryglenwright$
```

For your information

You can't give yourself access to a file or directory that you don't own. However, using the sudo command will give you five minutes of root status, during which you can change any (and all) permissions.

Important

Write-protecting a file doesn't mean that it can't be inadvertently deleted. To properly protect a file from deletion ensure the directory it's in is write-protected too.

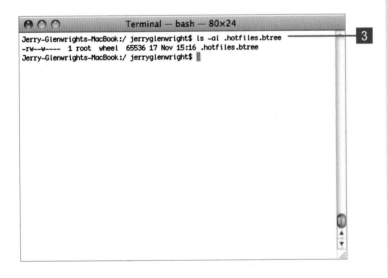

When you don't have permission

1. Type:
   cd /
   to make root the working directory. Now type:
   ls -al
   and, from the directory listing, choose a file or directory that is owned by root, say .hotfiles.btree (or some other root-owned dotted file).

2. Type:
   chmod g+w .hotfiles.btree
   and press [Return]. Darwin tells you 'Operation not permitted' – you don't have sufficient status.

3. Now type:
   sudo chmod g+w .hotfiles.btree
   to boost your status temporarily to root. Darwin will prompt you for your password and, if you enter it correctly, give you root status. The **chmod** command is executed. Check with **ls -al** (remember you can use the up arrow key to scroll through previous commands).

4. The power of sudo will last for around five minutes before prompting for your password again.

5. Reverse the action with:
   sudo chmod u-w .hotfiles.btree.

Working with files

When Unix made its appearance back in the late 1960s, arguably its most powerful and certainly its most novel feature was the way in which it addressed every entity as a file – whether a data file, a directory or a peripheral such as a printer or disk drive. Everything appears in the file system as a file and can be addressed and manipulated using standard file-orientated commands. You've learned how to manipulate directories, so now it's time to work with what they contain.

Copying files

1 The **cp** (copy) command is used to copy and rename files.

2 To make an identical copy of a file but with a new name (to create a backup, say), navigate to the directory containing the file and type:

cp myfile.doc myfilebackup.doc.

3 Alternatively, you can specify a path with the **cp** command. Let's say you have two directories in your Home directory: one called docs, which contains text files from a word processor, and the other called backups, where you like to store copies of the text files in case of a mishap. To copy a file but without renaming it from one directory to the other, type:

cp /docs/myfile.doc /backups

and an identical copy is created in the backups directory.

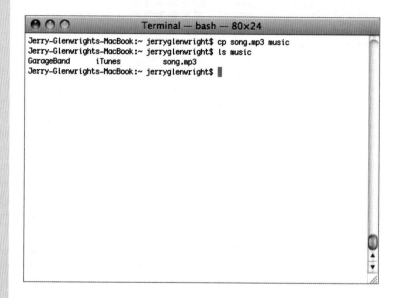

Working with files (cont.)

```
  ● ○ ○            Terminal — bash — 80×24
Jerry-Glenwrights-MacBook:~ jerryglenwright$ cp song.mp3 music
Jerry-Glenwrights-MacBook:~ jerryglenwright$ ls music
GarageBand       iTunes          song.mp3
Jerry-Glenwrights-MacBook:~ jerryglenwright$ █
```

4 Other possibilities include:
cp song.mp3 music
(copies the specified file from the current working directory to the Home, Music directory)
cp documents/file. txt .
(copies file.txt from Home, Documents to the current working directory as specified by the period)

… and so on. Use a dummy file and try copying it hither and thither in the file system to gain familiarity with the **cp** command.

5 **cp** will overwrite an existing file with the same name unless you use the **-i** flag for a warning prompt.
cp dummyfile1.txt dummyfile2.txt,
cp dummyfile3.txt dummyfile2.txt
will overwrite the first dummyfile2.txt unless you use the **-i** flag:
cp -i dummyfile3.txt dummyfile2.txt.

9

Working with files (cont.)

Rename a file

1 Use the **mv** (move) command much as you did when working with directories to rename a file.

2 `mv code.html index.html`

will rename the file code.html index.html in the working directory.

3 Beware: like **cp**, **mv** will overwrite an existing file called index.html unless you force it to warn you using the **-i** flag: `mv -i code.html index.html`.

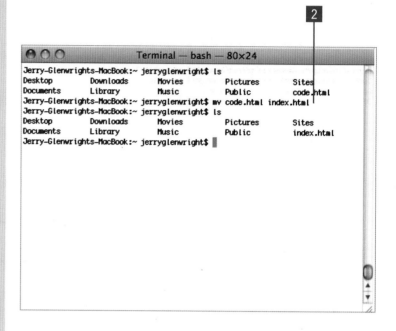

```
  ● ○ ○              Terminal — bash — 80×24
macintosh:~ jerryglenwright$ mv ~/documents/holidaypics/* ~/documents/slideshow
macintosh:~ jerryglenwright$ █
```

Wildcards

1 You can copy and move related files without laboriously specifying each name using the wildcard *.

2 To move (or copy, simply substitute **cp** for **mv**) all the digital pictures in a directory called holidaypics to another called slideshow, both in the Documents directory of your Home directory, use:

mv ~/documents/ holidaypics/* ~/documents/ slideshow.

3 You can use the wildcard to filter files too, so that

cp/textandpics/*jpg /digitalpics

will copy all the digital pictures with the jpg suffix to the directory digitalpics.

4 Use the **-R** flag to copy or move files and directories recursively.

9

Working with files (cont.)

Viewing a file

1. You can see what's in a text file using the `cat` command. Although `cat`'s principal purpose is to join ('concatenate') one or more files, using the command with just one argument – a single file – its contents are echoed to the standard output (Unixese for the screen).

2. For example, with a text file in your Documents directory called chapter9.txt, you can echo its contents to the screen by typing:
   `cat chapter9.txt`
   and pressing [Return].

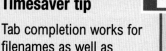
Timesaver tip

Tab completion works for filenames as well as directories.

```
000              Terminal — bash — 80×24
Jerry-Glenwrights-MacBook:~ jerryglenwright$ cat documents/chapter9.txt
Back when computers filled rooms and were attended by men (and a women or two) i
n lab coats and hushed tones, the operating system Unix was gradually currying f
avour among the cognoscenti. Built from the ashes of Multics (an attempt by seve
ral manufacturers to create a hardware-independent operating system to resolve t
he endless incompatibilities then prevalent), Unix was a bare bones OS which off
ered many unique features including security, novel file and peripheral organisa
Jerry-Glenwrights-MacBook:~ jerryglenwright$ █
```
2

For your information

Darwin requires that you type the complete filename – that is, including a suffix such as .txt, .doc or .html – so that it can recognise which file you're trying to manipulate.

Important

Unix reserves certain characters such as **&**, **|** and ***** for use in system-level operations or as prompts. There are workarounds such as using the backslash to escape the next character (tell Darwin not to treat it as special) and using quote marks to cause the character to be treated literally. However, other than inserting a space in a filename, as a novice user it's probably best for you simply to avoid their use.

In order to provide the seamless user experience that is the Mac computer, OS X must work tirelessly in the background coordinating your clicks and key-presses, the work of various applications that you have running at any given time and the exchange of information with other computers on a local network or across the Internet. To do that, the Mac itself is running dozens of system-based and largely invisible computer programs. Each of these and all of the applications you're running are known as processes in Unix, and each is allocated system resources and processor time.

The Darwin command line, for example, is just the tip of a very large Unix iceberg, all ticking away in the background, providing the display, processing typed input at the keyboard, playing digital music files, spooling data to a printer, communicating with other computers, and all operating apparently simultaneously (not actually, but that's how it's meant to appear). Even your typed commands cause processes to be created. Enter ls at the keyboard, for example, and when you press [Return] Darwin suspends the operation of bash and runs the **ls** process, sending its output to your screen.

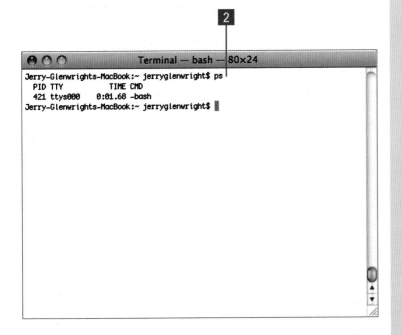

Processes

1 To keep track of all the processes, the system allocates each a unique identification number known as its PID (process ID). You can see a subset of the running processes together with their PIDs by typing **ps** (processor status) at the prompt.

2 Darwin displays the information associated with the bash process (the shell you're currently working with). From left to right, you can see the process's PID and the terminal it's running on (in this case, the console).

Behind the scenes (cont.)

Killing fields

1 At the command line, type:
`ps -x`
(the x flag says include processes not controlled by a terminal – in other words, system programs as well as those you're running).

2 Locate the Terminal utility under the COMMAND field and note its PID. Now type:
`kill xxx`
(where xxx is Terminal's PID) and press Return. What happened? Did Terminal crash? In fact, the application vanished instantly because you sent a kill signal to its PID. All other processes can be ended in this way too, instantly and fuss-free. Don't end Terminal in this way as a matter of course, however. Always leave the system neat and tidy by logging out correctly using [Control] + [D] or typing exit at the command line.

3 You cannot end processes associated with other users, unless you have superuser status (i.e. you're logged in as root).

If you've used any other type of computer previously, you'll be only too aware that, previously, when a program crashed usually the computer crashed too and had to be restarted. OS X brought with it a robust defence against crashes – user applications (word processor, browser and so on) are running as discrete processes beneath the Aqua interface deep in the underlying Darwin Unix. With rare exceptions, when a process crashes, it cannot affect any other part of the system.

Previously, you may have used the Force Quit option from Aqua to end troublesome or crashed applications, but you can also end processes direct from the Darwin command line too.

2

```
● ○ ○          Terminal — sleep — 80×24
Jerry-Glenwrights-MacBook:~ jerryglenwright$ sleep 10
```

Away from the limelight

1 Processes can run in the background as well as in the foreground.

2 Try this: at the command line, type:
sleep 10
and press [Return].

3 Sleep is a system-level command that causes bash to pause for 10 seconds. The prompt disappears and you're required to wait for 10 seconds before regaining control. The sleep command ran in the foreground and its effects were immediate and direct.

9

Important

Do not use the kill command indiscriminately, especially if you have superuser status – you could crash the computer and lose important data or even damage the file structure.

Behind the scenes (cont.)

4 Now try this: type:

`sleep 10 &`

and press [Return]. The ampersand (&) causes bash to run the process (AKA 'job') in the background. After displaying the job number (the figure in square brackets) and its process ID, the prompt is returned and you can continue. The sleep process is running, but it's running in the background, allowing you to continue.

5 You can run any number of processes in the background subject only to the limits of the system's resources though by running lots of CPU-intensive background processes you could slow the machine significantly.

6 A background process will end when its task is complete, or you can end with the kill command and its process number.

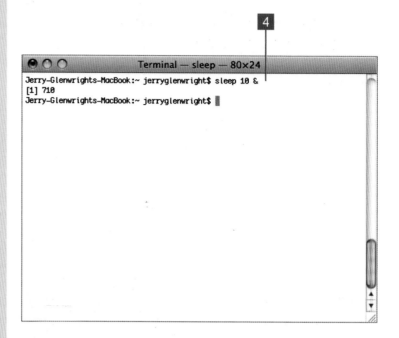

4

```
Jerry-Glenwrights-MacBook:~ jerryglenwright$ sleep 10 &
[1] 710
Jerry-Glenwrights-MacBook:~ jerryglenwright$
```

```
● ○ ○            Terminal — sleep — 80×24
Jerry-Glenwrights-MacBook:~ jerryglenwright$ sleep 1000
^Z
[1]+  Stopped                 sleep 1000
Jerry-Glenwrights-MacBook:~ jerryglenwright$ bg
[1]+ sleep 1000 &
Jerry-Glenwrights-MacBook:~ jerryglenwright$ jobs
[1]+  Running                 sleep 1000 &
Jerry-Glenwrights-MacBook:~ jerryglenwright$ ▆
```

Background and foreground

1 You can 'background' a process (computing at the geek level, you'll find many instances of weird 'verbs') already running in the foreground.

2 Try this, type:
sleep 1000
and press [Return]. Now press [Control] + [Z] to temporarily suspend the process and, when the prompt reappears, type:
bg
to background it.

3 Background processes can be returned to the foreground using the **fg** command.

4 Type **jobs** for a list of your running and suspended processes. The figure in the square bracket is the job number. To bring it to the foreground, type:
fg x
where x is the job number.

9

Important

When a computer crashes, there's no bang, flash or crunch of metal and plastic. It simply means that the machine has become confused and can't determine how to proceed. The result of a crash is usually that the machine locks up and is unable to accept input or act on an instruction.

For your information

You can see at a glance all the processes running and sleeping on your computer by typing **top** at the command line. The information is updated as you watch.

Timesaver tip

Type: **fg** without a job number to foreground the last backgrounded process.

Take control ▶

By now you should be reasonably comfortable with working at the command line. You've learned how to determine your location within the file system (and what a file system is!) and how to navigate directories, copying, moving and manipulating as you go, how to change permissions and even how to become the superuser – now you really are in control of the system.

Several text editors are available to you at the Darwin command line. The de facto standard editor available on every Unix system is vi, a full-screen editor (i.e. you can move up and down through text, editing as you go, rather than manipulating one line at a time, as with a simple line editor). vi is powerful (even more powerful in its Darwin incarnation 'vim', or, 'vi improved'), but its various modes and commands will be incredibly obscure to anyone used to using, say, iWorks Pages in Aqua. An alternative Darwin text editor, and one that is a little easier to get to grips with, is pico.

Text processing

1. At the command line, type:
   pico
   and press [Return]. To enter text, start typing. A summary of commands is listed at the foot of the pico editing screen. Enter commands using the [Control] key and the relevant letter: [Control] + [O] will 'write out' (i.e. save) your document and [Control] + [R] will read (i.e. open) an existing document. The summon help command, [Control] + [G], will probably be most useful to you at first.

2. For now, try the pico experience by typing a few lines of text in the editing window, and then press [Control] + [O] to save. At the prompt, type:
   testfile.txt
   or some such and press [Return]. The file is saved and you're returned to the editing screen.

3. Press [Control] + [X] to quit the program.

4. At the command line, type:
   ls- l
   to see the newly written file. View and verify its contents by typing:
   cat testfile.txt
   pressing [Return].

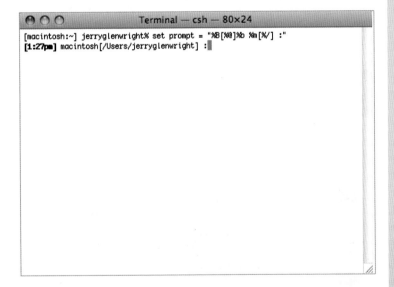

```
● ● ●                Terminal — csh — 80×24
[macintosh:~] jerryglenwright% set prompt = "%B[%@]%b %m[%/] :"
[1:27pm] macintosh[/Users/jerryglenwright] :█
```

See also

Terminal's preferences are well worth a rummage. You can change everything from the size and look of the Terminal window to the keyboard mappings.

Take control (cont.)

Customise the prompt

1. The default Darwin command line prompt displays the computer's name, your location in the file system and your user name (truncated if it's longer than eight characters), together with the per cent symbol, %, to show you're working with the bash shell (the shell displays a # when you're logged in as root).

2. Assuming you're in your Home directory (type: **cd ~** if not), at the prompt type:
   pico .cshrc
   and press [Return]. You've instructed pico to open the csh configuration file if it's found in your Home directory or to create a new one if not.

3. At the editing screen, use the arrow keys to scroll to the end of any existing text and type:
   set prompt =
   "%B[%@]%b %m[%/] :"

4. Press [Control] + [O] and then [Return] to write out the amended config file. Now press [Control] + [X] to quit the program and [Control] + [D] to log out.

9

Take control (cont.)

Now you're going to summon the csh shell, one of several shells available to Darwin and especially easy to learn and program. Select Preferences from the Terminal menu and click the Startup tab if it's not currently selected.

Shell swap

1. Check the command button at the Shells open with option and change bash to csh. Close preferences.

2. Type [Command] + [N] for a new shell. Notice that csh appears in the Terminal window title bar. Also notice your new and customised prompt: now you have a permanent (until you change it back) reminder of the time, together with the host name and working directory path.

3. Now use `pico` again to customise the prompt the way you'd like it according to the control codes (AKA 'escape sequences') listed on page 299 (use your favourite search engine to look for `+csh+prompt+ escape+characters` for more).

4. bash can be programmed in much the same way (arguably it's a little less obvious than csh), and any good Unix text will get the interested reader started in shell programming and scripting.

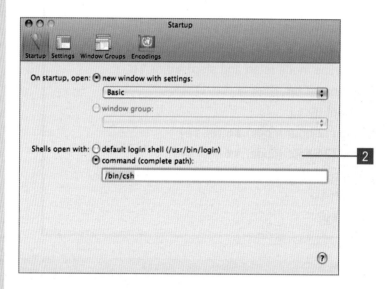

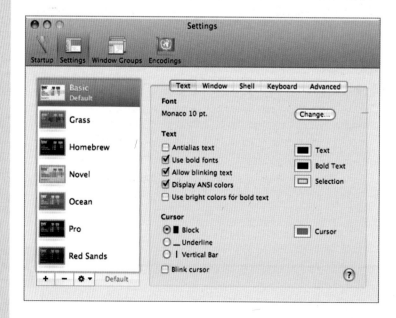

!

Important

Every shell has its own command syntax, and a script written for csh may not work as expected (or at all) when executed under bash. A solution is to use sh syntax – sh is the oldest Unix shell and a pointer to its location (`#!/bin/sh -`) as the first line of your script will ensure that the commands are interpreted correctly.

?

Did you know?

If you think pico and vi are obscure, try using emacs (type: **emacs** at the command line and press [Return]). Written in the days when computers filled rooms (well, cupboards anyway), emacs is described by the authors of its manual as the 'extensible, customizable, self-documenting, real-time display editor' and is about as obscure as it gets. For those who master its arcanery, however, there is vast power lurking within … but let your first command be help! ([Control] and [H]).

1 You can type commands at the prompt and have them execute in the foreground and background. You can also gather commands together into a file known as a shell script, complete with line spaces and comments (yes, just like a computer program) and have the shell execute them.

9

2 By creating a shell script, you can simplify complex or repetitive command line tasks. To execute the script, you type its name at the prompt and press [Return], just as you would any other shell command (in fact, many shell commands are scripts).

3 Create a directory called bin in your Home directory by typing: **mkdir ~/bin**. This will be the depository for your executable scripts.

4 Using pico, create a new file named stats in your /bin directory (i.e. at the command line, type: **pico /bin/stats** and press [Return]).

5 Now enter the following lines in the editing window:
```
#!/bin/sh -
#
```

Shell scripting (cont.)

```
clear
echo Hello
whoami
echo
echo You are in
this directory:
pwd
echo
echo This directory
contains:
ls
echo
echo The date is:
date
echo
echo
```

6 Press [Control] + [O] to write out the file and [Control] + [X] to exit pico. Back at the prompt, type:
chmod u+x bin/stats to give the script permission to execute (otherwise it's just a text file).

7 Now **cd bin**, type:
./stats and press [Return]. That ./ tells csh to execute the file as a script. See how even simple scripting can produce (relatively) impressive results? Use your favourite search engine to find useful sample scripts that you can use immediately or to help with developing your own.

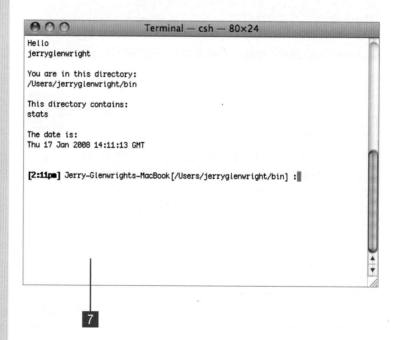

```
Hello
jerryglenwright

You are in this directory:
/Users/jerryglenwright/bin

This directory contains:
stats

The date is:
Thu 17 Jan 2008 14:11:13 GMT


[2:11pm] Jerry-Glenwrights-MacBook[/Users/jerryglenwright/bin] :
```

7

Based on what you've learned in this chapter, it's probably reasonable to assume that you consider the Unix CLI an arcane and obscure way to communicate with a computer, though it's probably also a reasonable bet that you're beginning to see why certain tasks are best completed at the command line – you have access to the guts of the machine and everything is laid bare for you to manipulate.

You've grown familiar with some of the basic Unix command structures and, over the next few pages, you'll be introduced to 10 further indispensable Unix commands and concepts that will help you pass from newbie to hoary old hand at a (key)stroke…

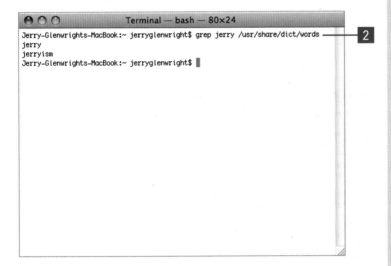

Jargon buster

Grep – The name 'grep' is said to derive from the combination of the letters used to search for strings when editing text in the Unix line editor Ed: g/re/p.

Useful Unix

Grep

1. Although the origins of its name are shrouded in the mists of time (but see below left, grep is a pattern-matching program that will search your computer for a string of text specified as argument. You can search for file- and directory names, a word, a sentence or a paragraph (or any other characters limited only by available memory) within one or more files or search for lines that don't match the pattern. Wildcards are permissible and you can also toggle case-sensitivity. The results of a grep search can be seen at the command line, or you can redirect the output to a file or even to another command.

2. Type:
   ```
   grep jerry /usr
   /share/dict/words
   ```
   and press [Return]. Grep prints its results to the standard output (i.e. displays its results on screen).

3. How about a real-world example? Let's say you're baffled by a crossword puzzle clue, the answer to which is a five-letter word beginning with j and ending in y. No problem for grep, type:
   ```
   grep '\<j...y\>'/usr
   /share/dict/words
   ```

9

A voyage of discovery with Darwin 303

Useful Unix (cont.)

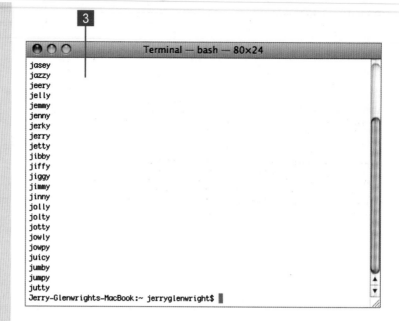

and press [Return]. Ah, jazzy!

4 The argument reads like this: find all occurrences of words that begin (\<) with j and end (\>) with y and have any three other characters in between. The * wildcard matches multiple characters so that grep `'\<j.*y\>' /usr /share/dict/words` will find all words that begin with j and end in y.

5 If grep's results are lengthy, you can redirect them to a file (**grep pattern search > filename**) or else use another Unix concept, the pipe, to redirect the output to the input of another command such as **more**, a convenient utility program that enables you to view text a line or a screen at time.

6 Type: **grep '\<j.*y\>' /usr /share/dict/ words | more** and use the [Return] key to move through the results a line at a time or the spacebar to view a screenful at a time. The | (i.e. [Shift] + [\]) is the pipe symbol. It connects output from one process to the input of another.

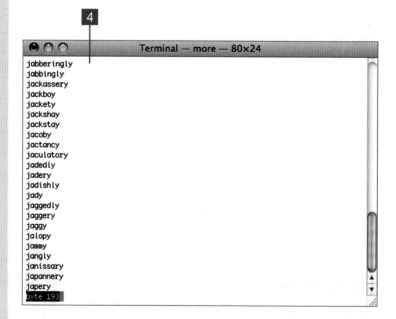

For your information

Use **man grep** at the command line for details of all the flags you can use with grep.

304

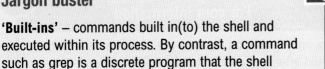

```
●●●                Terminal — csh — 80×24
[Jerry-Glenwrights-MacBook:~] jerryglenwright% alias songs ls -al Music
[Jerry-Glenwrights-MacBook:~] jerryglenwright% songs
total 16
drwx------+  6 jerryglenwright  staff    204 17 Jan 13:03 .
drwxr-xr-x+ 18 jerryglenwright  staff    612 17 Jan 14:24 ..
-rw-------@  1 jerryglenwright  staff   6148 21 Nov 11:55 .DS_Store
-rw-r--r--   1 jerryglenwright  staff      0 17 Nov 15:21 .localized
drwxrwxrwx   5 jerryglenwright  staff    170  3 Jan 16:03 GarageBand
drwxr-xr-x   6 jerryglenwright  staff    204  3 Jan 20:37 iTunes
[Jerry-Glenwrights-MacBook:~] jerryglenwright% ▉
```

Alias (csh shell)

1 The simple but useful 'built-in' command **alias** enables you to substitute convenient shorthand for a command that you use often.

2 At the prompt, type:
alias tunes ls -al Music
and press [Return].

3 Now, when you want a long listing of the contents of your Music directory, simply type:
songs
at the prompt and press [Return].

4 You can even replace existing commands with an alias of your choosing. Let's say you prefer always to use the all files and long listing variant of the list command ls. Try this: **alias ls ls -al**. Now when you type **ls** you'll see a long listing of all files. You can still use the **ls** command as originally intended, just put inverted commas around it like this: **'ls'**.

9

Jargon buster

'Built-ins' – commands built in(to) the shell and executed within its process. By contrast, a command such as grep is a discrete program that the shell executes as a standalone process.

Did you know?

In Unix (and therefore in Darwin), the screen display is called standard output, which is often abbreviated to stdout. The keyboard is called standard input and abbreviated to stdin.

Useful Unix (cont.)

Unless you're a glutton for punishment and actually enjoy typing command lines, it's sensible to use the up and down arrow keys to scroll to and fro through previous commands. Great shortcut, except what happens when you've typed in dozens of commands? It could take as long to scroll through them as it does to retype the one you want.

History

1 Meet History, another of csh's built-ins. History prints a numbered list of commands to standard output, together with the time they were used.

2 To redeploy a particular command, type its number preceded by an exclamation mark and press [Return]:
`!10, !72, !129`
and so on.

3 Use the exclamation mark with the first two or three letters to repeat the last instance of the command that started with those letters, wherever it features in the history list: `!gr` could be used to repeat
`grep '\<j.*y\>' /usr/share/dict/wor ds | more`

4 You can elect to see the last x number of commands by specifying a number with history:
`history 3`
will show the last three commands, for example.

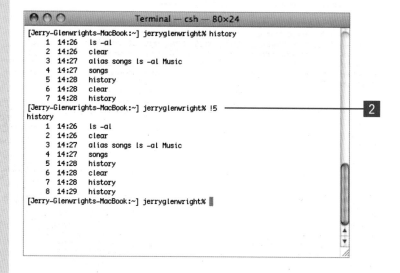

For your information

Unix operators such as pipes are known as 'daemons', named after the friendly helpful spirits of Greek mythology. Mostly, Unix daemons execute in the background and are invoked in response to requests from disk drives, printers, the mail system and scheduled housekeeping tasks.

Timesaver tip

Use the history built-in as a convenient way to check what you did when something unexpected happens (you might have to use [Control] and [Z] to suspend the untoward process and regain control of the prompt to issue the history command).

```
● ○ ○              Terminal — more — 80×24
total 3024
drwxrwxr-x+ 60 root          admin        2040 25 May 12:20 .
drwxrwxr-t  35 root          admin        1258 25 May 12:22 ..
-rw-rw-r--@  1 root          admin        6148 13 Jun 13:15 .DS_Store
-rw-rw-r--   1 root          admin           0 24 Sep 2007 .localized
drwxrwxr-x   3 root          admin         102 31 Mar 18:40 Address Boo
k.app
drwxrwxr-x@  8 root          admin         272 22 Jan 08:08 Adobe Bridg
e CS3
drwxrwxr-x@ 16 root          admin         544 22 Jan 08:10 Adobe Devic
e Central CS3
drwxrwxr-x@  4 root          admin         136 22 Jan 08:11 Adobe Help
Viewer 1.1.app
drwxrwxr-x@ 13 root          admin         442 22 Jan 08:13 Adobe Photo
shop CS3
drwxrwxr-x@  4 root          admin         136 22 Jan 08:12 Adobe Stock
 Photos CS3
drwxrwxr-x   6 root          admin         204  4 Jan 14:39 AppleScript
drwxr-xr-x  11 jerryglenwright admin       374  5 Feb 14:17 Audacity
drwxrwxr-x   3 root          admin         102 31 Mar 18:40 Automator.a
pp
drwxrwxr-x   3 root          admin         102 20 Sep 2007 Calculator.
app
:byte 118:1
```

More

1 You've just met more briefly while exploring grep. The more command lets you view a file at the standard output, a screen at a time.

2 Type:
more myfile
and press [Return] (substitute the name of the file you want to view).

3 more maintains a percentage counter display in inverse text in the lower left corner of the Terminal window to indicate where you are in the file. Press the [Spacebar] to scroll a screen at a time. Alternatively, pressing [Return] or the down arrow key scrolls a line at a time. The up arrow will move you back a line (i.e. towards the top of the file).

4 more's input can be piped from any built-in, shell script or program that produces output:
ls -al
/verylargedirectory
| more

5 You can search for text with a more's file by typing a forward slash and the character string:
/find this
for example.

6 Press [Q] to quit more.

9

Useful Unix (cont.)

Head and tail

1 A variation on file reading, head and tail is a convenient way to view the first or last few lines of a specified file.

2 Type:
head -5 myfile
and press [Return] and head will print the first five lines of myfile to the standard output.

3 Substitute tail for head to see the last five lines.

4 Using both head and tail with a pipe, you can specify a range of lines within a file. Type:
**head - 75 myfile |
tail -50**
to views lines 25–50 of myfile.

5 Step four is an example of a 'kludge' – a not very sophisticated workaround for a problem. A far more elegant solution (though one that requires far more effort to learn) for filtering files is the Unix stream editor Sed. Try **man sed** and give it a go ...

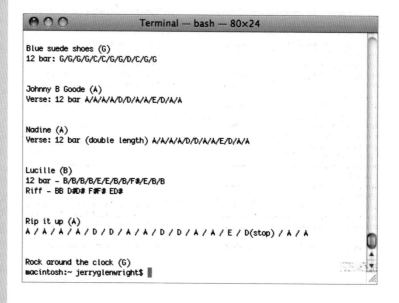

```
Terminal — bash — 80×24

Blue suede shoes (G)
12 bar: G/G/G/G/C/C/G/G/D/C/G/G


Johnny B Goode (A)
Verse: 12 bar A/A/A/A/D/D/A/A/E/D/A/A


Nadine (A)
Verse: 12 bar (double length) A/A/A/A/D/D/A/A/E/D/A/A


Lucille (B)
12 bar - B/B/B/B/E/E/B/B/F#/E/B/B
Riff - BB D#D# F#F# ED#


Rip it up (A)
A / A / A / A / D / D / A / A / D / D / A / A / E / D(stop) / A / A


Rock around the clock (G)
macintosh:~ jerryglenwright$ ▌
```

```
 ● ● ●              Terminal — csh — 80×24
[Jerry-Glenwrights-MacBook:~] jerryglenwright% cal 2 1962
    February 1962
Su Mo Tu We Th Fr Sa
             1  2  3
 4  5  6  7  8  9 10
11 12 13 14 15 16 17
18 19 20 21 22 23 24
25 26 27 28

[Jerry-Glenwrights-MacBook:~] jerryglenwright% cal 9 1752
   September 1752
Su Mo Tu We Th Fr Sa
       1  2 14 15 16
17 18 19 20 21 22 23
24 25 26 27 28 29 30


[Jerry-Glenwrights-MacBook:~] jerryglenwright% ▊
```

Cal

1 Ever wondered on what day of the week you were born, whether a week next Tuesday will be the 13th or what day Christmas falls on this year? You need cal, the Unix CLI online calendar.

2 At the command line, type: `cal` and press [Return]. cal prints a tabulated calendar for the current month. Now try this type: `cal 2 1962` and press [Return]. Cal prints a calendar for February 1962.

3 With a minute to kill, try this: `cal 9 1752`.

4 What happened to September?

5 Remember you can pipe or redirect the output from cal in the usual way: `cal 2008 | more` or `cal 2 1962 >> mysplendidyears.txt`.

9

Useful Unix (cont.)

Ending it all

1 Try this: at the command line, type:

`sudo shutdown -h 1430`

and press [Return] (substituting a suitable time for 1430). The Mac will shut down properly, closing all processes and ejecting any other users connected remotely (warning them first). Notice that shutdown (as you'd assume) is a superuser command: you need to precede it with **sudo**.

2 You can tell the Mac to shut down immediately by adding the argument 'now' (**sudo shutdown -h now**) or at a time and date some time in the next 100 years specified numerically in year, month, day, hour, minute format (**sudo shutdown -h 090213430** would shut down the Mac on 13 February 2009 at 14.30). You can also cause shutdown to restart your Mac now or later by using the **-r** flag (e.g. **sudo shutdown -r now**).

Although you are, by now, entirely familiar with shutting down your Mac from the Finder's Apple menu Shut Down option, the same can be achieved but with knobs on (what did you expect – this is Unix!) from the command line.

Let's say you're working on a text file at the command line and have a number of processes running in the background performing basic housekeeping tasks. You're needed elsewhere and, although you don't want to leave your machine running pointlessly, you don't want to stop the running processes either.

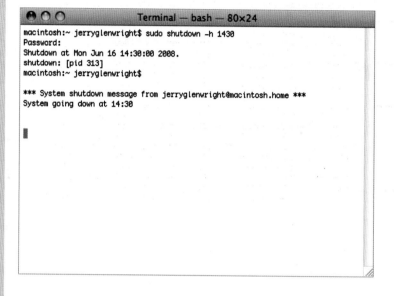

```
macintosh:~ jerryglenwright$ sudo shutdown -h 1430
Password:
Shutdown at Mon Jun 16 14:30:00 2008.
shutdown: [pid 313]
macintosh:~ jerryglenwright$

*** System shutdown message from jerryglenwright@macintosh.home ***
System going down at 14:30
```

```
●○○              Terminal — top — 80×24
Processes:  51 total, 2 running, 1 stuck, 48 sleeping... 222 threads   12:38:09
Load Avg: 0.03, 0.11, 0.13    CPU usage: 5.24% user, 4.29% sys, 90.48% idle
SharedLibs: num =   7, resident =  64M code, 1700K data, 4328K linkedit.
MemRegions: num = 6190, resident =  256M +  16M private,  141M shared.
PhysMem: 182M wired, 480M active,  29M inactive, 691M used, 327M free.
VM: 6514M + 373M  42344(0) pageins, 16(0) pageouts

PID COMMAND      %CPU   TIME   #TH #PRTS #MREGS RPRVT  RSHRD  RSIZE  VSIZE
323 top          3.7%  0:01.12  1   18    29    452K   200K  1044K   18M
317 Grab         2.9%  0:01.75  8  150+  313  4596K-   32M+   12M-  390M+
316 mdworker     0.0%  0:00.12  3   50    31    576K  5144K  2060K   31M
313 shutdown     0.0%  0:00.00  1   10    23    160K   188K   216K   19M
300 bash         0.0%  0:00.01  1   14    20    264K   184K   908K   18M
299 login        0.0%  0:00.01  1   17    55    272K   188K  1064K   19M
298 Terminal     2.2%  0:00.52  3  100   210  2120K+   15M  7340K+  345M
289 mdworker     0.0%  0:00.44  4   71    52  1668K  6092K  4012K   33M
169 LaunchCFMA   0.1%  0:06.80  2   80   250  9284K    12M    16M   422M
167 LaunchCFMA   2.4%  6:06.18  9  200   654   114M    34M   148M   891M
106 firefox-bi   1.3% 14:10.79 17  256   694    53M    30M    89M   452M
102 iChatAgent   0.0%  0:00.19  2   65    40   668K  3940K  2532K   286M
 98 usbmuxd      0.0%  0:00.00  2   21    26   200K   184K   696K   19M
 97 iTunesHelp   0.0%  0:00.05  2   53    46   508K  2864K  2320K   281M
 91 pboard       0.0%  0:00.00  1   15    23   164K   184K   584K   19M
 90 Finder       0.0%  0:05.51  6  182   326  5776K    25M    16M   367M
```

3 If you initiate shutdown but change your mind, locate the command's process number and use the kill command to end it. Remember, though, that shutdown is a superuser process. If you simply type **ps** at the command line you won't see shutdown. Use the **top** command instead and
sudo kill shutdown processnumber
to kill the shutdown.

9

Maintenance and troubleshooting

Introduction

OS X, especially in its latest incarnation 10.5 Leopard, is arguably the most robust operating system available to users of business and domestic desktop and laptop computers. Built on the rock-solid foundation of Unix and combined with a machine that Apple itself has designed and built, the operating system and hardware work perfectly together and you can certainly expect to use your Mac day in day out, year after year, and never see a system crash.

In the true spirit of the hacker approach (i.e. one in which a community of programmers and beta-testers create and maintain an operating system rather than a commercial entity working in isolation), Apple releases beta (pre-release) versions of OS X, its applications and utilities for the wider community to try and report bugs, a strategy that helps to iron out imperfections before they're unleashed on an unsuspecting public.

But, however solid a system is, a certain amount of scheduled maintenance is always a good thing, and there will be times when troubleshooting everything from a broken alias to a bad CD is required. Sensibly, OS X ships with many of the tools you need to keep the machine in tip-top condition and, what's more, you don't have to be a technician to make the most of them.

What you'll do

Use Software Update to keep your Mac in top condition

Get a snapshot of the system using System Profiler

Use Console and Activity Monitor to get system-level information about processor usage, running applications and memory allocation

Use Disk Utility to test and repair disks, volumes and permissions

Learn how to erase disks

Partition a drive

Online updates

The Internet makes for a perfect digital umbilical cord between you and the manufacturer of your computer. No longer do you fish it out of the box, put it on the kitchen table and gather the family around to marvel in isolated silicon bliss. Now, virtually every time you boot or launch an application, the Mac can connect to remote servers and check for and download updates.

Software Update

1 Software Update is the Mac's own updates utility, running silently in the background according to a preset schedule, checking for patches, new releases of system software and OS X applications. Generally the first thing a new Mac owner knows about Software Update is when its window appears onscreen to announce that updates are available and can be downloaded and installed. You can also run Software Update as a standalone utility and instruct it to check for updates.

2 Select Software Update... from the Apple menu. As the utility launches, it will show a dialogue confirming that it's checking for updates. If it finds any, you'll see New software is available for your computer, otherwise if your machine is up-to-date, Software Update will notify you and close.

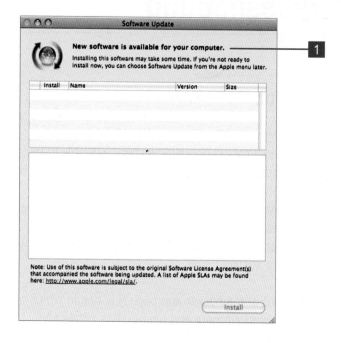

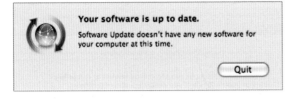

Your software is up to date.

Software Update doesn't have any new software for your computer at this time.

Quit

10

3 You can download and install these updates in the background and continue to work, though it may be that some system updates will require a restart. Some updates also require your password (the password that you set when you first set up the Mac). If you'd prefer not to bother, click Quit, otherwise choose the updates that you want (but there's no point in downloading, say, an iPod updater if you don't have an iPod) and click Install.

4 Software Update is minimised to the Dock and you can continue working.

Online updates (cont.)

Scheduling Software Update

1. Software Update does its stuff according to a schedule (unless you access the utility discretely), which you can adjust to suit yourself – overnight, perhaps, if you prefer to leave your Mac on standby rather than shut it down.

2. Launch System Preferences and select the Software Update pane.

3. Use the pop-up menu to schedule a frequency for your Mac to check for updates. Check Download important updates automatically so that your machine is fitted with essential security and system updates.

4. Check Now does exactly what it says on the button, though of course you'll need an Internet connection.

5. The Installed Updates tab displays a log of the updates you've installed during past sessions.

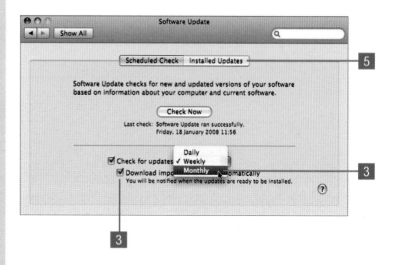

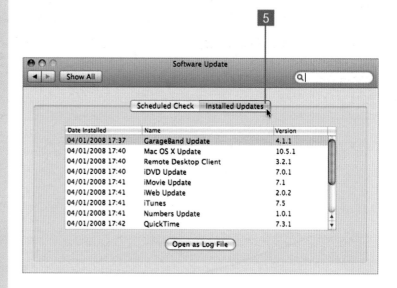

Online updates (cont.)

Customising updates

1 You can choose to hide certain updates – for example, if you do not have an iPod, then you probably don't need to receive future notifications about that.

2 With Software Update running, click on one or more updates in the list that you would prefer not to download or see again. From the Update select Ignore (or press [Backspace]).

3 If at some point it becomes necessary for you to acquire the updates that you're currently ignoring (e.g. you buy an iPod), select Reset Ignored Updates from the Software Update menu. All the updates that you missed will appear following the next check (use Check Now to acquire them immediately).

See also

You can also alter Software Update preferences by selecting the Software Update pane from the System section of System Preferences in the Dock.

Jargon buster

Patch – a snippet of computer code used to repair or improve system or applications software without a major rewrite or update.

Vital statistics

System Profiler

1 As well as providing a complete snapshot of your Mac's hardware and software (useful if you require telephone support from a computer technician), System Profiler helps when you're deciding whether or not your Mac meets the minimum requirements for an application.

2 Choose About This Mac from the Apple menu and then click the More Info... button to launch System Profiler. Alternatively, you can find and double-click it in the Utilities folder (**Applications> Utilities**).

3 Profiler offers three profile views – Mini, Basic and Full – switchable by pressing [Command] + [1], [Command] + [2] and [Command] + [3], respectively. When the utility launches, switch to full by pressing [Command] + [3] – no point in viewing a cut-price version of the available information.

You can use Software Update to view a log of the updates you've downloaded since acquiring your Mac and connecting it to the Internet, but what about the rest of the system? Use the machine for a few months and it'll be stuffed with all kinds of software casually downloaded and installed. The hardware is more or less fixed, of course, unless you install more memory or add an external disk drive, but how can you tell what's actually contained within the Mac's sleek outer case? No doubt you pored over a list of specs detailing hard drive size, graphics capabilities, the processor and the like when you bought the machine, but it's a safe bet that, within a month or two, and unless you're given to geekiness on a grand scale, you'll have forgotten all that stuff. Step this way, meet System Profiler ...

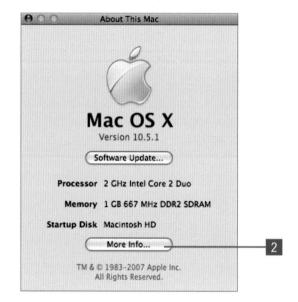

4 Profiler's window is organised in sections. On the left are the various parts of the system, the hardware, network and software, and on the right is an information pane. Select from the left and view on the right. Occasionally a further click in the right pane will split it and produce greater detail below.

5 Profiler opens with hardware overview. Click, say, Bluetooth, at the left to see comprehensive details of the Bluetooth installed on your machine. Admittedly, much of what's shown will be gobbledegook to the average owner.

Vital statistics (cont.)

6 ... however, there are some exceedingly useful bits and pieces here. Try this: select Disc Burning under Hardware in the Contents column and insert a blank optical disk. Profiler will tell you the range of write speeds supported by the disk.

7 Scroll the Contents list until Software comes into view. Click Applications. After a moment or two, all the applications – Apple's and any third-party software – you've installed will be listed, with details such as the version number. Now click on an application and Profiler will provide detailed information about it, including where it lives on the computer. This is useful if you're wondering whether to apply an update or patch provided by the company responsible for the software.

6

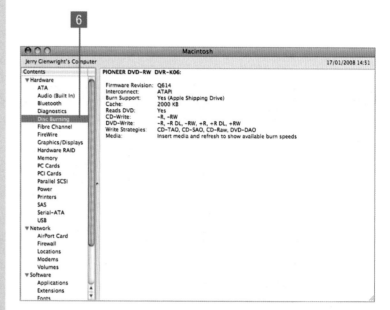

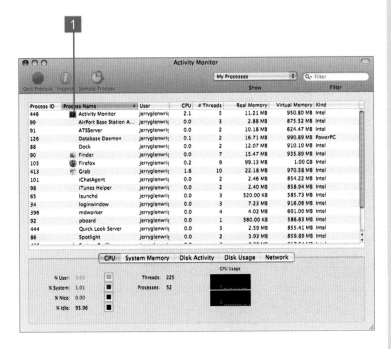

Activity Monitor

1 System Profiler offers an essentially static view of the machine – a snapshot – though of course you can press [Command] + [R] to refresh the profiles if you change anything while the utility is running. For a dynamic view of your Mac – a detailed look at all that's happening behind the scenes as it were, updated in real time (i.e. your time) second by second (actually half second by half second) – use Activity Monitor. OS X is built on Unix, and Unix is built on processes – stuff that's happening and the stuff of Activity Monitor.

2 Activity Monitor lets you view processes and determine what resources they're gobbling up on your Mac. You might, for example, use it to monitor the resources required by your Dashboard widgets – you'd be surprised at just how much processing power and network bandwidth (i.e. system resources) some of them swallow up. And every allocation of resources to items running in the background means less for the applications that you want to use in the foreground.

Vital statistics (cont.)

Getting closer with Activity Monitor

1 Locate Activity Monitor in the Utilities folder (`Applications> Utilities`) and double-click to launch it.

2 The window is divided into sections: the main part shows the current processes, a unique process ID for each, the percentage of CPU time in use and how much memory (actual and virtual) is consumed by the process. Processes are displayed in a hierarchy, with the most recent at the top of the list. You can reorganise the list – in order of CPU usage, for example – by clicking the appropriate heading twice (once to show ascending, and again to show descending order). With no other application running, probably the only process you're aware of actually starting is Activity Monitor itself, but you can see that all kinds of other items are active too.

3 And it doesn't end there. From the pop-up processes menu in the toolbar, select All

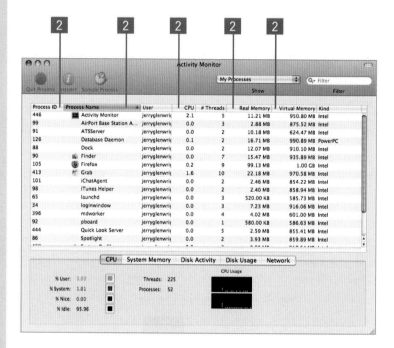

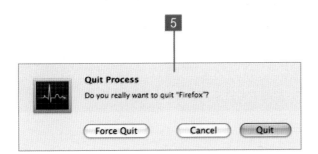

Processes – now you can really see what's going on! There are probably at least 20 or 30 processes. Some are yours, and some – the system processes used to make the Mac operate in the way that it does – are owned by root.

4   For a closer look still, click a process to select it and click the Inspect button in the toolbar. Use the Memory and Statistics tabs for more details.

5   Now try this: select Activity Monitor in the Process Name list and click the Quit Process button. A dialogue asks you whether you really want to quit. Click the Force Quit button, and the process is ended immediately, its resources are released and, in this case, you're returned to the Desktop – you just ended Activity Monitor. This function is useful to clear the Mac of what you suspect is a troublesome process.

Vital statistics (cont.)

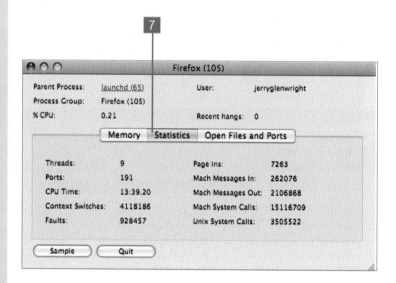

6 How dead is dead? For an even more final way to kill a process that's misbehaving or just to get close to the geek within you, select a process and choose Send Signal To Process from the View menu. Select Kill from the pop-up menu and click Send. The process is ended instantly without any dialogue or warning. Use the end process functions with extreme care – you could seriously interrupt the way your Mac is operating, crash the system, damage the file structure and wreak all kinds of other catastrophes.

7 The tabs in the middle of Activity Monitor's window enable you to monitor system memory, drive activity and usage and to watch data moving across the network. Click each in turn to see what they show.

8 You can elect to have some of this information show in the Dock – useful if you want to monitor the network, say, or an application while you're using it. Click Dock Icon on the View menu and choose what to display in the Dock.

Important

If you have administrator status you could probably compromise the Mac in all kinds of damaging ways by using Activity Monitor – take extreme care and don't do anything of which you're unsure.

Timesaver tip

For even faster access to System Profiler, hold down the Option key and select the Apple menu – About This Mac morphs into System Profiler.

Although floppy disks have long been relegated to landfill, computers remain slaves to their drives. And where there's a drive, there's the potential for lost data (even though the Mac's disk format is arguably the least likely to suffer problems). The hard disk *is* the Mac. When you boot the machine and see your familiar Desktop with that holiday picture of the kids as your wallpaper and aliases to your favourite applications arranged in just the way you like them, what you're looking at isn't the computer so much as the data on the drive – swap your drive for someone else's and the machine will look and feel like their machine – in fact, it'll be theirs. Although there's little you can do to maintain a Mac's hardware (and nor would you want to – that nonsense is for PC users), you can work with the hard drive to keep it in tip-top condition and to repair corrupted data.

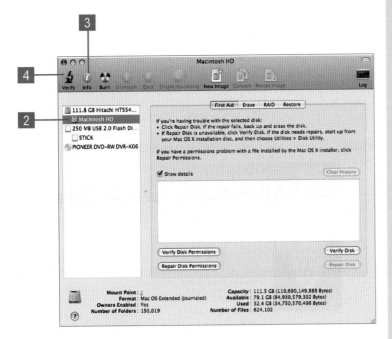

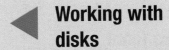
Checking drives and volumes

1. Disk Utility is located in the Utilities folder (`Applications> Utilities`). Double-click to launch the program.

2. At the left of the Disk Utility window you'll see a list of drives and volumes. Click the second in the list: it's your startup volume, the one the Mac boots from.

3. For a window with information about the volume, click the Info button in the toolbar.

Working with disks (cont.)

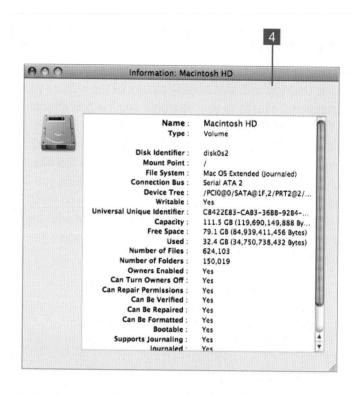

4 Now check the volume. Make sure it's selected and click the Verify button. Disk Utility runs a number of checks to verify the structure and integrity of the volume and presents you with the results in the main window. If all is well you'll see 'The volume XXX appears to be ok'.

5 Note that word 'appears'. Although Disk Utility is a capable program, there are some tests that it cannot perform. To go further, there are Apple and third-party utilities, such as Apple's TechTool Deluxe and Alsoft's Disk Warrior (**www.alsoft.com**).

6 If verifying detects a problem, you'll be notified, though it may be that you can't actually repair the problem even if it's within Disk Utility's capability. Why? Because you can't work on the startup disk.

7 To get around this problem, boot with your OS X installation DVD (insert the disk, restart the Mac and hold down the C key). Select Disk Utility from the Install menu and proceed as above, though now, of course, because the installation disk is your startup disk, you'll be able to repair the volume.

Did you know?

Apple was the first major computer manufacturer to adopt the 'new' 3.5-inch floppy when it became available in the early 1980s... and it was the first to abandon the floppy disk in the 1990s.

See also

For a while, many Mac users missed the convenience of the floppy disk, but, in this age of cheap 1 Gb memory sticks, there's nothing to commend the use of a 1 Mb floppy (less space by a factor of 1000). However, if you have important data on floppies that you want to retrieve, a USB floppy drive will readily connect to the Mac, and both Mac- and PC-formatted disks will happily mount on the Desktop.

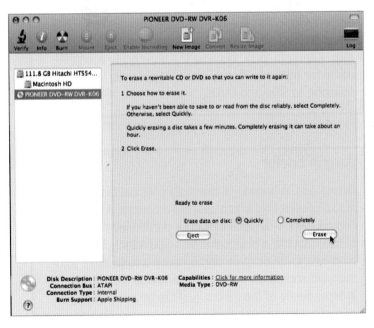

Working with disks (cont.)

Erasing optical disks

1 Your Mac's optical drive can work with rewritable CDs (and DVDs if you have a SuperDrive), disks that can be erased and used again. To erase a disk, you use Disk Utility.

2 Launch Disk Utility, mount your disk and click the Erase tab. Select it from the list and click the Erase Data on disc and Quickly. Then click Erase. The process takes a few minutes.

3 If the disk has been erased a number of times, or if you've had problems writing to it, click the Completely button, but be prepared for a wait... a full disk erase takes an age.

For your information

Although you can't use Disk Utility to work with the startup disk, OS X performs an automatic startup disk verify, checking the integrity of the file structure as the system boots.

10

Working with disks (cont.)

Partitioning a disk

1 A large external hard drive attached via USB or FireWire can be a boon if you work with big files such as digital movie clips. You can use a drive of, say, 500 Gb as one large storage space, or you can break it up (partition it) into two or three smaller volumes to help you manage and organise your files.

2 To partition a disk, mount it and launch Disk Utility. Click the Partition tab.

3 Choose the number of partitions you want from the pop-up Volume Scheme menu and select sizes for these partitions by clicking in each to select it and typing explicit figures into the Size field. You can also drag the window divider. Enter names for each partition and click Apply. The disk is partitioned according to the sizes you specified.

4 Partitioning destroys existing data, so make a backup if you're working with a drive that has an intact file system.

For your information

Disk or disc? Most computer terminology has American origins and, consequently, American spellings, such as program instead of programme, and disk instead of disc. Although 'disk' became the universally accepted name for hard and floppy disks, Apple uses 'disc' when referring to CDs and DVDs.

Jargon buster

Drives and volumes – a drive is a physical disk, the actual medium on which data are recorded. A volume is a 'logical drive' – an area of a drive partitioned to look and behave just like a physical drive – you might, for example, have two, three or more partitions on a large drive, and each will mount on the Desktop and operate entirely independently of the others, just like physical drives.

There are times – if the hard drive is corrupted, for example – when it would be extremely useful to start your Mac from a different boot source or mount the machine as if it were a simple external hard drive on another Mac. The most obvious example of this is one you've probably already used when you installed OS X on your new Mac – in that case, the alternative boot source was the install DVD. Using a variety of key combinations at switch-on, you can force your Mac to select from alternative boot sources, such as a network, a CD or a DVD, or to start in what's known as Target Disk Mode – as an external drive on a second Mac. Some of the startup options are useful when your machine is connected to a network – so that a technician can perform necessary maintenance or repair work, for example.

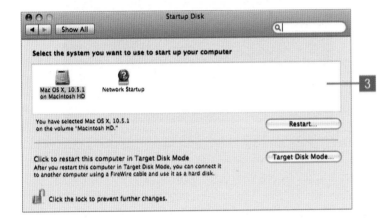

An alternative startup drive

Booting from the optical drive

1. You can force the Mac to start from a bootable CD or DVD (i.e. one with a system folder) at switch-on.

2. Insert the bootable disk and restart the machine, holding down the [C] key as it boots.

3. If your machine isn't bootable because the hard drive is corrupt or because OS X hasn't been installed yet, power up and wait until the machine attempts to boot, and then insert the optical disk. The Mac will recognise the disk and boot from it.

4. If the Mac refuses to boot from the disk and you're sure that it is bootable, try this: with the disk still in the drive, cycle the power by holding down the power button until the machine powers down. Power up again holding down [Shift], [Option], [Command] + [Delete] to force the Mac to scan for bootable volumes on attached disks.

5. By booting from the OS X Installation DVD, you can reinstall the system, should it become necessary.

An alternative startup drive (cont.)

Target Disk Mode

1 Using a simple FireWire cable, you can connect two Macs together in what's called Target Disk Mode and have one of them (the target disk) mount on the other as an external drive. Using Target Disk Mode, you can transfer huge amounts of data very quickly, sidestep Darwin permissions, or use Apple's Migration Assistant to transfer all your important files and settings from an existing Mac to a new one.

2 Connect the machines together via their FireWire ports using an ordinary FireWire cable.

3 Boot one machine as normal (i.e. not the one you want to mount as an external drive).

4 Press the power button on the other Mac while holding down its T key. After a moment or two, the FireWire symbol will be displayed on its screen and it will mount on the first Mac as a drive.

5 You can access the drive as normal, double-click to open it, and drag and drop data.

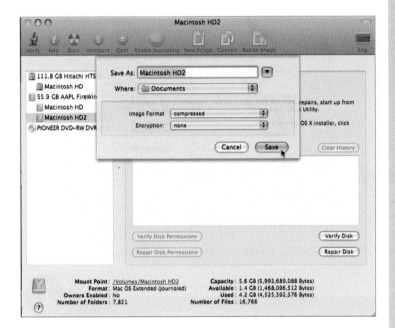

Cloning a disk

1 Using Target Disk Mode, you can clone an entire Mac hard drive as a mountable backup image.

2 With a Mac mounted in Target Disk Mode, launch Disk Utility (**Applications> Utilities**), select the target disk from the list on the left, and click on the New Image button on the toolbar. Name the image in the Save As field and use the pop-up Where menu to select a location to save it to (be aware that you could need many gigabytes of space, depending on the size of the disk you're cloning). Be sure to select the Compressed in the Image Format pop-up menu and choose an optional depth of encryption from the Encryption pop-up to protect the data from prying eyes. Click Save and prepare for a wait.

3 An exact copy of the drive is created as a mountable .dmg image, which you can use later in Target Disk Mode to recreate the original disk after a failure.

An alternative startup drive (cont.)

Migration Assistant

1. OS X ships with Migration Assistant, a utility to recreate your software settings when you acquire a new Mac. The program can be run as part of the OS X installation procedure, but an arguably better proposition is to run it when your new machine is up and running and you're happy with its performance and behaviour.

2. Migration Assistant is located in the Utilities folder (`Applications> Utilities`). Double-click the utility to launch it.

3. Follow the instructions detailed earlier to put the source Mac (the one you're migrating from) into Target Disk Mode and link the machines with a FireWire cable.

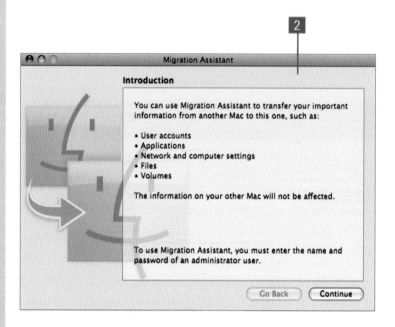

Migration Assistant

Introduction

You can use Migration Assistant to transfer your important information from another Mac to this one, such as:

- User accounts
- Applications
- Network and computer settings
- Files
- Volumes

The information on your other Mac will not be affected.

To use Migration Assistant, you must enter the name and password of an administrator user.

Go Back   Continue

For your information

Startup key combinations.

[Shift], [Option], [Command] and [Delete] – bypasses the primary boot volume and forces the Mac to search for an alternative boot source.

Option – shows system folders on all attached volumes.

N – boots from a compatible network server.

C – boots from an optical disk with a system folder.

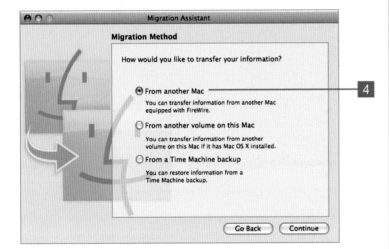

4 The process for migrating is essentially one of following onscreen prompts. Select a migration method and click Continue (for two Macs connected via a FireWire, this will be the From another Mac option).

5 Choose a user to migrate and select what to migrate – software and settings, network and time zone and so on. Migration Assistant will not overwrite newer applications on the target computer. Click OK to begin the migration.

6 When the process is complete, restart the target Mac.

Jargon buster

AirPort – Apple's take on the 802.11b/802.11g standard for wireless networking.

Application – is a full-blown software package such as a word processor or a movie editing suite. A utility is a small, generally one-task program geared towards solving a particular problem or else manipulating the operating system in some way.

Bayesian filtering – named after the 18th-century British cleric and amateur mathematician Reverend Thomas Bayes whose paper on probability theory published after his death guaranteed him a special place in the study of chance.

Built-ins – are commands built in(to) the shell and executed within its process. By contrast a command such as grep is a discrete program that the shell executes as a standalone process.

Bundled software – the programs and utilities included free when you buy a new computer or operating system.

Burning – the process of recording movies, music and data on to an optical disk such as a DVD or CD.

Cache – a special processor-only memory that 'remembers' recent operations thereby improving processing efficiency.

DHCP – Dynamic Host Configuration Protocol, essentially a method by which a computer is assigned all it needs to join a network and get online without an administrator having to specify each component such as network addresses, individually.

DLS modem – a device that connects your Mac to your phone line to enable it to use a broadband Internet connection.

Drives & volumes – a drive is a physical disk, the actual medium on which data is recorded. A volume is a 'logical drive': an area of a drive partitioned to look and behave just like a physical drive. You might, for example, have two, three or more partitions on a large drive and each will mount on the Desktop and operate entirely independently of the others just like physical drives.

Font – (AKA typeface), the alphanumeric and other characters displayed on the computer's screen (and reproduced on a printer) in a variety of shapes (known as 'families' such Futura, Gill, Din and so on), sizes and styles. The size of a font character is measured in 'points' (and known as the 'point size'), 72 of which make an inch (e.g. Helvetica Bold, 12 point, italic).

Grep – The name 'grep' is said to derive from the combination of the letters used to search for strings when editing text in the Unix line editor Ed: g/re/p.

Hard drive – what's hard about it then? Difficult to understand drive? Inflexible drive? The epithet 'hard' hails from an age when flexible 'floppy' disks ruled the backing storage world because they were cheap and largely disposable. Hard drives had – yes, literally – inflexible disks, far greater capacity but phenomenally larger price tags.

IMAP – Internet Message Access Protocol, used to access email messages from the Web.

ISP – Internet Service Provider, is the organisation that provides you with a dial-up or broadband Internet account.

On the wonk – deviating from the horizontal or vertical.

Patch – snippet of computer code used to repair or improve system or applications software without a major rewrite or update.

Phishing – the process of pretending to be a trustworthy entity (your bank) to acquire sensitive information such as account details, passwords and PIN numbers.

POP – Post Office Protocol, a system by which emails are retrieved from remote servers (that is, you connect to your ISP's POP server and collect your email).

Pop-ups – uninvited and often insidious browser windows, usually smaller and hidden behind the window you've chosen to view and which pop up automatically to offer some dubious 'service' or other when you visit a website. Where once pop-ups were a serious

menace to your surfing enjoyment (dozens could be lurking behind legitimate windows) modern browsers such as Safari and Firefox have excellent pop-up blockers offering virtually 100 per cent success in keeping them at bay.

Protocol – is the word used to describe the way two or more computers connect and exchange information. If both are operating with the same protocols, data exchange is possible.

RAM – Random Access Memory, a computer's memory chips.

Router – a device that shares a broadband connection between several computers via an Ethernet or wireless (or both) network. Routers generally incorporate a DSL modem.

RSS – Really Simple Syndication, a format for distributing frequently updated Web content, such as news headlines, podcasts and blogs.

SMTP – Simple Mail Transfer Protocol, the email-sending counterpart to POP.

Transition – a visual effect to link two scenes in a movie.

Volume – an attached drive such as the Mac's internal hard drive, a shared network drive, a pen drive and so on.

WEP – Wired Equivalent Privacy, an algorithm to secure a wireless network.

WPA – WiFi Protected Access, an algorithm to secure a wireless network.

Troubleshooting guide

Index